READ THEIR STORIES, JOIN THEIR JOURNEYS,
CELEBRATE THEIR TRIUMPHS

greenehouse
media that matters.

The Queens' Legacy

Read Their Stories, Join Their Journeys, Celebrate Their Triumphs

Cover design by: Michael Jackson
www.MasteryOfMarketing.com

ISBN: 978-0-9779034-3-6
Printed in the USA

Published by
FIG Publishing
An imprint of GreeneHouse Media
12138 Central Ave, Suite 264
Mitchellville, MD 20721
www.FIGPublishing.com
info@figpublishing.com

greenehouse
media that matters.

Once untold stories of The Queens' Legacy
Divinely inspired, God created her heavenly
Spiritually equipped with all the necessities
From tragedy to triumph, she figured out the recipe
From Sinner to Saint
Victim to Victor
Her nurturing hands helped mankind to endure
Winter, spring, summer, and fall
The joy and the pain, she's witnessed it all
Rightfully seated upon her throne
With grace and dignity she governs her home
From the brightest of days to the darkest of nights
She is the daughter of God, so Queen is her birthright
No matter the circumstance, or how daunting the task
Her story inspires and shall eternally last

~Mel Roberson

This book is dedicated to my mother, Rosetta R. Barbour, who showered me with unwavering love and devotion until the day she went home to be with our Lord. I am thankful for the legacy of helping and inspiring people that she left me and my daughters, Denise, Kianna and Kristyn.

As a result, we are truly The Queen's Legacy.

What is Your Legacy?

We would love to hear how you were inspired by the stories in this book. Please let us know how they affected you. Also, we invite you to submit your stories for consideration for use in future editions of *The Queens' Legacy.* For more information, visit our website at www.TheQueensLegacy.com.

Acknowledgements

It is with extreme gratitude that I acknowledge the following people for their support and assistance in the creation of this book.

Vera Cornish, thank you for round the clock access to you; for your incredible energy; and, for helping me to keep my eye on the prize. You've brought so many others to the table that have been a blessing to me and to this project and for that I'll always be grateful.

Michael Jackson, we did it! You have been an incredible partner, friend and muse for me. Thank you for all you've done. Your graphic and marketing skills are amazing. Thank you for using them to bless *The Queens' Legacy* and its authors.

Ryan Greene, thank you for having an incredible amount of patience with me as we worked through issue upon issue and for all you have done to bring this project to light. You are an awesome man and I look forward to working more with you in the future.

To the authors of *The Queens' Legacy*, you have helped to make this book project a raging success. Thank you for sharing your stories and being an inspiration for the readers and the other writers in this book. Your stories are inspirational and will impact the lives of many others forever.

To everyone who submitted their stories for inclusion in this book, we appreciate you. Although we weren't able to put all of the stories in this book, and we tried, I look forward to your possible inclusion in the next edition of *The Queens' Legacy*.

Because of the enormity of this project, we may have left out the names of some who contributed along the way. If so, I apologize. Please know that we really appreciate you very much.

Table of Contents

FOREWORD

I'll Always Love My Mama

KATRINA FERGUSON

If Your Whys are Big Enough, the Hows will take care of themselves.

My philosophy for life is, "If Your Whys are Big Enough, the Hows will Take Care of Themselves." Many people know me as the "WHY Lady." What they don't know, is what caused me to adopt this philosophy. Early in life, I needed something to hold onto; a place to hang my hat so to speak. A mindset that would allow me to continue moving forward in spite of the challenges I encountered.

Some of my challenges resulted from my parents divorcing when I was eight years old. Others were as a result of my getting pregnant in my freshman year of college. My parents, thinking they knew best for me, tried to force me to have an abortion. My father told me "Change your name, leave the state, we don't know you". My mother simply went along with him. My parents were highly educated with six Masters and three Doctorates between them. The path that I had chosen was completely contrary to the one they had chosen for me. And, like a lot of parents, they did what they thought they could to get me back on their version of the right path.

Still, I held my ground. This little baby growing inside me offered me something that until then, I hadn't received; unconditional love. No matter what happened, there would be a continuing cycle of love to envelope me and my baby for the rest of our lives, and I wasn't about to let anyone or anything interfere with that. School got tough with no family

THE *Queens'* LEGACY

support, so I packed my bags and moved to New Jersey to live with my cousin.

Shortly after my daughter was born, my mother came to visit. This was a surprise considering there had been little to no communication between us since I left Virginia. Little did she know that her first visit with her only granddaughter would end in her saving the baby's life. When she went into the room, Denise had choked and her breathing was obstructed. She was all sorts of shades of gray and blue. After I assessed the situation calmly and realized I couldn't bring her back, I started screaming. Fortunately, God had ordained that my aunt, who was a nurse, would be right outside. Having heard my scream, she rushed in, revived the baby and we went off to the hospital. Although Niecey-Poo was fine ultimately, Mom never recovered. She thought that her separating herself from her daughter in her time of need was why her granddaughter almost died. This is where we started building our world class relationship.

We did everything together; travelled, walked, talked, several times a day. We were the poster children for mother daughter-relationships. Not that we didn't have our ups and downs because we did. It's just that overcoming the near death of a child tends to minimize the issues. We were so close that no matter what happened, Mom was always there. With her bad wig and huge smile she was our family's favorite person. And not just our favorite, everyone that met Grammy loved her. All I knew was that I was going to be close to her for as long as we both lived; that I was going to make sure that my three daughters and I did everything we could to make her life brighter. We even sacrificed moving out of the state to stay close to her in Virginia; never living more than 15 minutes away, all the while singing the Intruder's song, "I'll Always Love my Momma."

My mom was spoiled and we all knew it. There were days that she would call me to just come sit with her. Because I worked from home, she thought I had the time. She would even call me to say that she wasn't feeling well and I'd rush to her side, only to find she just wanted company. When she realized I was on to her, she would wait until her high blood pressure medicine would run out and call and ask me to get it and bring it to her. This was our regular game.

When Mom called me the morning of March 6, 2002, two days after my recommitment to take my business to the next level, I took my time getting to her house. I went on three appointments, all of which were over 45 minutes away, yet I knew a positive outcome would change the face of my business. Little did I know that my life was about to be changed forever.

14

Mom called me three separate times. Each conversation, I told her the same thing. After I finish my appointments, I will be on my way. The last time I spoke to her, I heard something strange in her voice. As I was meeting with the HR Director of a Fortune 500 company, a check in my spirit told me that I had to get to Mom. I excused myself and ran out of the office building, hopped into the car and sped out of the parking lot on my way to see what was going on. As I hit the highway, I pressed '2' on my cell phone, Mommy's speed dial number.

Paul, Mom's husband, answered the phone. "Rosetta's down," he said. What? "The paramedics are here and it's bad." Bad? What does that mean? This time...this time she was serious! How could I be too busy for my mom? Unbelievable. As shocked as I was, I was angry too. Why didn't we have some sort of code so I would've known it was serious?

It was rush hour in the Washington DC Metropolitan area, the most challenging time to drive anywhere. On the shoulders I drove, speeding around cars, praying that there was some kind of mistake, believing that Mommy was going to be fine. In the back of my mind was that nagging remembrance that all of the women on my mother's side of the family died before the age of 50. More than a few times, I petitioned God to give me more time with my mother. She was 60 years old and I wasn't ready to let her go.

As I reached Interstate 66 going to Fair Oaks Hospital, I heard my mother's voice saying, "Slow down, I'm okay." I looked in my passenger seat and there she sat. Now my prayers turned to rebuking the enemy. This wouldn't be the first time that a loved one of mine had 'visited' me on their way out of the earth realm. I turned into the hospital parking lot, ran through the double doors and told the nurse at the desk that I was there to see Rosetta Barbour. She said, "go to room 29." Running down the hall, around the corner, to the room, I threw open the door. As my eyes adjusted to the sight and my brain received the information, I realized that they were unhooking my mother from the tubes and machines. She was dead.

"NOOOO!!" I screamed and collapsed right there in the middle of the floor. My brain was flooded with information from my eyes yet, I couldn't wrap my mind around the idea that when I spoke to my mother earlier that day, that was the last time. Out of nowhere a wheelchair materialized and the next thing I knew, I was being pushed down the hall to what I later realized was a meditation room. Paul was already there. As I have done at every stressful time in my life, I moved into problem solver mode and began to make phone calls to notify everyone of the news; get the kids to the hospital; get the loved ones and family members there too. How would I tell my girls, her sister, her nieces and nephews, the daycare

parents, the family? What about me? What would happen to me now? My mother was my safety net. Little did I know that in the coming months I would begin to understand the "Wind Beneath My Wings" song, as the wind had truly been taken from under my wings.

One by one my girls came in, my mother's pastors as well as mine. Best friends, sisters, everyone was there to see what had happened and to be a support to one another – we had lost Mom to me and Grammy to so many others.

True to form, I moved into survival mode. There were funeral arrangements to be made, people to notify, flowers to buy and that's what I did. I threw all of my time and energy into arranging the very best celebration of life I could . . . one that Mommy would have planned for herself. You wouldn't have even known that she was gone except that we couldn't keep our emotions in check for very long. Bursts of tears, people walking in the door with red eyes, anything could make us cry.

This was a major event in my life and I kept waiting for my mom to come. She never missed a big day. I would think, "Where is she?" and then I'd remember. And weep. And hurt. And be comforted by my daughters who were also crying. This was the hardest thing any of us had ever done.

After the funeral, I went right back to business; travelling, doing meetings. I didn't cancel any events. Flying on planes, I would think of mom and cry. Then I would pull myself together, get off the plane and go to baggage claim where out of habit, I would hit '2' on my phone. Only now, Mom didn't answer and I would cry as I listened to her voice on the answering machine. Then I would get to the hotel where I was staying and go to my room and cry some more. I'd pull myself together long enough to do an event; after all, I was a professional. Then I would go back to my room and cry some more. Thankfully I had no regrets. Mommy knew I loved her. Not only did I tell her, I showed her at every opportunity.

Several weeks later, I found myself at home, not going anywhere, not doing anything, just at home. As near as I could tell, I was in mourning. At least that's what the mirror said when it showed the reflection of swollen eyes, undone hair and unbrushed teeth. One particular night, after crying myself to sleep, I dreamed about mom. She looked so good. She had lost weight, her hair was done, and she was wearing a beautiful black dress, one that now hangs in my closet. Her facial expression was, well, angry. "What are you doing?" She scolded in my dream. "You've got these girls to raise; there are women all over the world that need to hear from you. I left too early. Get up, take care of your health and do what you were created to do." She proceeded to give me a list. "Get some pen and paper, you're not going to remember all that I'm saying" she added. And in my dream, I wrote down all the things that my mother told me that night.

The next morning, I woke up. Sad because I missed my mother, yet glad that she was all right. I had to get myself back up. Mom was fine, she was happy, I'd see her again. As I got out of bed to handle my morning constitutional, I stepped on a pad of paper – the notes that I had taken 'in my dream.' Now I thought I was losing my mind. How is it that the notes I took in my dream were now on the floor in my bedroom?

I called my spiritual mentor, thinking I was going crazy. He explained to me that the Word had become flesh. God wanted me to live on purpose, to do destiny and He used the voice of my mother to speak His will for me.

This project is a result of this interaction with my favorite woman in the whole world, she who blessed me with life, my best friend, my mother, my queen. God promised me that authors would be healed and readers inspired in this process; so for your inspiration, I present,
THE QUEENS' LEGACY.

In an instant, priorities can shift. As a

- Professional Speaker
- Successful Entrepreneur
- Author
- Trainer
- Life Coach

- Radio Personality
- Motivator
- Mentor
- Chaplain
- And more

Katrina Ferguson delivers a passionate, enthusiastic and entertaining message to both teach and encourage you to celebrate your individuality and breakthrough to become your 'greater self.' Her inspiring message is based upon lessons learned in her own breakthrough journeys. Ms. Ferguson is committed to helping others across the world apply these principles in their individual lives and relationships. In her unique, uncompromising style, she brings life changing principles and leadership skills that have inspired and motivated thousands across age, gender and industry lines. As such, Ms. Ferguson has been the subject of numerous articles and interviews and her story is currently being used all over the country to train and motivate sales forces of both public and private organizations.

Ms. Ferguson's acute understanding and ability to motivate people has enabled her to excel in the network marketing industry. Her keen awareness that conflicting demands, resource constraints and shifting priorities are challenges that must be overcome for success in today's global marketplace has placed her in constant demand as a presenter, motivator, and trainer of trainers by sales organizations across the nation.

Ms. Ferguson encourages everyone to be passionate and uncompromising in 'giving back' to the community and celebrating their ability do so. She is Chaplain for the WNBA Washington Mystics team and the Founder and President of *A Sister's Love*, a nonprofit organization, whose mission is to provide practical information, tangible and intangible tools to assist women and children in achieving while propelling them into greatness.

For more information, to purchase Ms. Ferguson's materials or to request an appearance, please contact The Ferguson Group at (888) 803-9373, or by e-mail: Katrina@KatrinaFerguson.com or online at www.KatrinaSpeaks.com, www.TheTotalWomanWorkshop.com or www.KatrinaFerguson.com.

The Queens' Legacy, an inspirational compilation of stories designed to inspire its readers to grow through what they go through so their greatness can show through. These authors have been inspired by women who have been queens in their lives. Some of the queens are their mothers, some other family members, some Civil Rights leaders, some themselves. The common thread being they have made deposits in our lives that are worthy of celebration and conversation.

Read their stories.

Join their journeys.

Celebrate their triumphs.

Change your life forever.

THE *Queens'* LEGACY

THE *Queens'* LEGACY

CHAPTER 1

Mrs. "A"

ADRIENNE WATSON-CARVER

"I am a trail blazer and a trend setter, enlarging my territory and walking with authority.
In every step there is passion, purpose and power!"

Born the youngest of four children and the only female child, I was definitely the "baby girl" of my family. My family's love and support gave me the courage to chase my dreams no matter what, determined to fulfill my destiny.

I could never share my legacy without talking about my parents, Earl and Inez Watson. Loving, supportive, committed, strong, loyal, and dedicated are words that I would use to describe them. I do not think one can find more dedicated and committed parents on the earth. I was raised in a very loving and nurturing family and my childhood years were full of memories of family vacations, holiday dinners, singing Christmas carols with my family by the tree on Christmas Eve, my mom's swim lessons and pool parties at our home, my dad coaching everybody's team and my mom serving on every parent committee known to man! In addition to loving us, my parents always seemed to be happy with one another as well. Seeing them cuddled up, holding hands, laughing together, or just watching television together was a regular occurrence and it still is today. Like all

parents, they had differences, but the love shown toward each other and toward me and my siblings far out weighted any problems or differences. My parents' loving example has influenced my relationships and my ability to connect with others. In fact, I have the same best friend that I've had since I was 3 years old and we are now a part of a circle of six women that have been best friends for more than 20 years. Four of us have been best friends for more than 30 years.

My mother is my greatest image of love. She is such an affectionate and loving person. To say that she is selfless would be an understatement. At a very young age I can remember my mom telling me that I was the most beautiful little girl in the world and that I could do anything. She would sit me on her lap and we would sit for hours singing songs, laughing, and having fun. And every now and then she would slip in a comment to let me know I was priceless to her. In her eyes, I saw my reflection smiling back at me. In her eyes I saw myself as one very special little girl with the sky as the limit. She said these things to me so often and with such passion that I believed her! I believed that I could do anything and I thought I was beautiful. Maybe not the most beautiful girl in the world, but definitely just as beautiful as anyone else, deserving whatever great things this world had to offer.

My dad was my athletic influence. He was also my biggest basketball fan. He would wear a special sweatshirt to all of my games. He had it made especially for coming to watch me play. On the front of the shirt it said "Dad of #22. Awesome A." On the back it said "shoot it baby!" Many of the parents called my dad "shoot it baby" because he would shout that every time I had the ball and was open for a shot. I owe my competitive spirit at a very young age to my dad and he encouraged me to always do my best. I listened to every word he said and I wanted to be just like him. He could dance, sing and was a great athlete, playing both high school and college basketball. He taught me how to play most sports and took pride in my athletic abilities. He nurtured my desire to be great. He always congratulated me and told me that I made him proud! As I looked at my dad through a child's eyes, he was larger than life. He was smart, handsome and well dressed! He was sharp as a tack and had his own swagger and style! He adored me so and I was so proud to be his little girl!

Both of my parents were strong disciplinarians with little tolerance for disrespectful behavior or low academic achievement. I was expected to have an unconditional respect for authority and to work to the best of my ability at school and whatever I did. Though my parents were serious about their children doing well in school, all work and no play never made sense to them. My mom and dad felt that sports and activities made a child well rounded and enhanced their social skills. My brothers and I always participated in several extra-curricular activities and my parents were always right there with us. Though I had working parents and have never experienced the luxury of a stay at home mom, I have always felt like my parents were right there, never more than a phone call or a few minutes drive away from me. My dad worked two jobs for most of my childhood life, but my mom and dad rarely missed a basketball or football game, concert, dance recital, bowling tournament, fashion show, school program, or anything else that we participated in. My parents are responsible for instilling within me, an unwavering confidence that has sustained me throughout my life. They are both responsible for the successful woman I am today. When the world rejected me, I always knew that if I could get home, everything would be alright because in my home, we were Watsons and we were all adored superstars!

Sports and the performing arts were areas of interest for me as far back I can remember. I have been singing and dancing since I was old enough to walk and talk. I started bowling, swimming and playing basketball at the age of 4. I loved to dance as a little girl. If there was a dance contest, you better believe I was front and center ready to get down. Most times, I came out victorious winning whatever prize they had for the best dancer. I also took ballet, modern and jazz dance lessons and fell in love with all three. I excelled in the performing arts and in sports, winning several trophies and awards for achievements in athletics, including an award for most outstanding middle school athlete when I was in the 8th grade. I also loved being in front of an audience speaking.   If there was a leading role or a speaking part in a school program, most times, I would be chosen for it. I was a class officer for all four years in high school. I was Vice President for two years and Treasurer for two years. I read the morning announcements over the PA system and was the coordinator of several school programs/shows. I was also the point guard for my high school's basketball team and I was team captain my senior year. I won the award for MVP both my freshman year in high school and my senior year as well.

But it was during my years as a member of the Woodlawn Middle School Gospel choir that my life changed forever. In the 7th grade, I gave my life to Christ and was born again after my choir director shared the prayer of salvation with us. Once I accepted Jesus as my Lord and Savior, I began to think differently. He was now my motivation and the love of my life. I remember being very excited about being saved and sharing the good news of Jesus Christ with others often. I carried this spirit with me to high school and sang with the Woodlawn High School Gospel Choir as well. That choir

THE *Queens* LEGACY

and my membership at New Psalmist Baptist Church in Baltimore, Maryland, grew me from a babe in Christ, into a strong young woman of God.

I graduated from Woodlawn High School and went on to graduate from Hampton University with a Bachelor's Degree in Sociology. At Hampton, I became friends with a very special group of girls during my freshman year and we are still close friends today. I reconnected with my love for dance while I was at Hampton, dancing with the Marching Band's dance line called "Ebony Fire". I went on to become Captain of the group my senior year. I was truly in love with Ebony Fire. It is one of my greatest college memories.

After graduating from college, I eventually found my way back to Baltimore and began working for an advocacy program for youth. I was employed as a case manager working with youth in some of the most crime and drug invested communities in Baltimore. I loved that job and I loved those kids! I felt blessed to be able to do such important work and my life felt meaningful during those years. I excelled there also. After being employed for a little less than a year, I was promoted to supervisor and was responsible for training and managing a team of seven case managers. I love being a supervisor and my staff and I were very close. During those years, I learned that I loved mentoring adults as much as I did children!

In 1995, I met US Congressman Kweisi Mfume at a festival in Baltimore. I became a close acquaintance of Mr. Mfume's during my teenage years while working with my mentor, Mrs. Pinnie Ross. She was a teen pageant director and charm/etiquette teacher. I was her assistant. She was also a mother figure to Mr. Mfume and he was her pageant MC when I first met him. He was the new CEO of the NAACP. Shortly after reconnecting, Mr. Mfume hired me as the National Director of the NAACP Back-to-School Stay-In School Program. It was the greatest job I ever had. I began speaking all over the country, conducting workshops and seminars, and meeting very powerful, influential people. Becoming nationally recognized as a powerful speaker all began with that job and I am so grateful to Mr. Mfume for the opportunity.

I was later accepted into the Masters of Divinity Program at Howard University and became a student there. Working, attending classes and working out at a local gym became my daily routine. In September of 1997, I met Stacey Carver, the man who later became my husband. After talking with him for a few minutes, I realized that I had seen him before, performing at a comedy club. He was a stand-up comedian. I quoted one of his jokes to him and he was so very excited. Today he will tell you that hearing me quote his joke, made him love me instantly! Two years later, we got married, September 6, 1999. We have been married for almost 10 years and have three amazing children, Stacey Jr., eight years old, Austin, seven and Aarin-Christina who is 5.

Supportive, fun, and loyal, my husband is the most amazing man I have ever met. Shortly after we began dating, we talked about all that we had in common. After we were engaged, we discussed the possibility of starting a business together after marriage. I was a model, dancer, trainer and coach, and he was an actor and comedian. After we were married, we started a company that booked comedians for all occasions. It was called Peanutz Entertainment. Shortly after we started the business, Stacey began to tell me that he thought I was far too talented to be working for someone else. He believed that I could use my skills as a dancer, model and mentor to girls to expand our business. I had been doing small fashion shows with my mother who was a women's clothing distributor and I, and a friend, started a small dance company that performed for weddings, church services, and parties. My mom named my modeling troop Studio "A" Models. People were constantly asking me to teach dance and modeling classes. Stacey encouraged me to give the people what they were asking for and he eventually convinced me to open what is known today as Studio "A" Modeling Etiquette and Dance Academy. Five years ago, we added a not for profit component called the Studio "A" Foundation. Through the foundation we have awarded more than $50,000 in scholarships to deserving students.

A few years after opening the studio, I became increasingly occupied with the business. Again, Stacey encouraged me to take the business to the next level by quitting my job and becoming a full time entrepreneur, focusing all of my energy on the studio. That was the best decision I ever made. Stacey's belief in me and my abilities amazed me. He is my blessing from God and I am a better woman because of his support and love. With each passing year my numbers grew and my services were not only in high demand, but I was being featured in local newspapers and on local television shows for my work with girls through my studio. In 2004, I appeared as a guest on the Oprah Winfrey Show after writing in to her staff. I had already appeared on the Today Show while working at the NAACP. Not long after my appearance on Oprah, I was featured on Maryland Public Television and other local station highlighting my work with youth.

In 2006, I was crowned Mrs. Maryland United States and was voted Mrs. Congeniality at the Mrs. United States Pageant. In 2007, I was crowned Mrs. Maryland America and placed among the Top 10 Finalist at the 2008 Mrs. America Pageant. I am also a former professional cheerleader for the NFL

THE *Queens'* LEGACY

Baltimore Ravens, a very successful pageant coach and a highly sought after speaker/workshop facilitator. I am humbled and honored to be chosen by God to speak a message of help, hope, and healing to all that are willing to listen. I give him all of the glory for my many gifts and talents and my prayer is that when others see me, they would give God the glory for the great things he has done both in me and through me.

Affectionately known as "Mrs. A", Adrienne Watson Carver is a "Super Woman"! This wife and mother is a gifted dancer, teacher, model, life coach, personal/professional development trainer, and motivational speaker/workshop facilitator. She is the Owner and Executive Director of Studio "A" Modeling, Etiquette and Dance Academy and the Founder of the Studio "A" Foundation Scholarship Cotillion Program in Randallstown, MD. She is a graduate of Hampton University where she earned her Bachelor's Degree in Sociology. She has also done graduate work in the Masters of Divinity Program at Howard University. Also a former National Director of the NAACP Stay-In-School Program, and Baltimore County Public School teacher, her passion lies with the development of America's youth. Contact Adrienne by e-mail at astudio@aol.com or visit her website at www.adriennecarver.com.

CHAPTER 2

I Am Because Of The "I AM"

AKILAH TUTT

Inner confidence, absent of arrogance, was an emotion I learned through the teasing of my two older, caramel colored siblings.

It was Friday, the 29th of June, when I entered the world from a Queen's womb. As an asthmatic infant, fighting for my life, my mother created a subliminal shield of strength that she believed I needed to endure the upcoming trials of my life. As I do not take my presence on earth for granted, I show reverence to the Most High in everything I do. By calling my soul and not my name, the Most High has given me the ability to carry out my purpose, which will naturally be completed through the observance of my passions.

My life's passions found me early. I dance. I write. I serve. I am the youngest of three, a graduate of Clark Atlanta University and an active member of my St. Stephen Christian Methodist Episcopal Church family. My message for young girls is "Nurture your soul as if it were your unseen oasis, allowing access to those that will handle it with unconditional love exactly the way you would."

Inner confidence, absent of arrogance, was an emotion I learned through the teasing of my two older, caramel colored siblings. They, along with a young school mate, made it clear that my chocolate skin was a darker hue

than theirs. I remember being outside the house one sunny afternoon, wishing I had never been born. These self-destructive emotions would visit several times throughout my adolescence and into my young adult lifetime.

Upon acceptance into Clark Atlanta University, I was beyond excited. Having spent the last four years committing myself to study, participation in extracurricular activities and holding leadership roles in numerous clubs and organizations while in high school, I had achieved my goal and was overjoyed at the opportunity to leave California. Without exception, in addition to the joy of the accomplishment, there came challenges. My mother and I began to argue. We had differing opinions about some of the roughest moments of our relationship. The argument was so heavy that I vowed that I would move away from California and never come back. When my family dropped me off in Atlanta, I was angry and hurt by the words the two of us had exchanged. I remember thinking, "Don't even cry!" Perhaps this was a situation that God allowed to make us realize the depth of each other's significance in one another's lives years later as I went through my own medical challenges.

Throughout my college years, I received the full benefits of attending an HBCU (Historically Black College or University). I followed the path of such greats as James Weldon Johnson, Ralph Abernathy, and Spike Lee. I had the privilege of being Hall Council President in the Homecoming Freshmen Hall Step Show. I was a dancer in a play, was on the basketball dance team, was accepted and pledged a sorority. I even dated a well-known spoken word artist on campus. Amid these activities, I was a familiar face around the campus, yet silent behind the mask of a constant social calendar of interactions. I distinctly remember crying on the steps of the dorm while a freshman, uncertain how I would afford the tuition to continue my education.

I remember working fifty, sometimes sixty hours, a week during the summer and watching my paychecks be consumed by the Student Accounts Office. Don't misunderstand. There were happy times too. The positive side included the fact that my relationship with my mother strengthened as the months and years passed. We put our mind and our money toward achieving the goal of my graduating from college. We connected through the trials and triumphs I experienced with my college sweetheart. The moments he and I shared were a perfect example of a solid relationship. The personalized poems, flowers, and sweets; we were the ideal wholesome and healthy young couple. However, the times I remember most were the Friday nights when I would lock myself in my room, lay across my bed and sleep. The course load and extracurricular activities were exhausting.

28

Major challenges surfaced after graduation. After giving my all, digging deeper within myself to give more, my college sweetheart and I decided it would be best to end our exclusive relationship. I was emotionally depleted. So much so that I would call my mentor, Katrina Ferguson, just to hear her inspirational voicemail, "If your 'whys' are big enough, the 'hows' will take care of themselves." This situation left me confused and looking for reality; wondering the past four years meant. Just as a tethered rope slowly unravels, I unraveled at each realization that the fantasy I had counted on as a little girl had deteriorated. My dreams were the same as so many other young women, to attend college, find my husband, embark upon a solid career and start a family. This dream lay in my subconscious mind as a distant dimension, slowly facing extinction. At odds about what to do next, I chose to move to Florida with a cousin who had often mentioned an opportunity at the United Way where she worked in Miami. Knowing that the Most High had not created me to be desperate, I felt I had no other choice than to move there to pursue my first post-college position with a non-profit organization.

After discussing this opportunity with my mother, who at the time still lived in Fairfield, California, she helped me to move across the country, including driving her car, packed to the ceiling with my belongings. The minute we got to Miami, my mother and I fell in love with the palm trees and tropical breezes. The disempowering emotions of insignificance and disappointment faded as we began to focus on my future with the United Way and living with my older cousin. My mother returned to California, excited about the possibilities for her baby girl, me.

Shortly after getting settled in Miami, I received word that my mother had been diagnosed with degenerative arthritis, would need to use a cane to walk and was taking narcotics. I was hurt and confused. I failed to understand how the woman I considered health conscious, happy, and my solid rock could be going through such pain and emotional turmoil. The passion for what I was doing in Florida waned. I missed my mama in the worst way. I knew I needed to move back to California, but also knew that I could not live with my immediate family for fear of slipping back into the zone of lack of motivation and complacency.

At the completion of my program, I moved back to California. Not into my parent's home, but into a duplex about twenty miles away. This created a slight distance between me and the toxic situation that I abandoned only four years ago. I felt it was the best thing for me to do under the circumstances.

Throughout all of this time, I secretly and silently kept my college sweetheart as a possibility for my future. That expectation was terminated when I asked to visit him and he told me no; he was intimately involved with someone else. The remnants of what I had hoped for and dreamed of were completely crushed. This reinforced my distorted opinion of men and, as a result, my relationship with my own father was strained.

My father was considered a "workaholic." His focus was on the dollar and providing for his family. While this can be appreciated and admired, it became a source of bitterness as frequently he was absent as a father figure and part of our family. The times that could have been shared as a family were interrupted by trips to casinos, his siblings, and isolated moments in his bedroom listening to personal development audio tapes. These things, although they went on for years, became apparent to me as I matured and were magnified in my mind after the breakup of my three year relationship.

The lack of communication about my father's actions and the resulting emotional state of the family were too much for me to handle, along with the demands of my work at non-profit operation. This soon led to an emotional breakdown. During this chapter of my life, I left my job after speaking my mind, all of it, to the executive director of the non-profit where I worked. Later I confronted my father about what I held inside for so many years. Words during this time period were shared under a cloak of bitterness and overdue tension. It was a time of detoxification and mental cleansing; getting many of the stifled observations off my chest.

This period in my life was one of pain, mixed with a self promotion, thereby freeing me from the shackles of silence that kept me from living up to my true potential. How absolutely amazing it is when the Most High weaves someone into the fabric of your life to pull you into the individual you were ultimately called to be. As I participated in 40 days of conference calls designed to help the listeners recognize their destiny and live on purpose, Ms. Ferguson repeatedly assured me of my self-worth, who I was created to represent, and what I was and wasn't to tolerate as a Queen destined for excellence. After attending her Total Woman Workshop© in Maryland, I regained a sense of awareness for myself and it is of those principles that I am reminded each day as I inspire my Daisy Girl Scouts, the children at school and the youth at church.

I enjoy immensely my career in Special Education. It baffles me how society mistreats people with disabilities. What is even more shocking is how children mistreat each other based on their differences. How unfair and unfortunate, especially since the Most High designed everyone. It is our responsibility to treat each other with love and respect.

To date, I am pleased to say that I have committed my life to the workings of Yeshua by being the best young lady I can be and by giving back to young girls through the Praise Dance Ministry at St. Stephen Christian Methodist Episcopal Church. It is a huge responsibility to encourage my dancers: "Nurture your soul as if it were your unseen oasis; allowing access to those that will handle it with unconditional love exactly the way you would." Youth today are faced with so many pressures and negative images created by the media. We need to help them understand that God comes first, then self, then school. Girls should not feel the need to have a boy to determine their self-worth. Because of my mother, Ms. Ferguson, and my relationship with the Most High, I now recognize my self-worth and share that wisdom with others.

Akilah Tutt is a Speech Communications graduate of Clark Atlanta University currently works in Fairfield, California in Special Education. Akilah loves dance and spearheads the Teen Praise Dance Ministry at her church, ministers in Children's Church and works with the Girl Scouts. Akilah can be reached by telephone at 888-332-8190 or by e-mail at akilahtutt@yahoo.com

CHAPTER 3

It Was Inevitable!

ALISHA STEWART

Isaiah 49:1 ...The LORD hath called me from the womb; from the bowels of my mother hath he made mention of my name

'Oh my goodness! What is that black mark on my baby's head?' screamed my mother during my birth.

'Maybe it came from all those blackberries you ate,' said my grandma.

'No', said my father, 'it is a mark of greatness.'

It was Christmas Day back in 1971 and I was five years old:

'ALISHAAAA...you march right back down to Sheila's house and get that baby doll! Why on earth would you give that doll away?' said my mother.

'Because, she liked the doll', I said.

'I just bought you that doll for Christmas, after you begged me for it... What on earth were you thinking?!'

THE *Queens'* LEGACY

'Mommy, I gave her the doll because I wanted her to like me; I wanted her to be my friend.'

I remember that scolding like it was yesterday. My mother always fussed at me because I was constantly giving my toys and clothes away. If somebody wanted it, I gave it to them, and my response consistently remained the same..."I just wanted them to like me."

At a really young age, I felt an extreme need to be liked and accepted by people. During my childhood, kids used to make fun of me, calling me "bucked-toothed", "ugly," "nappy head," or "the girl with the black mark." Let's face it...kids can be unkind and will say exactly what it is on their minds! All I knew at the time was if I wanted to avoid the name calling, I would try my best to do whatever it took to get them to like me...even if it meant giving away everything I owned. In reality, on the inside, my esteem was slowly dying because of the pain of what others thought of me. I just wanted to be accepted.

The Gift of Dance

Around the time I was two years old, my mother and father watched the Ed Sullivan variety show on Sunday evenings. Often, I would get up in front of the television and mimic the singers and dancers; but mainly the dancers. One particular night, my mother watched me as I moved with the group of ballerinas' choreography as they performed on the show – she looked at me with astonishment as I danced in sync and coordination with the ballerinas! That was when my mother realized my natural-born gift for dancing.

My mother enrolled me in the Art Linkletter dance school at the age of 3. Tap was my favorite: "Heel, toe, 1, 2, 3... Heel toe, 1, 2, 3... Shuffle, hop, step... Shuffle, hop, step..."

'Look Mommy, see what I learned today!' as I tapped on the apartment's balcony after my first day of dance class.

Because my mother was so excited, all I wanted to do for the rest of the day was stay on the balcony and practice those dance steps. Throughout my early childhood years, the kids constantly reminded me of my dreadful appearance, so all I had to hold on to was my dance.

My Role Model

My brother, Scot, played football and basketball with a local boys club. He became really popular because he was extremely talented in both sports. People admired him because of his natural athletic abilities and many assumed he would become a professional athlete. During this time, I realized a chance of being accepted and popular, so I joined the boy's club cheerleading squad. Often, I would dream about being a professional cheerleader...especially after seeing the Dallas Cowboy Cheerleaders' movie repeatedly. Throughout my youthful years, cheerleading became my world and my way of gaining self-esteem as well as the respect of others. Yet and still, feeling the punches of what others thought of me, I just kept the dream to cheer professionally to myself – hidden within.

False Perception of Acceptance

During high school I was extremely popular. I cheered throughout my high school years and was captain of the varsity squad my senior year. I enjoyed these times the most because people seemed to like me despite what others perceived as my flaws. I thought I was on top of the world! After graduating from high school in 1984, I attended Howard University and took a break from cheerleading. One afternoon, I was spending time with friends watching a major NFL football game on TV. And at some point during the game, they showed the cheerleaders performing in the end zone of the field. I remember as I was watching them perform, I said out loud and full of excitement "Someday I am going to be down on that field, doing exactly what they are doing!" And everybody in the room must have thought that was the most ridiculous statement because they laughed and made fun of me that entire afternoon. Needless to say, that was a long second half. I was really broken in my entire being that night about what my friends thought of me. It took me back to the place where I was as a child with no self worth. I cried and cried to the LORD to remove the pain...and instantly I experienced a major life transformation! As I reflected on what happened earlier that day, seemingly out of nowhere, a sudden Presence of strength and comfort consumed me. I decided to go for it..."I'm going to try out to become a professional cheerleader!"

Deliverance and Healing

Psalms 18:1-3

I will love thee, O LORD, my strength. The LORD is my rock, and my fortress, and my deliverer; my God, my strength, in whom I will trust; my buckler, and

the horn of my salvation, and my high tower. I will call upon the LORD, who is worthy to be praised: so shall I be saved from mine enemies.

I dropped out of Howard University during my junior year of college to pursue my dream as a professional cheerleader. I remember my parents asking, "Well, what about finishing college and getting your degree?" I promised them I would go back to finish school. The only people who knew about my pursuit were my immediate family members...my mother, father, brother and my boss. March 1989, I headed towards the tryout facility with inner strength and motivated by the voices of laughter. The arena was filled with approximately 1,500 potential cheerleaders. About 700 girls were eliminated that first day. The only thing I was focused on was the dream that was conceived inside of me. I did not know at that time God was delivering and healing me of my pain. I began to discover the beauty within me instead of dwelling on outward appearance. For some reason, gaining acceptance or being liked by others was no longer my concern. I endured three weeks, five days per week, and three hours per night of strenuous tryouts and lasted through two additional cuts. On the last day of tryouts, I was exhausted, but I refused to succumb to the emotional and physical pain that consumed me and it was overtaken by the inner strength of my dream. That day I became a member of the 1989 Washington Redskinettes.

I was blessed to be a part of a winning team for 3 consecutive years of cheering. The first year, the team made the playoffs, my second year they won the Super Bowl, and my final year on the squad they played in the American Pro Bowl game in London. What an awesome experience in such a short amount of time! The capstone to the entire experience was receiving honors as the first recipient of the prestigious Cheerleader's Director's Award during my last year on the squad. I am convinced it was all in God's plan for my life and in His perfect timing.

In remembering, the day everybody in the room laughed and made fun of me when I said "Someday I am going to be down on that field, doing exactly what they are doing!", a day I thought was one of the most humiliating times of my life, it actually turned out to be the one of greatest things that ever happened to me. The desire to dance was evident at birth as witnessed by my mother when I was two and manifested itself as a professional cheerleader despite enduring years of low self-esteem. It was inevitable.

A Call to Purpose

Although God blessed me to fulfill my childhood dream of becoming a professional cheerleader, there was more in me than just that dream come true.

Pastor Lucius Ross of Ward's United Methodist Church asked me about my dominant gifts on the same day I joined the church. I told him "I have a background in accounting and dance." He said, "Praise the LORD! I have been praying to God for a leader over the dance ministry!" And right then and there he laid hands on me and declared that a dance ministry would be birthed through me. And in 1997, I yielded to the call of being a Minister of Dance. I became the Director for both the Finance and Dance Ministries for five straight years.

Understanding and Fulfilling My Purpose

Let the people praise thee, O God; let all the people praise thee. (Psalm 67:3)

Through my encounters with experienced dance ministry leaders, they stress the importance of certain physical characteristics and mental stability that would distract the congregation from praise and worship. My dance ministry's criteria allowed anyone who had a willing heart to be a part of the ministry regardless of race, age, weight or insecurities such as low self-esteem. During this season, the dance ministry became the largest ministry in the church.

There was a Children's Dance Ministry, which included boys and girls from ages 3 to17. There were also adult ministries for men and women ranging from the age of 18 to senior citizens. The church family had a sense of freedom and a love for the ministry of dance. God would often show Himself strong through these vessels, healing and delivering His people while breaking yokes within our church doors and throughout the community. It was an awesome work of God!

While, I no longer attend Ward's church, that ministry lives on and I praise and give honor to God for His anointing and kindness in blessing me with that ministry. It was the foundation to my journey of purpose.

Revitalization

Ephesians 3:19-20

THE *Queens'* LEGACY

And to know the love of Christ, which passeth knowledge, that ye might be filled with all the fullness of God. Now unto him that is able to do exceeding abundantly above all that we ask or think, according to the power that worketh in us

My desire is to share with the world that there is hope and you, too, can overcome insecurities such as low self-esteem, lack of confidence or the need for acceptance while fulfilling God's purpose and plan for your life. I was truly blessed with the experience of living my dream as a professional cheerleader; however, the essence of my transformation was the discovery of self-love. All the love I wanted to receive became what I wanted to give. My impassioned and empowering call is to revitalize others to live their dreams. Everyone has a dream they can dance to. Dance your dance!

As founder and president of Alternative Resource Management Solutions (ARMS) – an Accounting and Information Technology Firm – Alisha Stewart leads the firm's management consulting business, which provides a broad range of services for Outsourced Accounting, Project Management Support, Risk Management and IT Security Assessments. Alisha earned her BS degree in Accounting. She has over 20 years of combined public and private accounting experience with small- to medium-sized businesses, including emerging and fast-growing companies, non-profit organizations as well as sole proprietors.

Alisha is also the founder of Vision Keys, a leadership and motivational company on the cutting edge of providing practical tools and information which inspire, teach, and empower individuals to live their best. Her passion is to empower others to believe they can live their dreams and achieve true victory in their lives.

A former NFL Cheerleader, Alisha has the spirited heart of a dancer. She is a member of Evangel Cathedral in Upper Marlboro, MD and she enjoys reading, swimming, and spending time with family and friends.

For more information or to contact Alisha, she may be reached via email at stewarta1@verizon.net.

CHAPTER 4

Talk To The Master And Stand Still

BEAVETTE LONEY

"The things we see now are here today, gone tomorrow. But the things we can't see now will last forever." 2 Corinthians 4:16 MSG

Raised in a Christian family, it has been instilled in me to persevere and give during oppositional times. I spent the majority of my life in the inner city where, many times, the living conditions outside our home were not as pleasant and peaceful as it was inside of our home. And I watched as my Grandmother – Emmie Lee Moore – aggressively worked, with the support of her husband, toward answering the cry of the needs in our communities. She involved herself with committees and led many neighborhood events.

She also took on numerous responsibilities, one of which consisted of being President of a well-known local club called the Friendly Helping Hands Club, for many years. I can remember the club members gathering in her home for meetings; however, my most memorable moments were during the holidays. This was the time when I could participate in their fellowship by folding clothes, separating food and preparing boxes for families. The Friendly Helping Hands Club sponsored many functions and events from church services and clothes drives, to visiting local mental health hospitals. I don't remember a moment when my grandmother did not do something to better the lives of others, even if it meant transferring funds from her household to theirs. And through it all, my grandparents – especially my

grandmother – managed to provide noteworthy service to the city of Baltimore and beyond.

Until her passing in 2006 at the seasoned age of 96, she remained active in the community and the lives of many. Never forgetting that her family came first, her acts of loving kindness toward us were a constant reminder that besides God, we were indeed "top priority" in her life.

My motivating fuel today, is the life experiences shared with me by my grandmother and mother. Some of which I watched with my own eyes. And others are conversations I recall as they reflected on their past. It amazed me the strength that they obtained to conquer the tasks before them. I wish I could sit down face to face with you to share each life-enriching event. However, I will share a little bit of one particular conversation regarding the birth of my mother, Beulah Horne.

After several successful pregnancies, each ending in the death of the babies shortly after their birth, my mother is the only surviving child and the final birth to my grandparents. That alone was encouraging to me! I thought to myself "would I have given up after the second child, not wanting to endure the pain of loss and disappointment?" or would I have taken the stance of my grandmother? "God, I have faith that you have heard my cry and will answer my prayers, granting me the desires of my heart. My faith shall not be moved by what I see!" She never said those exact words to me, but I can only imagine the strength, faith and authority it would take to continue in spite of so much disappointment and frustration.

I also reflect on the moments when time appeared to stand still, and there was no one in the room but my grandmother and I. The wisdom she shared and the knowledge she poured into me always centered around these words, "Talk to the Master and stand still." It took me a while to grasp the revelation of standing still. As simple as it may sound, this is a charge that takes TOTAL trust in the Lord and the power of His word.

Going through my own battles and storms helped me to realize what inner strength really is. In my life, it not only consists of the ability to "steal away" (as the elder folks would say) to refocus, but to believe in *myself*, trusting the power and abilities that God placed in *me* to fulfill His purpose for my life. Knowing the work He has begun, that shall He also complete.

It is understanding that God has placed in you the capability to achieve greatness, at whatever the cost – no matter what the goal or God-given desire may be. Whether, it is to be the first in your family to obtain a high

40

school diploma, ranging up to being the first to break barriers in your particular field or industry. Whatever the desire, God has fully equipped us for the lifelong task ahead. He has not only placed the desire within us but, he has already strategically planned every event and detail of our lives AND He has given us a passion to see that vision come to fruition.

By the age of 16, I was a mom to a beautiful baby boy. Needless to say, becoming a mother at the age of 16 was not so "beautiful" to everyone that knew me and my family. Not only did I have to endure the countless remarks of "you know better" from outsiders who did not have a clue to the roads that lead me to that point in my life, but now with immense responsibility lying in my arms, my life changed completely. [Although, I felt like I was a mother to my brother, who is two years younger, so being a responsible person was not a difficult undertaking for me.]

I must admit that parenthood to me is akin to making marriage vows. 'Til death, do you part! LOL (for those who do not send text messages or email, this means "Laugh Out Loud"). Once you become a parent, you are committed to the well-being of this person until one of you leaves this earth. And truthfully speaking beyond that, we are to leave an inheritance for our seeds' seed. "A solemn sacrifice," I tell my children, "you must make if you have plans of becoming a parent." This is what my mother taught me. I watched as she put her aspirations "on the back burner," so to speak, for my brother and me. And now she makes sacrifices for my children.

My mother is my prime exemplar of a devoted daughter, wife, mother, grandmother, godmother, aunt, and friend. All of my life, all I have seen is her commitment to God and her family. Her devotion towards my Dad (whom she has been with since the sixth grade!) is an example that I have applied to every area of my life. It has proven to me that love is a commitment. That love makes positive choices followed by the right actions that should be applied, regardless of what your emotions say you should or should not do. From her, I have learned so much!

She has educated me on how to "be a lady" at all times, to maintain a posture of dignity no matter what, to find joy in life when all conflict breaks loose, to bake cookies and cakes (smile), to sing my way through good and tough times, to live my dreams and to inscribe them with heartfelt passion. All this and more, I started learning during my teen parent years, and she still pours into me daily.

I know from my own experience that "all things work together for the good of those that love Christ Jesus and are called according to his purpose."

THE *Queens* LEGACY

Everything that I have endured has produced glory that is beyond my most supreme imagination. If anyone would have told me that the child I carried would be a mighty instrument used of God to preach the gospel, I might have believed them but then I would have questioned, "Why me, and why this way?" Being a mother is one of my greatest joys and accomplishments...and thanks to my mother, who is such a divine example, I love it!!!

I have no complaints about my life thus, far. I have many questions from time to time...as I am sure we all do. These words help to keep my life in perspective: "For I reckon that the sufferings of this present time are not worthy to be compared with the glory which shall be revealed in us." As I reflect back on the places I have been, the people I have met, and things I have accomplished, I have no regrets, because each and every aspect of my life has equipped me for where I am today as well as where I am going.

This is the same for you. There are times when we just cannot understand the "who", "what", "when", "why" and "hows" of our life. I rest assured, knowing that God who is the Author and Finisher of our faith shall finish the work He has begun. He will never leave me nor forsake me! I learned this during one of the most tragic times in my life.

In 1996, I married my best friend and out of this union a little girl was birthed. Two years, three weeks and four days later, I lost my best friend, my husband, and the love of my life; and my children lost their father to a violent street crime. I was left a young widow with two small children to raise. The emotional, physical and financial strain became too much for me to bear . . . or so I thought. What do you do when all that you have now appears to be gone in the twinkle of an eye? With no time to prepare; no place to run and hide; what do you do when you must confront the thing that you may have feared the most and you haven't a clue what the next step would be, could be or even should be? This is where I stood.

With the support of close friends and family sheltering me, I ran to the arms of my Master and stood still. Through His Spirit, I gained tenacity to roll up my sleeves and put my hand to the plow and not look back. I didn't say I lost the memories associated with the situation at hand or the person which the circumstance surrounded. However, in the course of this life altering incident I learned that I had Kingdom building to do. I had a charge to keep and God to glorify. I had a family to raise and life was not going to stand still and wait for me to catch up. During this time of turbulence, I had to make a choice. Isaiah 54:6 met me right at my front door: "for the Lord has called you like a woman forsaken and grieved in spirit, like a youthful wife when you were refused" says your God.

At the time, it appeared that I would not be able to overcome such a tragic experience. It was a difficult season to endure. Because of some of the trials I faced, I began to make preparation in every area of my life. I prepared for death in every way imaginable. I secured wills, obtained a grave plot with my name on it, prepared family members with instructions and so forth. Now, to you, it may sound as if I was preparing to take my life. That was never a thought.

Little did I know what was really taking place was what Paul said in Philippians 4:8, " I count all things loss for the excellence of the knowledge of Christ Jesus my Lord, for whom I have suffered the loss of all things, and count them as rubbish that I may gain Christ." I had begun to break ties with what I thought brought me joy and comfort; giving up my life as I knew it, to pick up my cross and follow the Lord. Laying hold of the circumstances at hand and not allowing the circumstances to lay hold of me. I had to fight like never before during this time and the word of God was my only weapon – and a MIGHTY awesome weapon, at that!

When I had to fight for peace of mind and my sanity, His Word is what kept me in perfect peace. When I had to fight to defend my character during this season, it reminded me that every tongue that rose up against me in judgment would be condemned. When I had to fight to keep food on the table and a roof over our heads, the Word and Spirit of God reminded me to "take no thought for tomorrow for tomorrow has cares of its own."

As a child I was never a bully. I enjoyed staying to myself, but once I was pushed to my limit I could definitely handle my own. Being the oldest child and the only girl, I found myself fighting boys to defend my brother. This was not a problem at all. Once I got revved up there was no stopping me! Again, even in those times I was being molded into the type of character I would need today. No fear...tenacity. I hear people say "God never wastes a painful experience." Everything that we have already endured in life and those things we have yet to endure, are all for a greater purpose and a broader picture than what is taking place at that moment.

Even the things that we can sometimes take for granted and sometimes overlook, the most infinitesimal thing...it is an important detail to God. Life is *not* just what you make it, but it is what God has already ordained it to be! You just have to be determined to walk it out. Remember, "There is a way

that seems right to a man, but its end is the way of death." Follow the Master Plan!

I now carry the baton that my grandmother passed to me and my family, leaving a legacy to be helpers one to another, to persevere and still give during oppositional times. Join me in saying, "We're not giving up!" How could we? Even when, on the outside, it looks like things are falling apart on us, on the inside, where God is making new life, not a day goes by without his unfolding grace. These hard times are small potatoes compared to the coming good times – the lavish celebration prepared for us. There's far more here than meets the eye. "The things we see now are here today, gone tomorrow. But the things we can't see now will last forever." 2 Corinthians 4:16 MSG

Continue to stand fast, being unmovable! Your eyes have not seen, your ears have not heard, nor has it been perceived in the heart of man the entire plan that God has in store for *YOU*. Be transparent; allow your life to be an instrument of praise unto God. Fulfill your purpose; leave this earth an empty vessel, having given your all.

Thank you to all the Queens that have made and continue to make deposits in my life. Mere words could never express my sincere gratitude to you all!

Teenage mothers, single parents, families of individuals lost due to street violence, young widows, the homeless and the disenfranchised...Beavette H. Loney's experiences have served to increase her sensitivity to such individuals.

KINGDOM LIVING, INC. is a non-profit, faith-based organization whose overall goal is to provide a comprehensive program of education and services designed to effectively promote the stabilization and social/economic advancement of the destitute and the communities in which they reside. To Beavette, KINGDOM LIVING, INC. is not just a non-profit organization committed to Restoring Lives and Rebuilding Communities, it is a ministry.

Beavette H. Loney is a native of Baltimore City. She presently resides in Baltimore with her children, Brandon and Bryonna. Evangelist Loney comes from a family who has been and still is active in the Baltimore community and beyond. Their activities have greatly influenced her by instilling a desire to serve.

Beavette can be contacted by mail at Post Office Box 28246, Baltimore, MD 21234, by e-mail at Beavette@kingdomliving58.org or visit her website at www.KingdomLiving58.org.

CHAPTER 5

What Kind Of Legacy Are You Leaving?

BEN POVLOW

My journey was a long shot, but I truly believe that if I can do it, anyone can. And now I am the living legacy of my mother and I know she would be proud.

Warning: do not read this chapter unless you are prepared to be inspired, motivated and amazed by the words you are about to read. My name is Ben Povlow and what I'm about to share with you has never been shared before. I am going to let my guard down and do my very best to allow you to feel my pain, my joy, my struggles, my excitement and my gratitude for all the things that have taken place in my life.

There have been many Queens in my life, but the one whose legacy stands out above all others in my life is without a doubt the one of my mother – Lorraine Povlow. She was a strong, hard-working, fun-loving, beautiful single mother. The leadership she provided for our family was second to none. She didn't have much to work with but she always managed to make ends meet. She consistently overcame obstacles to provide for her family and because of the way that she lived her life; her legacy will live on forever.

I do not come from a big family, but growing up all the family that I do have lived under the same roof at one point. Let me explain... I grew up in a small Philadelphia row-home and my mother was the only one who had

a job. I have one brother – Jon – who is one year younger than me, and if our mom only had to take care of us it might not have been that bad. But that wasn't my mom's heart. If she "had", everyone "had"...so she provided for her mother, her brother and his 3 kids. I am sure you would agree that this situation could be overwhelming for anyone. I guess you are wondering why she was the only one who had a job. Well, that's a good question...I've wondered that same thing! Beside my grandmother who was really sick for a long time before she died, the rest of us were only kids.

We were always on welfare so we got food stamps, government cheese and powdered milk, but if we ever wanted anything outside of the basic necessities, we had to figure it out on our own. I started working at a young age. I had a paper route; I bagged groceries at the local supermarket; I cut people's grass; I used to set up bowling pins at a local VFW; and, in the wintertime, we shoveled snow and there were usually some other odd jobs. Thankfully, my mom always set a good example of work ethic.

My mom loved to have fun. I remember as a young child going with my mom to Philadelphia Phillies baseball games, Flyers hockey games, monster truck shows and all kinds of other live events. She loved music – especially Elvis...she was a huge Elvis fan! I remember coming downstairs every Saturday morning and hearing Elvis coming out of the radio as she cleaned the house. I believe that the highlight of her life was the time that she got to go to Graceland. I remember how excited she was when she came back from there. We never could afford to go anywhere and I don't know how she managed to pay for this trip but however she got to go...she deserved it. I believe that these experiences that I shared with my mother ignited passion in my life – for sports, music and live events in general.

You only have one mother and when she is gone you cannot get her back. Become friends with your mother. Get to know her. Spend time with her and learn as much about her as you possibly can. Be grateful for all the people that you have in your life; not only your mother, but your father, your brothers and sisters, aunts, uncles, cousins, grandparents, friends and neighbors. You never know which conversation with them will be your last.

I have a lot of experience dealing with death. It feels like I spent my entire life going to funerals. The more people you know, the more people you know that will die. And death is not an easy thing to deal with. I have been close to it many times, myself. Thank God I've lived long enough to change the way I think!

"Crazy people" are more common than you'd think...I used to be one of them! Growing up without a father figure and having a very lenient mother seemed to be the perfect combination for a kid to start getting in trouble at an early age. When I was growing up, I was the kid that your parents told you to stay away from. After I got expelled from my first school (in third grade), the school system evaluated me and determined that they wanted to place me in a school for "bad kids". My mother wouldn't allow it! She knew I was better than that. She fought with the school board and told them that she would take me out of school altogether if they made me go there. She pleaded her case...and won. Afterwards, we had a long talk about what she expected of me and she told me how important it was for me to receive an education. I was never a big fan of school, but I went and made the best of it to make my mother proud.

Growing up I had two groups of friends, ones who went to public school and always got in trouble and ones who went to Catholic school and were actually getting an education. I went to public school my entire life so when I approached my mom and asked her if I could go to Catholic school she was pretty excited. There were just two challenges, however: 1) I wasn't Catholic, and 2) we couldn't afford it. That's when my mom said to me, "you can use the Social Security checks that you receive from your father to pay your tuition." [I never knew my father and he died when I was 10.] So that's what I did. I became Catholic and started paying my own way through high school. This was much different than anything I had ever experienced before. The only times I had ever been to church was Easter, Christmas and funerals. Not to mention, it was an all-boys school which I was definitely not a fan of. Trying to adapt to this environment was a major challenge. I got involved in sports and that kept me occupied for the first year, but by my second year I started getting into trouble again. Halfway through my sophomore year my mom was having regular meetings with the Principal. They wanted to throw me out halfway through the year but once again she had convinced them to let me stay. They agreed to let me finish out the year but they would not allow me back for another.

Around this time, Mom started getting sick. She did not have the energy to put up with what she called my "shenanigans". She began cancer treatments and before long she was in the hospital fighting for her life. I understood that the trouble I was getting myself into was only making matters worse and I wished I could explain why I was doing the things I was doing but I don't have that answer. She did everything she could to give me a solid foundation and put me on the right track but I continued to be that defiant kid that just wanted to run my own program. Looking back on it, I

wish someone was there to slap me upside the head and knock some sense into me...but there wasn't.

After getting thrown out of that Catholic high school, I ended up going to the public high school which I would've gone to several years earlier...it was all downhill from there. Up to that point I had only gotten arrested for minor things like underage drinking and disorderly conduct. But I will never forget the day that I had to tell my mom that I had been arrested for a felony. I remember her reaction; it was almost as if she wasn't surprised. She just looked at me and said "you have to grow up and be a man about this, it's no one's fault but your own, there's nothing I can do to help you." When I went to court, the judge put a house arrest bracelet on my ankle and sentenced me to a court-appointed school. This was a blessing in disguise...I was forced to get an education. Because of the curriculum of this school system and the credits that I had from the Catholic school, I was able to graduate from this school at the age of 17 in only nine months with a high school diploma and a certificate in building maintenance.

On January 4, 1994, Lorraine Povlow passed away at the young age of 46 years old from cancer. We visited Mom at the hospital as much as possible, but it was never enough. I only wish my mother could have been alive to see me graduate...she would have been so proud. At the time she passed away, I was 16 and my brother was 15.

My life was heavily influenced by the legacy that my mother left behind, simply because of the way she lived her life. She battled with cancer for over a year, leading up to her death. But she made an impact on everyone that she had ever come in contact with. She had a strong will to help others and because of that, when she was sick and our family was in need, the outpouring of support was overwhelming.

She spent a lot of that time in the hospital while my brother and I mostly lived by ourselves. There were some brief periods of time where we lived with friends and their families, but for the most part we were at home trying to figure out how to survive on our own. The place where my mom worked took up collections of food and clothing and brought us these things on regular basis. Likewise, her friends and our neighbors did everything they could to help us out.

After graduating I still didn't learn my lesson though... I continued to hang out on the street corners and drink, smoke, fight, steal and along with the many other bad habits I had developed. This led to me getting arrested more and more. Two months before my 18th birthday, I was sentenced to juvenile life which meant that I was supposed to be incarcerated until I was 21. Because of my age and the length of my criminal record I only had two options, a maximum-security juvenile facility or a traveling program called Vision Quest which had a bad reputation for being a very tough place to go. After being interviewed by both programs I chose to go to Vision Quest. Even though it was kind of tough at times, when I look back on it I am very thankful that I had an opportunity go there because it changed my life. Up until this point of my life I had never really been outside the city of Philadelphia. This program gave me an opportunity to see how beautiful this country really is and it inspired me to want to go back to these places but more importantly, the grief and loss counseling that I received re-ignited the desire for me to make my mother proud.

It took many years before I got serious about becoming a better person and pursuing my goal to leave a legacy of my own. But when I was 28 years old, a gentleman introduced me to a business opportunity that opened my eyes to the concept of personal development, and it changed my way of thinking from that day forward.

I was never a big fan of traditional education but I became infatuated with personal development. I began to read inspirational and educational books on a regular basis. I began to educate myself about computers and the internet, how to build websites and all of the systems that were connected to it. When I became aware of how I could make money on the internet I became persistent. I started out making a few hundred dollars per month and then it became a few thousand and now I am in a position where I teach these very skills to anyone who desires to learn them through my training company – Eagle Eye Training. I now have an online learning center and I also conduct workshops all around the country.

My journey was a long shot, but I truly believe that if I can do it, anyone can. And now I am the living legacy of my mother and I know she would be proud.

THE *Queens* LEGACY

Ben Povlow has developed himself into a successful entrepreneur and a motivational speaker. He currently owns several internet marketing businesses, including his training company Eagle Eye Training where he conducts live seminars and has an online training site that teaches people the skills that are required to generate revenue using the internet. He is also a digital media consultant who provides video technology that takes personal and business communications to a new level. Ben believes that everyone has the ability to take control of their lives and create their own economy.

Are you are someone who desires to have an abundance of great things in your life? Would you like to be trained and mentored by someone who is committed to helping you achieve yours dreams and goals? You can contact Ben for more information and find out how he can help you take your life to the next level. Ben Povlow is also available for speaking engagements, workshops and personal coaching.

Contact Ben by telephone at 215-268-6981, by e-mail at
BenPovlow@HelloWorld.com or visit one of his websites
www.EagleEyeTraining.com, www.BuildWithVideo.com or
www.BenPovlow.com

CHAPTER 6

The Sky Is The Limit

BERNADA NICOLE BAKER

Your dreams are possible and your future is filled with limitless possibilities

Let me introduce you to a young woman who once strongly considered taking her life. That young woman was in despair and felt as if the world was against her. She had felt the intensity of the pain of life's disappointments and frustrations. That woman knew firsthand what it felt like to be all alone in this big world. That young woman is me.

This woman may have once been you or someone that you know. The situations of life sometimes weigh us down and leave us feeling that all hope is gone. However, as a result of my faith in God, I can honestly say that if it had not been for the Lord, on my side, I simply do not know where I would be. Now I realize that I am stronger and wiser because of the struggles and misfortunes that God blessed me to overcome. I am grateful that I was privileged to have queens in my life that believed in me and encouraged me along my journey. Although my mother succumbed to societal pressures, I am eternally grateful that she blessed me with the gift of life.

My grandmothers, Geneva King and Katie Baker, worked extremely hard to keep me grounded in my faith. It was their prayers in the midnight hours that helped me to stay focused on achieving my dreams.

My stepmother, Joann Baker, taught me the importance of being a young lady and not settling for anything less than the very best that life had to offer. My mentor, Deborah Harper, taught me the value of standing tall, being the best that I could be, and staying true to my identity.

My mentor, the late Sheila Ward, inspired me to rise above the challenges that were strategically designed to detour me from achieving my destiny. Another of my mentors, the late Marsha Herring, believed in me and supported my dreams to effect the changes that I hoped to see in the world. Marsha supported my vision to work in order to positively impact the lives of young girls across the nation.

My Godmother, the late Gina Burce, equipped me with the essential tools to become the bold and vibrant woman, wife, mother, daughter and child of God that I was predestined to be. The legacies of these women who have touched my life, continues to live on in my heart and in the work that I do to serve others. As a result of the influential seeds that those queens invested in my life, my primary mission has become to empower teenage girls and women to discover their purpose, maximize their potential, and to triumph over the obstacles of life.

"Some people say I have attitude - maybe I do . . . But I think you have to. You have to believe in yourself when no one else does - that makes you a winner right there." -- Venus Williams

It is important for you to believe in yourself. If you do not then it is impossible to expect others to believe in you. My legacy as a queen has been uniquely crafted by my fortitude and relentless tenacity to succeed through the trials and tribulations of my life.

"You're the only one who can make the difference . . . whatever your dream is."
--Earvin Magic Johnson

Given the circumstances of my childhood, the presumption was that I life would end up as a mascot for a failure campaign. My passion for living was derived from my relentless desire not to become a victim of drugs and alcohol or any sort of abuse. I had become fed up with seeing women who had become helpless to situations that were within their control.

"You gain strength, courage, and confidence by every experience in which you really stop to look fear in the face. You are able to say to yourself, 'I have lived through this horror. I can take the next thing that comes along.'... You must do the thing you think you cannot do." --Eleanor Roosevelt

As I reflect on my life's experiences, challenges, mistakes, and lessons learned, I reckon that even I could not have hired a more skilled architect to sketch the blue prints of my life. It is amazing how we, as humans, are so quick to "judge a book by its cover." Looking at me, you would never guess that I have personally experienced the traumatizing pain of my mother's out of control drug addiction, her being shot in the heart by drug dealers, domestic violence, homelessness, and many thoughts of suicide. I have had to fight, sweat, and shed buckets of tears. Through it all, I had to thank God for keeping me in my right mind. I believe in the dictum, "Life is only 10% of what happens to you and 90% of how you react to it." I was determined with all of my heart not to allow circumstances to determine the outcome of my future. One of the greatest lessons I have learned is that the trials of life only come to make you stronger and what does not kill you will only strengthen your faith.

"For I know the plans I have for you, says the Lord, plans to prosper you, to give you hope and a good future." (NIV, Jeremiah 29:11)

My experiences have taught me to recognize similarities between me and some of the mighty men and women of the Bible. Like Joseph, many of my life's experiences left me feeling alone, in a pit and betrayed by my family. Like David, I learned the hard way that God would fight all of my battles. Like Esther, my journey started with humble beginnings and now I have the opportunity to walk in my authority as a queen. The instructions that God gave Joshua to 'be strong and courageous' are the instructions that I live by. Joseph, David, Esther and Joshua are all exemplary role models who left transforming legacies in the Bible. Sure enough, everyone has a story to tell. The primary difference is how hard we are willing to work in order to triumph over the obstacles of life.

There is a very meaningful statement that I like much: "Excuses are tools of incompetence and anyone who uses them rarely accomplishes anything." God has a way of orchestrating his plan for our lives. Contrary to popular belief, even if I had the opportunity, I would not change anything about my life. It was through my trials and tribulations that I evolved into the spiritually grounded woman that I am today. I will not quit until I attain all of my dreams and goals. In my heart, I know that God has predestined a

path for me to follow that will result in my leaving a transforming legacy to my people.

Attitude determines altitude. When life gives you lemons, you must choose to make lemonade. We must teach others, especially our youth, not to become victims of their circumstances. Through it all, I have never felt sorry for myself as I always knew that brighter days were ahead. I am a midwife on a mission to help others give birth to the potential and passion that lies within them. I could have chosen to mask my hurt, pain, frustration and despair by giving up on my desire to succeed in life. However, I intend to be the agent of change that I desire to see in the world.

The most profound legacy that I would hope to impress upon you is to trust God, even when the road ahead is not clear. 'Anybody can do just about anything with himself that he really wants to and makes up his mind to do. We are capable of greater things than we realize.' My life demonstrates that dreams do come true. This is not what I heard about or someone else's story; this is my life's journey. You, too, have the potential to rise up against the circumstances of life and achieve your own hearts' desires. The time has come for you to begin to imprint your personal legacy on the world; therefore, I exhort you to begin to write your vision and make it plain. Put your plan into action today and refuse to allow procrastination or fear to prohibit you from being and doing all you were created to be and do. I encourage you to plan purposefully, prepare prayerfully, pursue persistently and proceed positively. Always remember, there are no limitations to what you can achieve, except the limitations within your own mind.

It is your responsibility to believe in you. It is your duty to know who you are and who God has called you to be. You must rise tall against the storms of life and forge ahead trusting God every step of the way. The late, great Rev. Dr. Martin Luther King Jr. said, "The true measure of a man is not how he behaves in moments of comfort and convenience but how he stands at times of controversy and challenges." The ultimate decision to overcome the challenges of life is up to you; either you can choose to be empowered to move to the next level of success or you can allow them to overtake you.

Your challenges will force you to step outside of your comfort zone and into the world of the uncertain or even the unknown. Challenges will cause you to dig deep down within and utilize the strengths and abilities that you would otherwise have never known existed. Challenges that create struggles are powerful step ladders; if they were not apparent, you would not appreciate the victory in the end. Challenges deliver a myriad of disappointments, heartaches and failures and, in the midst of it all, you have to keep moving towards fulfilling your dreams. It is important that you push beyond what you feel, fight back your tears and stand tall in the midst of adversity. It is the challenges of life that will force you to operate in your maximum potential.

I encourage you to understand that despite what you have been through and regardless of who has caused you pain, today is the day that you must decide to allow God to heal the wounds and wipe your tears away. After you have suffered for a while, He will strengthen, settle, establish and perfect you. Be encouraged at this very moment to embrace the fact that the disappointments, failures, mistakes and setbacks do not define your destiny. "If you want your life to be a magnificent story, then begin by realizing that you are the author and everyday you have the opportunity to write a new page."

Your dreams are possible and your future is filled with limitless possibilities. You have the potential to obtain every dream and vision that lies inside your heart and soul. You can make it and you have the power to move every mountain that attempts to stand in your way. You are gifted beyond measure, an extraordinary person and, most importantly, you are destined for greatness. Believe in your heart that the sky is the limit and there are no boundaries to the limit of success that you can achieve. To accomplish anything in life, you have to be passionate and aggressive. See what Thomas Edison has said, "If we all did the things we are capable of, we would astound ourselves." To get to a place that you have never been, you will have to do something you have never done. Eddie Robinson said, "The will to win, the desire to succeed, and the urge to reach your fullest potential are the keys that will unlock the door to personal excellence."

"The world is waiting for ordinary people like you to do extraordinary things. I look forward to seeing you at the top. Until we met again, be encouraged to triumph over the obstacles of life, to achieve your dreams and maximize your potential in all that you do! Go confidently in the direction of your dreams. Live the life you have imagined." --Henry David Thoreau

"She has been troubled yet not distressed, perplexed yet not in despair, persecuted yet not forsaken and cast down but not destroyed." The obstacles of life tried to hold her down, but "No weapon that formed up against her was able to prosper." --Bernada Nicole Baker, MBA, MPH, MDiv.

THE *Queens'* LEGACY

A native of Chicago, Illinois, Rev. Bernada is a sought after motivational speaker, educator, counselor, life coach and workshop facilitator who seeks to inspire others by sharing her testimony. She is the CEO of B' Encouraged Consulting, Inc. Rev. Bernada Nicole is the Founder of The Sisters in the Spirit International Ministries and The Princess Within Foundation. She is a member of The Association for Pastoral Counselors, Toastmaster's International, The National MBA Association and Alpha Kappa Alpha Sorority Inc. Rev. Bernada serves as the Georgia State President for The Teens N Power International Ministries.

Rev. Bernada is the quintessential model of a tenacious, anointed and influential leader of the Joshua Generation. Rev. Bernada Nicole earned her Master of Business Administration and a Master of Public Health Degrees from St. Xavier University at the tender age of 23. Rev. Bernada received her Master of Divinity Degree from McCormick Theological Seminary in Chicago, Illinois, and is currently pursuing her Ph D in Community and Social Services. She is affectionately known as the Midwife of Motivation, because of her commitment to helping others give birth to the potential that lies within.

You can reach Rev. Bernada directly by phone at 773-425-0890, by e-mail at bernadabaker@yahoo.com or by visiting her website at www.sisterinthespirit.org or www.theprincesswithin.org.

CHAPTER 7

A Lesson In Forgiveness

CHERYL PULLINS

The ultimate question for me was "Why?"
Why had the woman who gave me life given me away?

Going over it in my mind, I can recall one of the most pivotal moments in my life: the day I learned my brother and sister were my very own next door neighbors. Yes, you read it correctly. Through this chapter, I will take you on a journey of fear, rejection and low self-esteem to a triumphant destination of restoration, victory, forgiveness and love.

At a very young age my birth mother decided that it would be in my best interest if she allowed someone else to raise me. She was a young teenager who wanted to see and experience the world, but she also wanted to put me in the position where I was in a stable environment where I could grow up and experience life like any child. As a result, I was given to a much older woman who had already asked my birth mother if she could take me and raise me. After a few months of asking, I was finally given to live with the woman who later adopted me and raised me as if I had come directly from her womb.

Time had passed and I grew up to this point in my life (1975) thinking that the woman who had been taking care of my every need (food, clothing, shelter and anything else a young woman would have needed or wanted)

was the woman who had given birth to me. Imagine the sinking heart of a twelve-year-old girl who comes home from school and is told by her "mother" that she was really adopted and that the children who you've been playing with, spending time with and living right next door to are your brother and sister!

You have to understand the impact of this moment. The homes which my sister, brother and I grew up in were attached to one another – your classic inner-city row homes. My sister and I used to talk to one another through our bedroom windows because they were directly across from one another. We used to throw stuff back and forth into one another's rooms through the windows. The ones I was developing a bond with already shared a bond with me. I don't know if I can adequately convey the emotion of this moment which plays in my head every now and then, but I can remember it as if it were yesterday.

As much as I had acted as if this startling announcement didn't impact me, from that day until many days following it, my perception of me and the world around me was changed, and it was not good. There were subsequent feelings of both neglect and rejection. As the months and years passed, I began to question many things and people who were a part of my life. Were the people that I knew as my aunts and uncles really my relatives? Was the one person I knew as my brother really my brother?

The ultimate question for me was "Why?" Why had the woman who gave me life given me away? Was I not good enough, pretty enough or smart enough? Did I not fit in with her plan? All of these questions began to mount and the search was now on to find the woman who birthed me into this world. But wait...where was I to begin? From the day I was told that I had been adopted (and for a long while after that), there was no further discussion about my birth mother or the circumstances surrounding my adoption. I certainly didn't think or feel that I could approach my adoptive mother about my birth mother.

To me that was a recipe for conflict, not only on the outside between the two "mothers", but also an internal conflict within myself. I certainly couldn't appear to be disloyal to my adoptive mother, but I had a definite interest in learning about my birth mother. Life for me continued with unanswered questions and unresolved issues.

From age twelve to almost age eighteen, I didn't have any information concerning my birth mother, except that she lived in California with her husband and their three children. At this point, I don't know if the man she is married to is my biological father or if the three children they had were children she gave birth to or not. The only thing I did know was that the woman who gave birth to me was living her life in California, raising and taking care of a family that didn't include me or my brother or sister who lived right next door. Imagine my thoughts now... What was so different about me that I couldn't live with my mother and family?

One summer afternoon I was sitting at home entertaining a friend, and the doorbell rang. I answered and there were two women standing before me. One woman looked familiar and the other I had no idea who she was. I went back into the house to let my adoptive mother know that she had visitors. She let them into the house, seated them in the den and then came to me and said, while pointing to the den, "That is your mother". At this point I am 18 years old. This was my very first recollection of seeing my birth mother. The visit, needless to say was quite awkward. Here was a woman who looked like me and had given birth to me but in my mind, we had nothing in common. We basically spent the afternoon looking at photos of me when I was younger.

Years rolled on and we both made attempts to connect with one another. But for me, fear and the thought of being rejected again had a mammoth grip on me. My thought was that at all cost I was going to protect my heart. I certainly wasn't prepared to be turned away "again" from the woman who had given birth to me. Now this wasn't something that I "knew" she would do, this was something that I "thought" she would do, based on our past history.

I had allowed the impact of my history with her to defeat my quest to have a growing relationship with my birth mother. For another twelve years we worked to bring life full circle. We tried to keep in touch on a consistent basis, but life always happened. During this time period there was only one visit, which didn't go very well, I married my childhood sweetheart and my adoptive mother, Susie, passed away and I gave birth to two beautiful daughters, Valerye and Julianna.

It was after the birth of my youngest daughter that I really began to feel something within myself that desired to have my birth mother in my life. I had finally reached a point in my life where I felt I was ready to have a relationship with her. In the summer of 2000, I invited her to come spend time with me and her granddaughters. Things were not going well between me and my husband during this time, which made the visit a little awkward; however, my birth mother and I spent some wonderful time together.

During this visit we had to break down walls and barriers in order to have an open and candid conversation about what took place some thirty years

ago. There were many tears shed during this time but they were tears of cleansing. It gave my birth mother an opportunity to tell her story directly to me. The one thing I never thought of until that conversation is what my birth mother had to live with all of those years. Imagine having to live with knowing that you gave your children to other people to provide and care for them and you could have no contact with them.

Imagine living life and everyday in your heart and mind you carry the distant memory yet ever-present thought of the children you birthed into the world. Imagine having thoughts that the children you gave birth to might not ever forgive you for what they could have perceived as the worst thing that happened to them. Imagine living life and not being able to forgive yourself. I could continue on and on with a list of things which I realized my birth mother had been living with for all of those years.

The visit with my birth mother had my heart pricked and I knew I would have to do whatever it took to not only develop and have a relationship with my birth mother, but to also help to encourage my children to develop a relationship with their "new" grandmother. Not only that, but I would have to forgive her for giving me away thirty years ago. I prayed consistently that God would heal my heart. I allowed the Word of God to massage my heart. I openly acknowledged to God that I was harboring fear, bitterness and unforgiveness in my heart. I began to wake up and say, "Who am I to harbor these things in my heart against another person? Of all the things God has forgiven me for, I have no right to not forgive another person." I certainly was in no place to judge another person...even my birth mother. I spent time listening and reading about love. Agape – the Godly kind of love. The kind of love that loves unconditionally, and loves "in spite of", expecting nothing in return.

Fast forward a little bit and let me update you on the impact that operating in love and forgiveness has had on my life. I am the oldest of my mother's six children. I now have a relationship with two sisters and three brothers. My sisters Lorraine and Angelique are more precious to me than they could ever know. My brothers Troy, Sean and Vernon have become brothers who watch for and care for their oldest sister as if we all grew up in the same household. For the past fifteen years my mother, Lea Marie, has become an active part of my life. We talk, laugh and share on a regular basis. I spent a year living in California within walking distance from my mother's house. I was one of my mother's supporters as we went through the sickness and death of my father, who I earlier referred to as "my birth mother's husband" (that is another story for a different book).

When I remarried in September 2008, it was my mother who came and spent three weeks with me, two of which she helped with all of the last-minute details. Life for the both of us had finally come full circle because that is what God promised. He had already determined that Lea Marie and Cheryl, mother and daughter, would take their different paths to learn the impact of forgiveness, the power of a mother's love and the tenacity of a daughter's desire to honor the woman who gave her life, now affectionately acknowledged as "Mom."

Cheryl A. Pullins, a native of Philadelphia, PA, began by serving pastors and their ministries on the Executive level. Cheryl is the Founder/CEO of Pullins Enterprise LLC, which holds several companies, including Pullins Media Group (PMG), Pullins Publishing, PMG by Design and several other companies and projects which are under development (including a data collection service, consulting companies, several books, as well as a purpose coaching company which will launch Fall 2009). In partnership with the Suber Media Group, Cheryl is also the Founder and Editor-in-Chief of LIVE Magazine, a publication targeted toward Christian women and focusing on luxury living for "Kingdom-minded" individuals.

Cheryl is the proud mother of two daughters, Valerye Marie and Julianna Christyne and has recently acquired two additional children, Zachary Jr. and Deardra, along with three granddaughters. Cheryl currently resides in Columbia, Maryland with her husband, Zachary.

You can contact Cheryl by e-mail at capullins@liv-magazine.com or editor-in-chief@liv-magazine.com.

CHAPTER 8

Thank God For Second Chances

CHRISTIANA "CHRIS" BRIDGES

Look out world; my last years will be my best!

Thank God for this opportunity to share my story with you. Until 2007, I didn't think I had a "story" until I was asked to deliver a commencement speech. I asked God to reveal what was so interesting about me and why would anyone want to hear my story. Well, it didn't take long for me to stop minimizing God's work and to realize that like many other women, I had experienced achievements, disappointments, victories, hurt, fear and many other emotions over the 43 years of my life. It's funny how we can identify other people's accomplishments and achievements and not see our own. Maybe it's how we've been taught to recognize success in others by their degrees, titles, awards or something like that. I'm no different than other women and on the next few pages, I will share a little about my life's journey.

My parents divorced when I was a teenager. I remember not having much of an opinion nor, quite honestly, a strong feeling about the matter. All I cared about was me. I planned to go to college and only cared about how their divorce would impact my plans. Well, the divorce did impact all of us. My father moved out and my life changed. After a short time, it was just my mother and me in the house and without my father's influence I began to make inappropriate decisions as a teenager. When I graduated from high school, everyone expected me to attend college and

become a successful woman. I had the grades, the maturity and the drive to do just that. However, it didn't turn out quite that way. Instead, I fell in love. Rather than packing my bags and heading to a dorm, I got engaged and moved out with my boyfriend. At 19 years old, I was married with a high school diploma. A year later, I had my first son. Three years later, we had our second son. So there I was a 23 year old wife, mother of two and still only a high school graduate.

Several people in my life tried to convince me that marriage at 19 wasn't the best idea and life had so much more to offer. I thought I had already lived and was ready for a lifelong commitment. Truth be told, I didn't understand the connection between "commitment" and "marriage", so in my mind, if it didn't work out there was always divorce.

My first job out of high school was at a prestigious law firm making about $13,500 a year. That was in 1985 and the money wasn't bad at all. As a matter of fact, we purchased our first home when I was 21 years old. Don't get me wrong, I loved my life, but I knew deep inside that I needed more than a high school diploma. I was still the same girl that graduated from high school with a plan for college who was destined for more.

In 1992, with no ideas as to how I would work a full time job, be a wife, mother and now, a college student, I enrolled at Strayer University. What I did know was that I had to figure it out if I wanted to move ahead in my career and provide a better life for my family. After four years of evening and weekend classes, I graduated Magna Cum Laude with a Bachelors of Science degree in Business Administration.

From there, my career took off. After 12 years in law firms, I moved into sales at Xerox Corporation. Wow, I thought I had really arrived. I went from a controlled salary to income based on my efforts. As a matter of fact, I still have a copy of the first $10,000 check I received. My degree opened the doors, but God provided the increase. I thought I was really doing something. I was making a name for myself in the industry, making more money than I ever imagined and completely focused on me. All the while, my marriage was falling apart and I neither saw it coming nor prepared my heart to stop it. I thought I was climbing the corporate ladder; come to find out, I was really sliding down on the other side.

After about two years of separation, reconciliation and separation again, I was divorced, without a home, husband or full custody of my children. Through this ordeal, I was still one of the lucky ones, because my children had a great father who was committed and dedicated to them with his time and finances. But it is not the same to live on one income instead of two. With all of my career accomplishments, I was starting over in my personal life, moving into an apartment and learning how to budget. More importantly, I had to learn to accept responsibility for my decisions.

My parents were divorced and so were most of the couples I grew up knowing. I thought separation and divorce was the norm. As a matter of fact, I hand only seen maybe a handful of examples of good marriages. I didn't have an understanding of God's Word or a revelation of the sanctity of marriage. Nor did I consider the impact of my choices on my children. The boys were young at the time and had to spend about a year in counseling after the divorce. They were confused, hurt, sad and in some instances angry. Yes, that was probably the most difficult time for all of us and a consequence of my decision.

As a family, though separate, we made it. Each month and each year got better as the boys grew accustomed to our lives. We knew as parents that they needed each of us and that no matter what, together we would still be 100% parents. This may not be an ideal arrangement for everyone, but it worked for us even with the growing pains. The boys are now 23 and 20 and doing very well. The oldest, Robert, is a graduate of Towson University and Cameron is a sophomore at Morehouse College. Thank God for His grace and mercy over their lives!

Thank God for second chances. In 1997, I met my husband, Fulton. We were married in 1999 and had the perfect blended family. Fulton also had two sons and when we got married the boys were 13, 12, 10 and 7 years old. Had I given birth to them all, I could not have planned it better. Life was great...so I thought.

Although this time around, I had a much better understanding of the covenant and commitment of marriage; I still didn't expect to have to work so hard. Fulton and I, like every other couple, had our challenges. At times, I thought I was being punished for the things that I did wrong in my first marriage. Through it all we continued to grow together as a family, and in both of our careers.

Fulton and I moved up quickly, positioning ourselves in the highest tax bracket, earning over half million dollars annually combined. Life was really good! Money was a means to bless ourselves and others and was not a contributing factor to any of our concerns. When I was 36, my wonderful husband asked me to have his baby. At that time, my youngest birth son Cameron was 13 and my youngest stepson, Stephen, was 11 years. That

just didn't make much sense to me, since we had the perfect family already. So I ignored him. The next year, through much prayer and struggle, we decided to have a baby. For some, providing for the desires of my husband's heart was the ultimate act of submission; to others, it was straight crazy. Either way, I agreed. What I didn't realize was the amount of time, money and pain it would take to make it happen. My tubes were tied after my youngest son, so we chose In Vitro Fertilization. We had no idea that it would involve two rounds of the procedure costing about $25,000 out of pocket; require minor and major surgeries, daily shots and a blood clot.

In 2006, our daughter Taelor was finally born. Six weeks later, I stopped the daily shots for the blood clots and thought, "Thank God it's finally over." She was beautiful and the angel that God promised us. She completed the family – four boys and a girl! At this time, I was Vice President of Business Development of a global organization and at the height of my professional career with a new baby. Here I go again, starting life over. But it was still good.

When Taelor was about five months old, I started experiencing health challenges. It wasn't until after the fourth hospital admittance, heart surgery and draining the equivalent of a two liter soda bottle of fluid from my heart and lungs, did the doctors finally diagnose me with Lupus. For about 45 days, I struggled with the side effects of this disease. The doctors believed the Lupus was dormant in my body until the trauma and drama of having a baby caused it to awaken. Wow. What a consequence to what I thought was an amazing accomplishment. Now on top of being a new mother at 40, with a 20 year gap between my oldest and my youngest children, I have Lupus.

For a season, the Lupus aggressively attacked my body. With much prayer and good medical treatment, I have lived a normal life for the last three years. Praise God! Although I have a responsibility to my family to know my body and this disease, I refuse to let Lupus determine who I am or my destiny.

After surviving the highs and lows of 2006, I was longing for a change. I guess in a way, I wanted to make sure I was giving my daughter what I thought I had not given my sons, which was more of me. I didn't want to look up years later and realize I missed something with her because I was more focused on my achievements. As a mother, it's an incredibly tough balance. In 2007, I did the unthinkable; I resigned to be home with Taelor. At least, I thought that was the reason for my resignation. Just a year earlier, Fulton started Nirvana Real Estate & Mortgage Services, Inc. I figured that since I was home with Taelor, I would help out a little with the business. That was my plan, but not 'The' plan.

At two years old, we enrolled Taelor in a learning environment. Therefore, with my extra time, I decided to support my husband and the family business full-time. This gave me the opportunity to use my experience, skills and education to assist my husband to fulfill the vision that God has given him. Although as entrepreneurs we are not yet enjoying the same financial success as we did in our careers, it is more rewarding to provide employment and opportunities for others.

In 2008, God showed me that he had something bigger for me. We launched Nirvana Credit Services to raise awareness of the impact that credit has on your financial freedom. I had no idea how important this business would be in today's economy. I just knew that I was passionate about helping people and giving them the hope and encouragement to achieve their dreams. Knowing that God has given me the wisdom, resources and compassion to do what I do, I love my job today. God is a restorer and He gave me a second chance at marriage, children, career, but most of all life.

Look out world; my last years will be my best!

Christiana "Chris" Bridges is the President of Nirvana Credit Services, a personalized credit consulting company, located in Camp Springs, Maryland. Chris is committed to educating and raising awareness of the impact of credit and how it affects our financial freedom. She strongly believes that, "If we know better than we would do better." Chris is passionately dedicated to spreading the news about credit restoration through client consultations, seminars and workshops. She is also the author of "Your First Step to Credit Restoration".

Prior to starting Nirvana Credit Services, Chris has held several senior level positions in the corporate industry and retired in 2007 as Vice President of Business Development. In addition to running Nirvana Credit Services, she is the Chief Operating Officer for Nirvana Mortgage Services. It is a business

that she operates with her husband who is also committed to assisting clients to make their dreams of homeownership become a reality.

Chris is a graduate of Strayer University with a Bachelor of Science in Business Administration, which she achieved as an adult student raising two small children. She is also a wife and mother of five ranging from three to twenty-three years old and speaks from personal experience of overcoming obstacles, reaching her goals, and walking in God's purpose for her life.

For more information about Chris Bridges or Nirvana Credit Services please contact her by phone at (301) 423-7772, by e-mail at credit@nirvanaservicesinc.com or visit her website at www.nirvanacreditservices.com.

CHAPTER 9

To Change The Fruit, You Must Get To The Root

CHRISTY SPARKS

When a rose is covered in mud, because of its delicate petals,
it takes gentle cleansing to see its beauty.

My journey begins with me standing in the hallway of our home with my three year old daughter as she screamed, demanding my time. My frustration was intense. Inside I could hear myself screaming, "I HATE YOU!" Realizing that those weren't thoughts for my daughter, I went to my bedroom, fell to my knees and with tears flowing I prayed to God asking, "Where is this coming from? What do I do?" What I experienced as a child, I didn't want to be my legacy to my children.

God allows people and situations into your life to bring healing. As I was on my knees asking for direction, I was afraid. Although my daughter is a blessing from God, I too needed some attention. I needed to feel love rather than the emptiness and loneliness I was experiencing. I didn't want my daughter to experience what I had as a little girl. My pain, as a result of generations of abuse would not be passed down to my children. The buck stopped here.

THE *Queens'* LEGACY

As I started attending a healing retreat, my eyes and heart were opened to my responsibility to be the change I wanted to see in my life. As I started finding answers to my questions, I realized that I was simply not happy. I couldn't understand what I was feeling. On the outside, my life appeared very normal. You would have thought that I had it all. On the inside though, I was hurting.

As I hoped for a quick fix, I started peeling away the layers of my feelings – much like one would peel an onion. Thinking that all I had to do was to look at it and be done. This wasn't so. I've heard that life is a journey, a process even. It's like putting the pieces of a puzzle together. One by one, we have to take it in little pieces even though the pain and hurt is sometimes overwhelming. The puzzle isn't finished until we have touched all the pieces and placed them where they belong thereby creating the image that we want to see. The picture God intended us to be and to have. This wasn't something I could do on my own. I needed support. Oftentimes, it's easier for those on the outside to see the whole picture of our lives and the beauty behind it as they are not emotionally involved. Much of the time, the one who lives the puzzle ends up feeling stuck and frustrated.

One day at a counseling session, I found myself in a cocoon of frustration created by the memories buried deep in my psyche. I didn't intend to bury them; however I did have to survive. As I sat with my counselor, separated from my husband, I told her that the thought of even kissing him made me feel sick to my stomach. I continued to explain that it would be like picking up dog poop and squeezing it in my hand. Through deep conversation, I had a life altering experience. We discovered that my feelings were the result of my being sexually molested. The realization that I had suppressed these feelings for so many years caused me to leave in tears. It felt like I was in a dream. Could all this be true? It would be only through the process of time that I would e able to absorb this realization and come to grips with it all.

In order to change the fruit in any situation, you first must get to the root. I started asking my family questions and found that at a very young age, I had been abused by my grandfather. I didn't know what exactly happened. I just knew that it severely hurt my sense of trust and self respect. My innocence had been stripped away at a very young age and as I result, I felt very vulnerable. A child trusts that family will treat them well and love them - not hurt them. The boundaries had been broken and that made me angry. How could someone you unconditionally trust and love hurt you in that way? I had buried the pain of this situation as far down as possible, hoping that it would go away. Instead it resurfaced for healing that I so desperately needed. I continued seeing the counselor and started to write my feelings in a journal.

When a rose is covered in mud, because of its delicate petals, it takes gentle cleansing to see its beauty. I began to realize that I am that rose. Someone covered me with their mess. I didn't feel worthy. I didn't feel beautiful. I didn't even respect myself. I hadn't set healthy boundaries and had a hard time telling people no. I needed cleansing. That process started with my dealing with the pain. I did so the same way that you deal with death. Although I knew it wouldn't be easy, my children deserved a healthy and well-adjusted mother. Even though I had decided to move on, I knew it wouldn't be easy. I was overwhelmed and wanted to crawl into a hole. As I continued to think of my daughter and son, I realized that they were worth it.

If I didn't do this, who would? Suffering and pain was not what God had planned for me in my life. So I kept moving forward. As I grieved the loss of my childhood and agonized over school and career decisions, I realized that my whole life was based on decisions I made at a young age. It was time for me to take responsibility for the decisions that I had made and, although it was not my fault, stop blaming myself for what happened. I had to forgive my grandfather and stop asking "Why me?".

Sister Celica helped me to start healing from the anger. She taught me that there is a healthy anger and that I needed to accept it. That as long as I didn't inflict pain on myself and others, I could grow past my anger. As I continued writing in my journal, the feelings moved from my head, to the paper and ultimately out of my life. I had to stop giving the abuser control in my life. I had to move from being the victim to being the victor. I constantly reminded myself that I was worthy, beautiful and a precious gift from God and that with his help, the mud would be removed and would emerge the beautiful rose underneath.

As part of this process, Sister Celica took me down into a basement where there were mattresses on tables. She handed me a bat and told me that I had to get my voice and my power back. That until I gave that little girl her voice, the abuse would continue to have power in my life I started to hit the mattress. I felt like a stone with no emotions, afraid of what might come out. Sister Celica encouraged me and told me that I had to express my anger. That this was one of the biggest parts of my healing process yet my words were still frozen. Then she started talking to me as if she were my grandfather. Then the tears and words starting coming out. "How could you do this to me? I trusted you. I loved you. You hurt me. You can't hurt me

anymore. You can't touch me anymore!" I just keep crying, "NO MORE!" After I finished, she handed me a white rag, a symbol for innocence and purity, as she told me to continue saying all that needed to be expressed. I was twisting it tighter and tighter, finally throwing it down to the floor. Sister Celica said that I was done. That as a result, my grandfather would no longer have my power, that I am a victor, a beautiful rose and a child of God. I felt relieved as the anger that I carried for more than 28 years melted away.

Sister Celica took some blessed oil, prayed and anointed me. She gave me the oil so that I could anoint myself and my kids. She gave me a daily prayer written for those that had been hurt by physical, mental or sexual abuse. I was excited to be done with this entire situation. Little did I know that there was one more step on my journey to healing - the last and most important step of forgiveness. True healing, freedom and power come from forgiving. This took a while for me to process. To sincerely forgive was going to be a challenge. Yet I wanted the freedom to move forward.

On a business trip, I travelled to the area where my grandparents lived. Since my grandfather had died, I let my grandmother know that I was coming by. Although I didn't intend to tell my grandmother what happened, as we sat on her front porch, I started to share with her.

God put it in my heart to visit my grandfather's grave up the street from my grandmother's house. Having written a letter of forgiveness, the following morning we went to the cemetery. I read the letter to him, forgave him, tore up the letter and buried its pieces in the ground to signify my letting go. I was so thankful for that experience.

Looking at my life and the people that I've allowed in it, I have come to realize that I haven't always chosen the best men. Oftentimes finding myself in the same place, longing to have an incredible relationship, a life partner, a man that will love, respect and treat me as the queen God created me to be. Somehow I continue to accept relationships that are the exact opposite. There was another piece of the puzzle that I had ignored. I had to forgive myself. Constantly I have to remind myself that I am worthy of the respect and love and that I can respect and love myself before I can attract the person into my life that will treat me the way God intended. God meets all my needs and has helped me to turn my experiences into stepping stones that lead to breakthroughs.

As I lay aside the baggage of my past, I fully expect to have success on another level. Having been cleansed, the true gift that God has placed inside me shines through. The gift that comes with loving myself and trusting the process and the blessings that come along the way. I realize that all of the people in my life are there for a reason, season or a lifetime. My responsibility is to recognize who is there for what. Am I going to mess up? Sure. However, no matter what happens, with faith and action, I will overcome. Life is a journey. Every day I grow stronger and am grateful to be on the right path. The path I chose to assist me in finding God. The spiritual path where I walk with Him, love Him and live my life through His purpose.

In closing, there is the story of a man stuck in a hole screaming, "Someone please help me out." A person walked by and said, "Here is a check that will help you out." He said, "No silly, this check will not help me out." He kept screaming, "Someone please help me out!" Another person walked by said, "I will pray for you." He said, "Prayer is awesome, but prayer alone will not get me out of this hole." Becoming very discouraged, he continued screaming, "Someone please come help me out!" Another person walked by and jumped down in the hole. He said, "Ok, now you idiot there are two of us stuck in this hole." He said, "No I've been here before I can show you the way out."

My experiences, both good and bad, have helped me get where I am today; a place where I can better help people reach their dreams and goals as a result of my journey and life events. I am breaking old patterns and leaving a legacy for my kids; a legacy that teaches them don't give up, just get up. Draw a line in the sand, create your dreams and write your story. Purpose to use your story to help others and that is where life and purpose really begin.

Christy Sparks is a single mom and successful business coach helping individuals to achieve their goals and dreams. Prior to establishing her coaching business, Christy spent six years as a massage therapist. You can contact Christy Sparks directly by telephone at 573-795-4595 or by e-mail at csparksppl@gmail.com.

CHAPTER 10

God Has The Last Say

MINISTER DAWN R. CARTER

The miraculous story of my conception and birth is a constant reminder for me of the power of faith and God's love for His broken-hearted children.

God has an unusually awesome sense of humor! Think about it...can you recall hearing someone say something will never happen and then that very thing happens anyway? Not to mention when relatives or close associates work hard to chisel away at your dreams. Just before they succeed, God opens a door and allows your haters to watch you soar farther than even you imaged. Yes, God has an unusually awesome sense of humor! God and I shared our first laugh while I was growing in my mother's womb (Surprising...I know...lol).

I was blessed to share the DNA of a shy, committed, hard working woman named Dora W. Carter, my Queen. My mother had a strong desire for motherhood ever since she was a little girl growing up in Welch, West Virginia. She thought about it and hoped for the chance to experience motherhood as soon as possible. To her surprise she experienced medical challenges during her 20's that almost destroyed her dream. Her medical

challenges were so great that she experienced the heartbreaking miscarriages of three sons. The medical complications worsened during the last miscarriage to the degree that her doctor told her she may never have children. This mind blowing news crippled her spirit and caused her to withdraw from the world and even from prayer time with God. As years, months and days passed by, she could not shake her desire for motherhood.

One summer day in 1977, after a lengthy period of silence, my Mom fell to her knees and told God how angry and hurt she was that he had taken her three boys from her. She cried out to him and exposed her inner hurts over each lost. As she prayed, she felt a jolt of boldness rush through her. She said to her Lord and Savior, "I am gonna ask you one more time for a child. If you answer my prayer, I will raise that child to serve you. I will be the very best mother I can be to that child!" Momma said after she prayed, she honestly left the prayer on the altar of God's heart. Approximately six months later she learned that she was pregnant. As one might imagine, she did not get excited right away because of the past three failed pregnancies. It was six months later when she finally got excited. To encourage her heart, God allowed her to feel her baby's first strong kick while sitting at her work station. Her desk drawer was pulled out and resting on her lap as she organized her area. All of a sudden she felt a hard kick and the drawer slammed shut. After this shocking experience, she began to allow her heart to embrace the fact that God had finally answered her prayer.

The miraculous story of my conception and birth is a constant reminder for me of the power of faith and God's love for His broken-hearted children. Since childhood, I can recall several moments that I looked at my mother with pride and amazement. I am proud that she never gave up on her dream of having me. In awe as I look back over my life and can connect with the very message from the prayer she prayed, on that summer day in 1977. She promised to raise her child to serve God and to be the very best mother she could be. That's exactly what she did. My mother and I are living witnesses that God will always have the last say! No matter what discouraging news someone tells you or how far off track from your goal you may feel. God always has the final say! It's almost as if he is saying (with a smile), "You thought it was over...I think not."

This particular miracle has taught me five key points that have helped me stay focused on the positives when life appeared to be full of negatives. Prior to understanding the miracle of my birth, I used to feel doubtful about achieving my goals. I used to feel a sense of stress and lack of inner strength. You may question how I could feel such negativity after such a blessed birth? My response would be, like most people, we do not always immediately embrace our miracles until God brings us into a situation that makes us see the value of our miracles. Too often we look at the people or situations in our lives and criticize them or take them for granted until God leads us to a point within our self development where we find the joy and beauty of the miracles that we did not notice. Here are the five key points that helped me to feel the joy of the miracle:

Know Your Value: God has created each and every one of us with different gifts and talents. Our gifts and talents should not be denied, ignored or forgotten. We have a purpose!

Understand Divine Timing: There is a difference between our timing and God's timing. Considering the fact that He is our creator, we do not know the fullness of what we need in order to fulfill our dream. We have no idea who we will meet along the way that will help us achieve the goal. We have no idea what lessons we need to learn in order to become strong enough to carry the dream out. Because of this, we must learn to embrace patience and trust that God knows when the time is right.

Be Vulnerable Before the Lord: God wants to know our inner thoughts. He wants to have a close relationship with us. He appreciates the respect we give him when we bow our heads to say grace before eating, but he desires to help us where it hurts most. Like my mom, we have to learn to share our hurts and disappointments with God. God wants us to come to him, exercise our faith and allow him to lead us. As we journey with God he reveals himself and his power to us.

Prepare and Get Excited In Advance: I thank God for the mirrors he placed in my life. Those mirrors include family members; mentors; friends; sorors; and mentees all of whom have encouraged me over the years (too many to name...I LOVE YOU ALL). On countless times my mirrors have spoken into my life and told me where they see God taking me. They have encouraged me to do what I do well and have told me how to strengthen my weak areas. As a result of them sharing their observations, I have discovered my purpose. Their feedback has helped me to prepare for my destiny. Now that I understand where God is taking me, I am excited as my purpose unfolds.

Be Open For the Unexpected: The birth of a beautiful 8 lbs. 4 oz. baby girl was a total shock to my mother! She was and still is in awe of how God decided to answer her prayer. Like my mother, we make plans yet often they do not materialize as we planned them. Once we place our petitions before the Lord, we need to be open for the unexpected. He has an

awesome way of answering our prayers while blowing our minds all at the same time. This is why I celebrate the beauty that can be found in chaotic situations. I believe that without the mind blowing storms of life, we would take God's miracles for granted. We would not need him to be GOD if everything in our lives occurred based on our plans.

No, my life is neither perfect nor have I lived without hurts. I have simply embraced the fact that God blessed my mother to birth me. As a witness and product of this special miracle, I realized that I have a choice. I can embrace this miracle and learn methods that will allow me to enjoy this blessing or I can focus on the negatives that life comes with and miss the joy of my journey. As I began to realize that God did not have to let me be, it became easier for me to embrace the joy of my life. He could have taken me as he did my three brothers. Instead I was allowed to live.

I have chosen to honor the legacy of my mother by celebrating what God has done for us. By remembering what He did, I am inspired to rise as HIGH as my spirit will allow. My friend, like my mother, we all have a desire or dream within. Don't quit. Regardless of how long it seems to take, do not quit. God has not forgotten you. As long as He allows breath in our bodies, we still have a chance to see our dreams come true. Knowing this, I can publicly thank my mom for not giving up on her dream of having me.

Minister Dawn Carter is a native of Washington, DC. In 2007, she was ordained as Deacon in the Christian Methodist Episcopal Church. She obtained a Master's degree in Adult Education from Coppin State University in 2008 and is currently a Manager in Coppin's Office of Admissions. She is passionate about encouraging and mentoring her students and other people to reach their fullest potential in spite of life's obstacles. She has received several awards of recognitions for Mentoring and Leadership and was featured with other Historically Black College Campus Queens in *Ebony Magazine (April 1999)*. She is a proud member of the Ministerial staff of St. John CME Church in Washington, DC and a member of Delta Sigma Theta Sorority, Inc. You can contact Minister Carter directly by e-mail at sangchild4god@yahoo.com.

CHAPTER 11

Complacency Is The Enemy Of Success

DENISE MCMILLAN

My mom explained to me that people do make mistakes, but the trick is to learn from them and not make them bigger and more complex.

When you think of single parents, you think of irresponsible excuse-makers, lazy people, or bad parents who have bad kids who eventually turn into irresponsible excuse-makers, lazy people, and eventually parents who have bad kids, who will continue to perpetuate this ugly cycle. Do you realize that children of single-parents can be raised to be happy, healthy, well-adjusted adults? I didn't.

Pregnant at 16, I had my first daughter at 17. My family supported me and to them I am eternally grateful; but what I longed for, what I really wanted, was a dad for my daughter. To me, my being a single parent was my first failure in raising her. I wanted a partner, a companion. But no matter what I wanted, I was in it alone and all that mattered was that my baby would love me no matter what.

T'Nyce was born on April 7, 2001. Weighing in at 8 pounds, 5 ounces, with cheeks the size of softballs, I was in love at first sight. I brought her home and we spent our first night in my mom's room. The next morning, I woke up proud of my little daughter and confident about the future. Her first night home from the hospital, she had slept through the

night! Mom's sleepy glare startled me and she told me the truth. I had ignored her all night. My mom got up to feed and change her. When she woke me up, I snapped, yelled and went back to sleep. Some would call that some sort of postpartum depression. I called it another failure. How could I do such a thing? One of the first times my baby needed me and already she knew she could not count on me. (Funny, to this day she still thinks she has two moms!)

I knew I had to do right by my daughter. The next day, I went to Social Services and got everything we qualified for: formula, money, child support, daycare, and housing. I was home-schooled for six weeks and then went back to public school. That lasted less than one week, my temper was too volatile, likely due to sleepless nights, a crying baby, and that postpartum depression still lingering.

While living with my Grandmother, her words of wisdom didn't register, but the seeds planted in my spirit would soon bring forth fruit. "Denise, depend on NO one but you, finish school, and get your education," is what I was told. I would think to myself, "finish school AND depend on myself? But I just got kicked out and I'm on my way to pick up my food stamps. Living off the government is way easier than 'depending on me'. I have no job, no credit, and no home – all I have is this little baby, and she needs to eat."

While she was living, I didn't pay her much attention. When Grammi died, when my daughter was 11 months old, it both devastated and awakened me. Did I want my daughter growing up, doing and living like I was? I knew that's who she would look up to first – me. I could do better, I *would* do better. My mom, the motivational speaker, stayed in my ear, "You can do it." "You can take care of yourself." "You can finish school." I don't know if that was because she wanted me out of her hair, or what, but it worked.

In June 2002, I graduated high school with a 3.5 GPA. My head was high at my ceremony and my fat little baby even seemed proud of me. When I went outside, my graduation present was in the parking lot - a purple Mazda Millenia with leather seats and a sunroof, thanks to my mother. Little Chunky Butt and I rode off into the moonlight.

I worked a number of jobs, doing a little of "this" and a little of "that", but it never seemed enough. On a trip to Cancun, I noticed that the airport screeners at the airport seemed to have sweet jobs. So I went home, looked them up online and applied. Two months later I had a job at Reagan

International Airport as a TSA Screener. I had just turned 18 and the freedom that came along with that was overwhelming.

There was a guy at our pier, let's call him James. James was 27, and he seemed dorky to me, but all the girls at our terminal wanted him, and it became a competition. I was determined to "win". I did. I moved in with James in November of 2005 and he proposed in January 2006. He wasn't really for me, but he was older, he had a car, he had his own house, and at the time, that's all I wanted.

After moving in, I discovered he had another thing -- a temper. James thought he and I should have some twisted father/daughter relationship. If James said jump, I was only to ask "How high?" Anything else would be a problem. Well, I wasn't looking for a jerk of a father who enjoyed using, abusing, embarrassing and hurting me, so I got out. And after I moved out, I discovered I was pregnant. How could I be so stupid to do this again??! Once again, I rolled with the punches.

Living in Maryland and working in Virginia, I commuted and took my fat baby to daycare in Virginia. After work I went to school and went home exhausted, in pain, tired and feeling overwhelmed, but each day I woke up and did it all over again. The knowledge that I was doing something good for my family, for my daughters, for our future, kept me moving. I created a calendar with the equipment the new baby would need spaced out on it. Every two weeks, on payday, I bought the baby items from the calendar. I was determined to do it myself. I was blessed to have family and friends who cared for me so much that when I burned out, they took my daughter and gave me time to rest and recharge so I could keep moving. The key here was to *keep moving*. Life waits for no one. Kids won't stop growing up so you can 'get yourself together'. Do your best, and if your best isn't good enough, remember God doesn't give you more than you can bear... so do better.

Tamaya was born on October 17, 2004. In the room with me were my mom and my aunt. Her dad was nowhere to be found. He knew when I went into the hospital and I even called him when she was born. Still, he was a no show. A month later, my name had reached the top of the Section 8 and there was a townhome available for me. In December 2004, I moved into Greene Hills Apartments. Excited to have my own place, I almost immediately moved in my high school sweetheart, let's call him Donnie. Donnie seemed like a good guy – good with the kids, quiet and easy to be around. Donnie was also lazy.

In the beginning stages of a relationship, that is a simple thing to overlook. But as you mature and it seems only one of you is maturing, a decision has to be made. Am I going to take care of a grown, able-bodied man in addition to my children? Should I support him never trying to advance himself, being complacent not making enough money to take care of himself, let alone a family? The problem was I didn't begin to seriously think about this until the evening before our wedding.

My mom explained to me that people do make mistakes, but the trick is to learn from them and not make them bigger and more complex. Mom (my "right hand") told me if I decided not to marry that man, she would stand at the church the next day and tell everyone no wedding was happening. As the mother who had been involved in abusive relationships where I was told no one would want me with two kids, I decided I would go through with it. Donnie was none the wiser. He didn't feel the knot in my stomach when I said, "I do."

After we got married I became more and more prosperous and he became more and more of an anchor. I wanted out of Greene Hills. I wanted a newer, larger vehicle. I needed to be around people who wanted "more", yet I found myself around someone who was complacent. Complacency is the biggest contributor to failure. Become complacent and you will never go anywhere. Being around someone who was complacent made life a constant struggle; internally, I wanted more. I wanted my kids to have more. I wanted them to be able to play at the neighborhood playground and not step on condoms or needles. I needed to prove to my babies that there was more to life than doing hair for $20 and loaning money to people in the neighborhood who would never pay you back. Everyone doesn't make cigarettes with marijuana leaves. Whole families should not all live in separate homes in the same Section 8 neighborhood. It's complacency. That's why it's been the way it has been for so long. Everyone was complacent.

My marriage was difficult for other reasons, too. I was looking for and thought I'd found my prince, when in reality I had happened upon a pauper who didn't even see his own potential. Looking back on it, there were plenty of signs I should have noticed before allowing him into the space belonging to me and my children. He still lived at home with his mom; he had been kicked out of college; and he had a son that he was not allowed to see. The flags even went beyond just him... he had major issues in his family. There was mental illness, major infidelity and more dysfunctions than I choose to mention here. These flags were so ridiculously blatant that I was blinded by them. I couldn't believe it could be that bad. Hindsight is a "you-know-what" when it comes to these things.

Despite the flags, the pomp, and the circumstance, Donnie and I had a baby girl in January of 2006 who, at 5 pounds, 11 ounces, was premature with numerous accompanying issues. She was released 10 days after her birth but was returned quickly to the hospital as a result of her health challenges. Her hospital stay turned into two transfers, four hospitals, innumerable doctors, specialists, and nurses. Some I remember for their distant and cold attitude, even blatant disregard for my wishes. However, most of them I remember for their true concern and help saving my daughter's life. Taylah was finally released from the hospital June 27, 2006. Cautiously I returned home and watched my daughter grow stronger. (At three, now she's the Big Mama of the group, constantly making her presence known and never allowing herself to get the short end of the stick.)

Shortly after Taylah was released from the hospital and her father saw she was well, he stepped out. I found out. We fought. I took him back. A year or so later, he slipped back into old habits and had a new "friend" at work that I sensed he was a little too close to. This was the second and last time. He had to go! In theory it was that simple. In reality it was much more difficult.

The Fairfax County Court became like a second home to me. He moved in with his girlfriend and has not looked back. Although he had father/daughter relationships with all of the girls, the kids did not hear from him for nearly six months. It wasn't until child support was established that he wanted to come back around and talk about getting back together. That might have been a viable option before, but I had grown leaps and bounds since he left. With the income from a promotion at work, I was able to move out of Section 8 housing, get my own townhome, go back to college and get off of ALL government assistance. I couldn't go back to complacency.

Today, although I am proud of the accomplishments to date, I'm still striving. I work every day and take care of my babies every night. On the weekends, I look for new educational opportunities to share with them; to teach them new things. And I teach them the same thing that was taught to me – "good enough" is never enough... you can always do better. And you, the reader, can do better, too. Remember, complacency is an enemy to success.

THE *Queens'* LEGACY

You can contact Denise directly by e-mail at denisealena_02@yahoo.com or visit her website at www.DeniseAlena.com

CHAPTER 12

Adversity Has Its Advantages

DONNA RUSSELL

The pain will go away, the bruises will heal and you will be happy and whole again – you may be bruised but you're certainly not broken.

I was born in 1956 on the island of Nassau in New Providence in the Bahamas, the third of five girls born to my parents before their separation and the end of their marriage. I faced the challenge and disappointment of being left in Nassau to be raised by grandparents while the other siblings departed for Freeport, Grand Bahamas, the second city in our chain of archipelago islands. At first, I didn't understand God's purpose and will, and much disappointment set in. Although the reason I was left behind was a noble one – I had passed a general examination requirement to be accepted into a government High School on a scholarship program – I still felt deserted and forsaken.

As it turned out, being raised by my grandparents was the perfect preparation for my spiritual journey, which began early in life. My grandparents, who were both Christians, believed strongly in church participation and in Bible reading. Subsequently, my duty each evening was to read to them from their favorite psalms. By the time I departed Nassau and joined my family in Freeport, the Word was imbedded in my heart as well as in my memory. Looking back, I would say it ensured my very survival.

God had begun His work of separation and sanctification in my life. All through my life I continued to read the Bible and attend church, and I felt that I was a pretty "good" person, until age twenty when I came to realize that my grandparents' faith was not sufficient, and that I needed to accept Christ as my personal Savior and Lord. Thus, the covenant and protection of the 'Living Word' was in place to fortify me, and form the foundation for my survival through the trials and tests to come.

I graduated from High School at the age of eighteen and married my high school boyfriend the next year. This was the start of a journey into physical, emotional and mental abuse and of a co-dependent relationship with a man with alcohol and other substance addictions, which continued for thirty-one years. My life became a never-ending cycle of highs and lows; of hope sometimes, and despair at other times; of wondering if God was really real and if His Word was true.

I lost my first-born daughter to a condition I could barely pronounce, but in layman's terms, her lungs collapsed after I had carried her to full term. This led to a period of sorrow, grief and emptiness that I endured with a smile on my face, but with a deep feeling of loss inside. My faith in God and His Word gave me the courage to carry on even when life seemed most unbearable. Three other children eventually came into the marriage, and I chose to raise them as my own. Even though adultery was a "part of the journey" for my husband, I choose to remain in covenant with God and faithful to my marital contract.

I was tempted to turn to man and to lean to my own understanding and reasoning, but I resisted and made the decision to trust in the Lord with all my heart. Because of this, I know that a woman can remain pure and undefiled and not buy into this world's system or yield to the desires of the flesh. It is possible to survive your trials and bring glory to God. There is victory after being delivered from the adversity, but God is also able to keep you from experiencing the adversity to begin with. This is my testimony.

I reigned over the feelings of disappointment, anger, bitterness and a desire for revenge and retaliation by learning to manage my thoughts and emotions positively. I allowed the higher values of 'agape' love and forgiveness to ascend, and the strong urge to put 'self' on the throne to descend. I learned to reign over compromise for the greater good of a Godly legacy for the generations to come. Self-gratification is very short-lived, but the consequences can have negative implications for generations. Far too many of us make decisions and choices without regard for our responsibility to the next generation, and never learn the valuable lesson that our lives inevitably affect and influence the lives of others – born and unborn.

We are commanded to leave an inheritance for our children's children, so why not leave a Godly, righteous one? The truth is, it is not about us, but it is rather about those who will be helped by our stories and struggles. Our lives are only a small part of a larger puzzle; and although that part is small, it is very significant. I would venture to say that we have all had the experience of putting a puzzle together and realizing at the end that one of the pieces is missing – and the picture is incomplete.

One of the important lessons that I learned on this journey was that I was spending too much time being frustrated and discouraged by the [lack of] results of my efforts to change my husband. I knew that he needed to change and I thought that it was my job to make sure that he did just that. After many futile years of trying to change him, I learned the hard way that it was not my job. I could not control him, but I could control *my* thoughts, *my* emotions and *my* attitude – this became a full-time job for me.

I had to learn that as "good" as I wanted to be all of the time, I still needed the Lord to change me – I could not do it by myself. So the more I trusted on Him and relied on His help, the more I was able to yield myself to Him and allow Him to do a work in me. My circumstances did not change, but I was better able to handle them. The truth is that we truly are not able to prevent some of the situations in our lives from occurring, but we can always choose how we respond to them.

It takes two "whole" persons to have a successful life together. I learned that some of the expectations I placed on my husband were unfair. Men are not able to make us complete, fulfilled or whole; only God can do this from within. Too many of us women look to men to validate and approve us and to decide our worth. This is a common error. I believe each person was designed specifically and especially by God for His unique purpose. Only He can fill the void in our lives when we enter the right relationship with Him and accept His love, acceptance and approval. With this perspective, we are ready to embark on the process of becoming the "help meet" to embrace the design and purpose of our mates.

I have come to accept that I am valuable and original and that I do have something to contribute to the world, even if my circumstances might indicate otherwise. I learned that my joy and strength came from my faith in God and my happiness did not depend on my circumstances. I can enjoy my life *in spite of* and not *because of* negative circumstances, but this had to be a daily choice. I am entitled to be happy and safe, and I choose to keep

growing...becoming better and not bitter, even in adverse circumstances. The peace that I carried on the journey came from within as I learned to accept, forgive and love myself.

The key is to make these decisions, not just once, but on a daily basis. We must trust, respect and love even after continuous lies, distrust and disappointments, understanding that we are not alone in experiencing these trials and tests. I was not being singled out. I have survived, and I'm able to stand as a testimony to the fact that there is truly life after emptiness, aloneness and pain. I started to believe that the struggles that I faced and overcame could possibly inspire other women to not quit, and to use each difficult encounter to build a foundation to rise higher and higher. The key is to not build up walls and harden our hearts, but to remain vulnerable and soft. Walls serve to keep others from hurting and abusing us, but walls can also keep us from experiencing the joy, peace, laughter and love that can eventually replace the pain and hurt.

I did not plan for my life to turn out the way it did. I could not have designed it this way in my wildest dreams (or nightmares), but I can learn to be grateful, thankful and content. I can still continue to dream big and have hope of success and a better life. We need to allow God to truly reign over the hurts, habits and hang-ups that we all will eventually face and trust that He will bring us out victoriously each time.

I decided not to become a victim, nor to continually ask, "why me?" I learned to accept that God would not allow me to suffer more than I could bear. As I learned to cast all of my cares on Him, so He bears them. There are no problems that are bigger than God. I would encourage others not to look at the size of the problems, but at the greatness of the Almighty God. Know that if you can believe Him, all things will work together for good.

The pain will go away, the bruises will heal and you will be happy and whole again – you may be bruised but you're certainly not broken. A bruised, stomped on, kicked, spit on and crumpled $100 bill does not lose its worth and value because of the misuse and abuse. Diamonds endure tremendous pressure, heat, rubbing and extreme "processing" before they display their brilliance and shine. Even though it's covered up and buried, its beauty and significance remain intact. So can it be with your life, as you realize that having a spirit of unforgiveness, hatred, revenge, mistrust and anger can trap and enslave you and keep you in bondage, thereby allowing the trail and pain to last that much longer.

Acknowledge and accept that you are experiencing these emotions, evaluate what good can be learned and what growth and strength can be gained, and then let go. It may be a slow and painful process, but it can be achieved. Be willing to change what you can. I experienced my biggest frustrations when I tried to change things that were not mine to change. I learned to stop doing so much and decided to become more of what God expects, and to do what it took to effectively represent His kingdom, as He showed me each day the joys of living in hope with no regrets.

My motive is to show others that they truly are more than their jobs, occupations, situations and circumstances. I want to encourage them to believe in themselves; to know that they were created with special talents, gifts and abilities that they can develop, nurture and invest for the glory of our Creator. We should focus more on God and less on ourselves. We can trust that He knows how to accomplish His plans, and we can avoid discouragement and self-pity by serving others. Everyone should find a passion worth dying for, and live for it.

Be creative in finding the time to get away from the chaos of your daily duties to spend quiet time with the Lord. Have a hunger to continue learning and growing and developing in all areas for spiritual, familial, financial, social and intellectual balance. This could mean reading as many books as possible per month on a subject that are of interest to you, and learning from the experiences of others. There's a wealth of knowledge and wisdom contained in books. Be sure to keep a personal journal, and have a measurable, written plan for your life. Never underestimate the potential inside of you.

Overcoming adversity calls for personal discipline and the willingness to work to maintain a positive attitude. There are no challenges in life that cannot be overcome. Everyone has the potential to change – all that's really required is the earnest desire to change, persistence to overcome all obstacles, finding people who want you win and are willing to help you achieve your goals, and prayer. These elements can come together to create a solid formula for success.

Having practiced these strategies, I know that they are doable. One of my favorite quotes states that "a person's life will transform in direct proportion to the alteration of one's mind." Another favorite quote of mine states that "a man's progress in life is directly related to his continual pursuit of excellence." It is important to note that it is your responsibility to choose this path, and not leave it to chance. The Bible clearly states that we must renew our minds – that means getting back to the original plan and blueprint of God – back to thinking and creating like Him. It means continually pursuing His plan for our lives ...even from the very beginning.

THE *Queens* LEGACY

Donna has been part of a Leadership Development Team for three and half years, Donna Russell is an avid reader and a believer in personal development. Her passion is to serve, motivate and inspire others to pursue their dreams. Donna loves meeting people and sharing her faith. She is very active in her local church and has served as an elder there for fourteen years.

Donna was born in Nassau, New Providence in the Bahamas, and, at age 52, she is an Export Manager with a private organization. She resides with her husband Ivan of thirty-two years in Freeport, Grand Bahamas Island. She has three adult children – Tanya, Tameka and Ivan Jr., and five beautiful grandchildren.

You can contact Donna directly by mail at P.O. Box F-40221, Freeport, Bahamas, by e-mail at domarussdr@hotmail.com or by phone at (954) 246-3136 or (242) 373-9530.

CHAPTER 13

I Leave You Love

DR. EVELYN BETHUNE

I am Evelyn and the first female grandchild of Mary McLeod Bethune.

I am Evelyn and the first female grandchild of Mary McLeod Bethune. I was born in Daytona Beach, Florida, during segregation, by the grace of God and the prayers of my maternal great grandmother, Sara Jones. She prayed me into this world when the white "doctor" who was supposed to assist my mother with a difficult delivery, walked out on us as she lay in the delivery room trying to push me through pelvic hip bones that would not dilate. She should have had a cesarean-section but remember, she was a black woman in 1952, giving birth in a hospital that had little or no space for black people. The doctor said that he was tired and left my mother in the care of a black midwife who would not give up on us. With her help and the prayers of my momma Sara, my mother agonizingly pushed me into this world and lived to talk about it.

Many people have told me this story as I was growing up. They would always say that every sick person in the "Colored Ward" got healed that day because Momma Sara got on her knees and lifted up a prayer so powerful that God had to hear it and because she was a true prayer warrior,

THE *Queens'* LEGACY

my momma and I lived. The story also goes a bit further to say that I came into the world unmarked by the trauma of my birth, not screaming, but with a smile and eyes wide open. The elders would say "She was looking ahead of herself, seeing the unseen"; which was another way of saying that I came into the world already knowing, I would just have to remember.

When I think about that statement today, I know that I have insights and don't remember a time that I did not feel the presence of God in my life, even when I placed myself far from Him. This story is also a reminder to me that I have always been a fighter, unwilling to give up, even when the odds appear to not be in my favor. I call this 'In *the spirit of Mary McLeod Bethune.*' God's almighty hand continues to guide me back to the right path and help me not be afraid.

Years after my grandmother passed, I have memories of sitting in the darkness of our house, because the lights had been turned off, looking out of the window of my parents bedroom at the lights of the college, the president's house, the dining hall, and science building, and wondering why everyone seemed to benefit from the work of my grandmother and my daddy, except for our family. When our lights would get turned off because of my parents already stretched resources, we didn't understand how there could be so much and yet so little. When my father was forced to retire on a $50 a month pension, we did not understand.

Where was the care and compassion from the college to which he had given his life to help his mother realize her dream of providing an education for the descendants of the enslaved Africans? As he recovered from a stroke that nearly took his life, attempts were underway to distance him from the college that carried his last name, Bethune-Cookman College. This was the place where as a child, he had sold magnolia blossoms to tourists to help fund its growth, made ink from elderberries, raised chickens for food and grew vegetables. He traveled the country, singing with the choir to help the college built on prayer become real. Yet the very institution that should have nurtured the descendants of its founder, pushed us away like unwelcome step children.

How do you come to a place of peace in your very soul when you see the legacy left to you being stolen away? The journey to the answer is a true tale of God at work. It is the story of Mary's grandbabies...out of the darkness of slavery into the light of freedom. You see, one does not always have to have a visible shackle to be enslaved. Sometimes the enslavement comes through fear and anger. This true story of coming out of that darkness into the light of freedom is a story of love and family and how the strength of our ancestors is with us and guides us to the restoration of stolen legacies.

For about 10 years, I struggled with how to tell this story, trying to get other family involved. Yet I could not get all the pieces to come together and one day God said, " I did not give it to them, I gave it to you".

I must remind you that *BETHUNE: Out of Darkness into the Light of Freedom*, is my story, my point of view and my memory of events, as well as a lot of my feelings, good, bad, ugly, spiritual, and sometimes indifferent. It is told from the standpoint of living the day to day with my parents, my brothers and sisters, my nieces and nephews and feeling what they felt. I have seen the impact of my grandmother on our lives. Her imprint is deep and wide.

My very first memory of my grandmother, Mary McLeod Bethune, called Mother Dear by our family, is with my Cousin Georgia and Cousin Lucille in the kitchen of Mother Dear's house. The morning air in the kitchen was always filled with the smell of fried southern ham (bone in), fried eggs and grits with the red gravy from the ham, hot biscuits with real butter and apple butter jelly. The back door was always open and there was always a place for me and my oldest nephew Donald, son of my oldest brother, Albert Bethune, Jr. I loved the chatter of Mother Dear, Cousin Lucille and Cousin Georgia as they prepared for the day. They never seemed to feel that I was in their way.

I hear my grandmother's voice as she told stories to the neighborhood children at story hour on Saturday mornings. I can also remember the gentleness of her touch as she would sit me on her lap to simply be my grandmother. The smells of her house and love for family are a part of the comfort that comes in the memories.

At the age of three, I was making the trip to Mother Dear's house pretty much on my own. Mommy would stand in the door of our house and watched me as I crossed the street to Mother Dear's house. We all lived within shouting distance of each other. I was also still sucking my bottle and I usually arrived with bottle in hand and curiosity on my mind. I loved to sit under the table in the kitchen or in the office under Mother Dear's gigantic desk. Now some of you may be wondering why a three year old would still be sucking a baby bottle. Thank God my mother was not into child psychology and did not feel that I would suffer brain damage or have a warped personality if allowed to suck my bottle until I got ready to stop.

Although looking back on some of my early adult behavior, she may have been mistaken. However, I was about 5 years old when I decided to give up the bottle. By now, I was fixing it myself and I think I liked it because I could drink my juice lying down and not spill it on my clothes. I never took it to nursery school, but once I got home, it was me and my bottle. The summer that I gave up my bottle, we were going on a train ride to Philadelphia, and I did not want to be seen on the train with it, so I threw it in the woods next to our house. We were in Philly about two weeks and I never asked for that bottle. Immediately upon returning to Daytona however, I requested my bottle and mommy said, "If you want it you'll have to go into the woods and get it." I immediately gave it up and moved on to drinking out of a cup.

About a month after my third birthday party, I can remember the bells on the campus of Bethune-Cookman College tolling in recognition of Mother Dear's death and the feeling of sadness in our house for a very long time. For days after the tolling of the bells, there were many people in our house. The coming and going, early and late went on for a time and then stopped. On one particular day there was great story telling by those who came and I remember sitting on my daddy's lap as he talked about the building of Bethune-Cookman from a one room shack to the institution left by his mother. He had many stories to tell about his life as the only child of the great Mary McLeod Bethune.

My mother, Elizabeth Sterricks Bethune, was twenty years younger than my father but the love they shared was epic. She was the smartest woman I know, with a compassionate heart for others and fierce spirit. Her love for us was undeniable yet she also believed in discipline and the showing of respect. My mother often told us how "Madame Bethune" initially was not in favor of her son, Albert, Sr., being involved with her. After all, to Dr. Mary McLeod Bethune, she was a high school dropout, leaving school in the 12th grade to get married and give birth to my oldest sister, Theodora. She was also a divorcee, living in the projects with what many would have viewed as a lower social standing than many of the socialites vying for his attention. Time however would change the mind of Mary McLeod Bethune because other than God, there was nothing she loved more than her family.

What set her apart? What gave her strength to move mountains of racism and open doors in the arenas of education, the Federal Government, economic development and community organizing? When it seemed the most impossible, she did her best work. Her faith in God was unceasing and her willingness to serve others unquestionable. The story of our family is a story anchored in the strength of ancestral Africans who did not give up, and in their struggle, gave us strength. They marked our DNA so that strength would be passed from generation to generation; even today this legacy continues.

My grandmother was far ahead of her time in her vision, focus, and ability to lead our people. She placed the well being of the people far ahead of any ideas of self. Growing up in her shadow was sometimes the hardest aspect of my life and other times the most rewarding. I have learned patience as well as how to forgive. My faith has gone from a surface requirement to a deep connection with God that allows me to truly be at peace even in the midst of great difficulty. Throughout this life experience however, we were blessed with parents who taught us by example to give to others, to share no matter how little we might have, to love deeply and to trust God. What an injustice to ignore this opportunity to speak from my side and talk about the beauty, the heartache, and the incredible strength of spirit in growing up Bethune.

There have been times in my life that I deeply regretted the choices that I made. I used to believe that the only person I hurt when I messed up was me. I have come to fully understand this is not true. Even when I was very naive or when I felt that nothing I did mattered, or that I must heal the world at my own expense in order to be worthy, or when I got caught up in bad behavior or bad relationships because I was angry or hurting, the end result was the same. We must learn early to "stop, look, and listen, *BEFORE* we cross the street". It is my belief that God always gives us a sign when we are headed in the wrong direction. We simply choose to ignore that uneasy feeling because it is something we really want. We work it out in our heads.

For a long time, the attempts to separate the Bethune family from Bethune-Cookman College after my grandmother died, adversely affected how we accepted the mantle of legacy. It adversely affected the way we felt about a place that to us, will always be sacred ground. Our grandmother is buried there. I hope that there is healing in the telling of our story.

I say all of this in hindsight, because as a child, I had no idea what it meant to be the granddaughter of one so great, in the eyes of so many, and there was no handbook on how to travel this road. Our grandmother accomplished more in her lifetime than would ever have been expected. Conceived of Africans who were once enslaved in this country, she was the product of greatness, a link to the royalty never to be visited again in the home land of her parents. My great grandparents, Samuel and Patsy McLeod, endured the degradation of enslavement, without losing their

strength of character, the dignity of their lineage, and their great ancestral love for family ...We, the BETHUNES, are cut from that cloth and no matter what, it is that blood that flows in our veins and thus, like the story, the healing begins

Dr. Evelyn Bethune, an original Floridian, has lived Houston, Texas for the past 8 years. She is the granddaughter of Dr. Mary McLeod Bethune, educator, activist, advisor to four United States Presidents, community care giver and international peace advocate. Bethune grew up in an environment that demanded awareness of world issues and participation in the solution to these issues.

As a political scientist and community activist, her dedication led her from Atlanta, Georgia, to Calhoun Falls, SC and on to Houston, TX in order to continue her work as a full time Missionary. Since that time she has established after school programs, developed curriculum for children of promise and worked to form collaborations with groups and organizations to stabilize at risk communities across the country.

Attend seminars with Dr. Evelyn Bethune and learn about personal development and self esteem building as it relates to solid economics and the importance of exposing young people to community activism, professional development, small business development in the urban communities, rites of passage for youth and adults.

Dr. Bethune can be contacted through Ms. Traci Boyd, Nascence Media at (832) 368-2826 or by mail at PO Box 3343, Houston, Texas 77253 or by e-mail at docbethune@marymcleodbethune1875.com.

CHAPTER 14

The Reality Of Recovery

GINA PEARSON

*My continuing passion is to part a curtain, that invisible veil of
indifference that falls between us and that blinds us to each other's
presence, each other's wonder, each other's human plight.*
~Eudora Welty

More than any of the other social and moral maladies, childhood sexual abuse has one of the most enduring and injurious effects on a person's life and soul; affecting and, in some ways, infecting the victim's perceptions of "self" throughout the individual's life. This is intensified when the perpetrator is biologically connected to the victim and often loved. The mixed signals and confusion can be overwhelming.

As children, we were both victims. I was a victim of his rebellion and his desire to control and to satisfy his lusts. He, in turn, was a victim of someone else's infliction of the same desire upon him, in addition to the spirit that commanded his surrender to it. I am of the firm belief that "hurting people hurt people". I also believe we all do what we know to do, given our history, our mystery, our misery and our ignorance.

When I became a thought in the mind of God, there was hesitancy in the earth realm in the mind of Catherine Guillory Gauthier, whose womb would be used to incubate, accommodate and nurture the human entity of

Gina Marie. Having already said yes to co-creating five other children, Catherine reluctantly agreed to accept the challenge of birthing yet another child. Gina would be her sixth of nine. Driving herself to the Charity Hospital neonatal unit in Lake Charles Louisiana, to deliver one whose spirit demanded entry into the earth unexpectedly early, Catherine delivered Gina – this restless spirit being embodied by only 4 lbs. 6 oz. of human flesh. Requiring special care in the ICU, she remained in the hospital for weeks while Mother Catherine returned home to care for her five other young children.

Having the stamp of rejection implanted in the womb and being cared for by the neonatal nurses equipped with the knowledge to protect my delicate life until I was able to survive on my own, I longed for the profound simplicity of my mother's touch. But with five other children and the environment relating to them to tend to, there was little time left for doting time from mom who was already overworked, overwhelmed and often overlooked.

Those initial stages of my life would set me up to begin a war not only for my physical existence, but also for my very soul. The battle began for my peace of mind. Insecurity, fear, rejection and a sense of abandonment were some of the hindrances and challenges that would demand that I discover courage within myself to face, confront and ultimately overcome. Later, I would learn how what some perceive as generational curses would impact my life and battle to steal my legacy. I had to take a stand, draw a line in the sand, cancel any assignment to mentally, morally or spiritually edit the God-ordained contract I signed in my pre-incarnate consciousness and reality.

My mother was the wife of an only child and adult alcoholic, who himself, lost his father to murder at the young age of ten. Together, housed in a six-room, wood-framed house in one of the poorest communities located in southwest Louisiana, they struggled against what seemed to be insurmountable odds to raise their nine children. The stress of her life was made more complicated by an absentee husband.

Feeling fragmented, frustrated and at times, sorry for myself, as a child, I began to be influenced by fear to forfeit any possibilities of freedom. With the impostors of fear, guilt, shame and anger mixed with feeling cramped, crowded and deprived fueling me, I resorted to stealing, manipulating, and being contentious and critical of others. The rage was building within. Possessing such inner angst would be the beginning of many self-sabotaging habits and behavioral patterns.

It would take years before I became dissatisfied enough to recognize and stand against the self-sabotage initiated by sexual violation and begin to recover my dignity – my sense of value and worth. It would be still more years before I would discover my voice and declare to my abuser along with my self-imposed oppressor that "enough is enough!"

My mother knew the power of affirmation and would often encourage me along those lines. As a child, in an effort to be a support to her, I would assist with the daily chores, and consequently, I was given the name "Cinderella". When the three older girls left for college, I remained home with my four brothers and assumed the chores of my sisters. Through my mother's encouragement, I began to learn that "I had value; I had a place in the world; I had something to offer others". Gradually, I began to feel that I was unique, with no duplicate; that I was born an original and was not going to die a copy. I was the only one of "me," as we all are originals. Yes, I was bruised but certainly not broken.

As I continued evolving in consciousness, I would further recognize that I did have a contribution to make to the world – to the lives and actions of others. I began to see and declare that I was a woman of intentional dignity. Slowly the process of recovery had begun. For me, like many others, it took almost an entire lifetime to recover from such childhood trauma.

In an attempt to protect the heart of a little girl who was injured before the age of accountability, and after many years of struggling with fear, rejection, low self-esteem, insecurity and mental torment, my desperation drove me to find the answer through discovering my state of spiritual bankruptcy. I found my freedom and peace through acceptance of the Father's love, through learning to love and accept myself, and through the forgiveness of myself, my abuser and others.

In the sacred text of scriptures, Jesus is recorded to have said in **Matthew 10:39**: *"He that finds his life shall lose it: and he that loses his life for My sake shall find it."*

As a young adult, a college friend introduced me to transformational learning, in her attempt to support me in freeing myself from my destructive behavior patterns. I immediately learned the gift of dealing with my issues and facing my truths, owning and honoring them. More recently, I am discovering why inspecting, interrogating and excavating our lives is crucial to our very existence. I have discovered that dealing with issues diminishes the curtain that hides you. Failing to deal

with issues diminishes your dignity and, in many ways, robs you of your sanity. Deep inside, I somehow knew that, when I faced myself and soul realities, I felt lighter. But to hear and feel the affirmation in my spirit, helps me understand why I have had this passion to pursue peace and find my freedom. As I grew spiritually, I discovered that peace was my inheritance and to possess it would require me to contend with the invisible.

I adopted for myself the words of the Apostle Paul in **II Corinthians 10:4:** *"The weapons of our warfare are not carnal, but mighty through God to the pulling down of strongholds; casting down imaginations, and every high thing that exalts itself against the knowledge of God, and bringing into captivity every thought to the obedience of Christ."*

Overcoming the exploitation of my innocence was a necessary choice, in order to maximize and fulfill my God-ordained purpose and to recover my soul. I decided to bury the "victim-conscious Gina". In order to dance the dance of life more skillfully, I am developing discipline in my thought life, as I remind myself that I am *not* that which was inflicted upon me. Rather than being a victim *of* circumstances, I decided to become a victor *over* them. That realization plays a part in propelling my forward motion, and gives me such hope to encourage others who are surviving childhood traumas such as sexual abuse.

I now know that my identity is not my past. My past does not define me, but in consciousness, I have chosen to allow it to help refine me. The position of influence and impact that I hold in public ministry also inspires me to and indeed *insists* that I continue to consciously transform my life. My capacity as a high energy, "make-it-happen" temperament serves me well as I serve my family and others. I am enjoying the diligent "stretch" of discovering and recovering **who I can be** for others as I am simultaneously discovering **who I am** and **why I get to occupy my particular space and place in the earth**. I have grown to know that this journey is not all about me, except for how I fit into the "whole".

Transitioning through the cycles and seasons of life can bring great opportunities for growth and change. When I became a student of the rigor of transformational education, I gained the tools that equipped me to submit to the awareness of what was stopping and stagnating me – those things to which I was blinded. I became aware of those habits in my life that hindered or impeded my relationship with God and others. Through study of scripture, investigations of scores of supplementary materials and submission to my own consciousness of the Christ principles, along with feedback from others regarding my automatic behavior patterns, I have become more equipped to face life's encounters with greater ease and excellence. Yes, adjusting to the seasons of life is a sovereign process and I was desperate to learn the skills to sustain and support me through the sacred shiftings.

As I reflect on the trauma and drama of my past life, I choose to embrace a statement by Diane Ackerman: "I will not dishonor my soul with hatred, but offer myself humbly as a guardian of nature, as a healer of misery, as a messenger of wonder, as an architect of peace."

Today, I enjoy a restored relationship with my brother, who was my abuser. He has apologized and repented to me, and I have forgiven him. We chat almost daily and genuinely love each other very much. We are restored...to God be the glory!

As a trauma survivor, I move forward in life to complete my journey walking in rhythm and to the beat of forgiveness, knowing that I am a crown jewel of God's heart – a virtuous woman, a crown to my husband; and queen mother to my children, Prince Julian and Majeste' Amour.

As a devout Catholic and a fervently praying woman, my mother did all she could to raise us to follow her example of reverence for and desire to more fully know God. She taught me at a young age the value of self-discipline and hard work. She remained faithful to daily mass and praying the rosary regularly as a family throughout our upbringing – teaching us to rely on God. Being emotionally abandoned, feeling uncared for and neglected, as a wife, did not hinder her unmitigated focus on her children.

On October 29th of 2007, my daughter's twelfth and father-in-law's eighty-second birthday, while battling for her life, she declared to her girls as we stood at her bedside that she was tired. Shortly thereafter, she surrendered her spirit to the Ultimate Rest. Having no other option, I released her, knowing her legacy would live in the rich lessons she taught her nine children.

As a woman and forever her baby girl, I committed to appropriating and practicing the spirit of gentleness, faith and faithfulness I witnessed in her, including her courage, her determination, her wisdom, her frugality, and her love. It lives on in the earth through her daughters, my sisters – Charlene, Madeline, and Iris. And it is my passion to make its rich

deposit into my daughter, Majeste' Amour, and to all I am privileged with the honor of blessing with this legacy of victory.

How P.H.I.T. (Physiologically Healed Internally Transformed) Are You?

- Are you aware that your **unhealthy** secrets are robbing you of energy and life?
- Are you walking in unforgiveness?
- Are there truths you can begin to replace with the lies you believe about yourself?
- Are you participating in destructive behavior patterns and cycles?
- Are you interested in discovering how to become an observer of yourself, get feedback on how you are showing up in the world in order to support you in living your life?
- Are you convinced that you are living a life that contributes to a legacy worth leaving?
- If you answered **YES** to one or more of these questions, it's time to get P.H.I.T with Gina!

Gina Pearson is the Founder and CEO of P.H.I.T. 4 Life (Physiologically Healed Internally Transformed), an organization committed to inspire excellence in individuals in every domain of their lives.

As a Certified Transformational Leadership Coach, Gina designs and facilitates workshops and seminars that promote the transformational discipline. Her audiences include small groups, corporations and community organizations. The emphasis of her work brings attention to the value of collaborative partnership required to facilitate social change and create healthy relationships beyond the boundaries of race, culture, gender and other "-isms" in the work place and in the community.

To learn more about Gina, visit her website www.ginapearson.com or email **PHITness Coach Gina Pearson:** PHIT4life1@cox.net

CHAPTER 15

My Journey To Spiritual Restoration

GURMAY E. DARLINGTON

God put something in me before He formed me.
He made me in the correct time and season because He knew that I could
handle the tribulations.

MY LIFE BEGAN WITH TRIALS AND TRIBULATIONS

At the age of 3 months, I was poisoned by an older cousin who didn't like me because of the color of my skin. I was seriously ill and hospitalized for months. I suffered medically, socially, and academically and was diagnosed with enuresis, bedwetting, until the age of 16.

ENDURING THE LONELY YEARS OF SEXUAL ABUSE

I lived with my grandmother and because of frequent bed wetting; I slept on the living room floor. My grandmother's male friend, Young, also slept on the floor beside me and began sexually abusing me almost immediately. Physically I fought my abuser for years; and some nights I had

THE *Queens'* LEGACY

no strength. This was reported to my grandmother immediately who smacked me and responded that I was lying about that God-fearing man. She then ordered me to continue sleeping on the living room floor. I dreaded coming home, let alone going to bed. Sometimes I would sneak into the bedroom with my blankets and lie on the floor. When my grandmother found me, she would send me back to my bed where my abuser was always waiting. For many days and nights all I could think about was when was my mother coming to get me and why she was not protecting me and whether I was going to be sexually abused that night as well. I became withdrawn, isolated and unable to trust adults. This sexual abuse ended when I was reunited with my stepfather, mother and siblings.

I remember distinctly that it was a Sunday and as I was playing with my pretend doll house, another family friend, Happy, came to visit and began to talk to me. Soon after that he began to inappropriately touch me. I took a Carnation milk can and hit him so hard on his forehead that it was immediately swollen. He began to scream and yell that I was a crazy girl and that I would amount to nothing good. My mother began to advance with a belt in hand and I ran outside. When my stepfather came in from work, my mother reported the incident and I came when he called my name. He picked me up and began to beat me. I fought to get loose as I yelled that Happy was touching my private part. He continued to beat me and I bit him until he loosened his grip on me.

FROM BEING ABUSED TO ABUSIVE RELATIONSHIPS

My first male friend was charming and nice and wanted marriage when I turned 16. He asked permission from my great-grandmother who was my guardian. He presented himself to be attentive, kind, and very loving – at least until he couldn't get his way. He would try to buy my love by giving me his paycheck, which I always refused. He did not want me to have any friends or to have any relationship even with family members. I began to feel smothered and suffocated which caused me to stop making marriage plans because he became possessive, jealous and demanding especially when he saw me with anyone else. If he saw me speaking to a male, he became violent and went crazy.

Once he came towards me and demanded that I leave with him; I refused and he threatened me. The next day, I was at a party with family and a male friend of mine was there. The male friend who wanted marriage approached me and demanded I leave with him. He then proceeded to pull me and I began to struggle and eventually he let me go. He again threatened me and later that day, beat me severely with his fists while my uncles and cousins observed and only laughed. He was a professional boxer. He came by many times later to apologize but I never even spoke to him again.

My four siblings and I were relocated to Brooklyn, New York where we were reunited with our parents and two other siblings. My two siblings did not like me, especially my sister. There were always fights and arguments in our one bedroom apartment. They made me feel like a stranger and as though I did not belong there. They complained that they had to share their things and suggested that I should return to Guyana, South-America, where I was born. I began to feel isolated and lonely and spent many nights crying. My sister took a special interest in abusing me. She frequently stole my money and even my bank book and went to the bank, forged my signature and drew my money out. My sister stole my clothes and shoes and gave these items to her friends because she couldn't wear them because she was too fat.

I became engaged in continuing education classes and extracurricular activities at school just to avoid the tribulations with my sister. Most nights when I returned home, she would have already eaten up my dinner and would tease me until we started a physical confrontation. I would try to ignore her by reading or watching television or doing extra home work for which I later got credit. She would switch channels on the television or turn the lights off and use profanity. I don't know how I managed in those days without losing my mind. Then, to compound matters, I was dating a nice guy to whom I was able to tell my problems.

That same month that I graduated from high school, I became pregnant. My sister suspected my pregnancy and she really became vicious. She would place pins and needles in bed on my side and when I lay on the bed and got stuck she would laugh hilariously. This continued right through to my seventh month of pregnancy. Quite unfortunately, that nice guy was not that nice. He began to engage in adulterous relationships with other women and verbally abuse me. When I called him during the delivery of his child, his whereabouts were unknown. I actually worked and attended community college until two weeks prior to the birth of my baby.

At age 21, I graduated with an Associates of Arts Degree and moved with my baby into my own apartment. The baby's father continued with his adulterous relationships and, in addition, began to physically abuse me and on one occasion I almost lost my left eye because I was hit with a bottle as I was drinking wine from a Tupperware glass in celebration of his birthday.

THE *Queens* LEGACY

He too was jealous and was always accusing me of having affairs in spite of his loose life. Although it took a while, I ended this relationship.

WHEN ENOUGH IS ENOUGH

Years later, I met an older man and was engaged to him. We started a business and shortly afterwards I found out that he was cheating me. He emptied the business bank account, stole my debit card and I became penniless. I found out around the same time that this finance was also having an adulterous relationship. This man began to threaten me that he was going to leave because he felt unappreciated. One day I came in from work and he moved because he needed a break. The next day I contacted a moving company; packed his stuff, and in three days, moved his things right out of my house and into storage. I went to the post office and removed his name from my address. I went to the bank and closed the business account down. Then I went to an accountant and closed the business structure and restarted another one in my name only. I called a towing company and had his car towed off of my property and I changed my locks, mail box keys and code to the house alarm.

A few years later, I met my husband who promised me the world. Prior to marriage we both went before the Pastor for counseling and I specifically stated the five things that I would not tolerate: abuse, adultery, dishonesty, a husband that does not function as the head of his home, and dishonesty. My husband swore to love and cherish me until death. Our wedding vows were broken in less than a year; he was having an affair. When he was confronted, of course, he became abusive and pulled my hair and held it for a good five minutes.

The second time, he was caught and confronted, he hit me in my chest and for a minute I thought that that was my last breath. He is a truck driver and I went out on the road with him when I found out that he was having another affair. I confronted him and he yanked my hair so hard and held it. I had to struggle to get free. I called 911 but they were unable to assist since I was in West Virginia and I did not have an address. This made him even more furious and he began to use profanity and threatened me. He then proceeded to push me out of the 18-wheeler truck while he was driving. The first opportunity I got I jumped out, penniless.

At times he refused to speak to me for weeks and still, during those times, he would demand intercourse. On one occasion, I refused and that made him so angry that he raped me. I fought him and that made him angrier. I grabbed the house phone to call 911 and he knocked it out of my hand and left the bedroom. He returned and walked towards me, pinned me down with his hand while he held a butcher knife to my chest and clearly told me that the next time I called 911, he would kill me. The abuse continued and I was forced to file a police report and petition the court for a restraining order because my life was in imminent danger.

LIVING THE GREATEST YEARS EVER

God put something in me before He formed me. He made me in the correct time and season because He knew that I could handle the tribulations. Once I repented and changed my mind, God began to work His plan to restore me to my rightful place. As an Ambassador of the Kingdom of God, I understand that I do not have to accept pain, abuse, suffering, mediocrity, poverty and trouble.

God's desire is to restore me so that I am able to take dominion and authority over the birds, fish and the earthy realm and the very things that were once perceived to have authority over me. Daily I seek a relationship with Our Heavenly Father. As a Kingdom citizen, I am victorious by the power of the Spirit of God who resides in me. As I continue to put God's interests first and to represent Him faithfully, He will take care of my interest. In His word, He says that once my heart is right towards Him, He is obligated to orchestrate the affairs of my life. The tribulations, abuse, and trials were not for me.

God was only using them to get something through me because of His assignment on my life. Remember, a tree can't taste its fruit. I developed a thirst for wisdom and to know what God's word says about Kingdom living, marriage and relationship. God stepped into my tribulations and brought His order and I continue to glorify Him. Righteous living comes from suffering in trying to do the right thing. God allows people and things to leave my life in order for the right things to come into my life according to His plan.

Our Heavenly Father is not obligated to fill a vessel that is full. Our Heavenly Father ordered me in 2006 to write about my life as a testimony to free other hurting people. This year His desire and will is being manifested in the earth. God told me that after I've done all I can I must stand and I now continue to stand on His word. Finally, I confessed that it is not my will but His perfect will that will be done through me.

THE *Queens* LEGACY

Gurmay was born in Guyana, South America, and relocated at age sixteen to Brooklyn, New York. She received degrees in Social Welfare from Adelphi University and in Social Work from Fordham University. Gurmay is currently a Psychotherapist. Previously, Gurmay was a Teacher and completed teaching requirements from Medgar Evers College, Staten Island College, and the United Federation of Teachers. Gurmay has attended Les Brown University and completed training to obtain designation as a Certified Seminar Speaker. Gurmay's commitment is to help you make your life a daring adventure.

You can reach Gurmay directly by phone at 704-906-1400 or by e-mail at efffrigefraser@gmail.com or visiting one of her websites, including www.myspace.com/fraserenterprises, www.youtube.com/herzlberbice or www.gurmay.mentorsclub.com.

CHAPTER 16

I Am An OVERCOMER!

IYABUNMI MOORE

I forgive myself, and others who have sinned against me. Today I eliminate guilt and judgments from my thinking. I am positive, happy and appreciative!"

I've been blessed. Actually that is an understatement. I have been extremely blessed. This isn't to say that everything in my life is exactly where I want it to be at this point in time, or that everything has always gone my way. Like most people, I am not who I was and I am not who I am going to be. I still have plenty of growing and developing to do. But I am excited about my future and where God is taking me. I hope you are excited about your future as well. If you aren't, just hold on. By the end of this chapter you are going to need to put on some sunglasses. I am here to tell you that your future is so bright that you need to wear shades. What He has done for one, He can do for all.

Growing up, I was blessed to live in a household with my parents who were great role models. They always edified me and caused me to believe that there wasn't anything that I couldn't do. Both my mother, Jerri Stewart, and my father Zik Stewart, have been great influences in my life. Being their daughter has made me who I am today. My parents grew up on the poverty stricken streets of Baltimore. Both were poor but didn't really

know it until they were grown. My mother worked as a school teacher and my father at Bethlehem Steel until they were both bitten by the entrepreneurial bug in 1982.

So what does their background and upbringing have to do with me? Everything. You see, their bug bites were contagious. As an only child born in 1971, I watched my parents cultivate their God-given potential so much so that by the mid 80's, my mother was making $85,000 a year in her part-time business. Needless to say, she left her $25,000 a year teaching job and went into business full-time with A.L. Williams. At this time, my father joined her and by year three, they were earning a six figure income. Year six saw them reach $50,000 per month!

Seeing their achievement helped to give me a positive outlook on life. It expanded my vision. I believed that if they did it, I could do it too. Their belief that you could make money or excuses, but you couldn't make both is a part of my philosophy today. I grew up seeing the Law of Responsibility, 'If it is to be, it's up to me!' All around me I saw hard work, love, persistence and goal setting. Still I had to pave my own way through life.

Herein begins my story. I am sure you or someone you know can relate to the following glimpses into my life of obstacles, blessings and God's grace. It starts off being a little off track, but ends up being right on point. I am on my way to my date with Destiny...and so are you.

If I had a half of a cent for every woman who has suffered from sexual abuse, I'd probably be a billionaire. Thank God my abuse story isn't worse than it is – still, being forced to have sex with your 17 year old cousin against your will, being too scared to move does damage to your emotions. Five years of feeling...yuck...gross and fifteen years of guilt. Why didn't I scream? Why didn't I get up? Why didn't I do *something*, *anything* to make him stop? Oh how I wish I could go back in time. Thank God that time is a healer. If you have been abused, proclaim this with me,

"I AM AN OVERCOMER!!!"

In 1993, I married my high school sweetheart, Kevin. We met in 1983 when I was a cheerleader for his little league football team and started dating in the tenth grade. God has truly blessed me with a great spouse. Unfortunately, we started acting like we were married before we actually were. If you are a young, unmarried lady reading this chapter and are in a sexual relationship or contemplating one, PLEASE trust me when I say, do whatever you have to do to wait. Put on a chastity belt if you must. You will never regret waiting and there are many regrets if you don't. Just a year after we got together, I was pregnant.   As a teenager, I knew that fornication was a sin. I also knew that abortion was too. Although I wanted to have my baby, I was forced into an abortion by my emotionally devastated father. From then until now I think about that baby. If you have ever regretted a decision you made hat affected your life or someone else's, you must forgive yourself. You need to be released from it. Proclaim today,

"I forgive myself, and others who have sinned against me. Today I eliminate guilt and judgments from my thinking. I am positive, happy and appreciative!"

In 1989, I was off to Hampton University. This was the time when my relationship with God deepened and became more personal. Being on my own without my parents nearby, created a dependence on God that I hadn't had before.   My freshman year I had a 4.0 grade average. I was proud of myself and so were my parents. After that first year. I considered how I might relocate to the Hampton Area and get a job down there. Those plans quickly changed.   The summer after my freshman year, I was pregnant again. This time I told my parents what I had planned to do. I would have my baby and not go back to Hampton. My mother pleaded with me to go back. She said that she would take care of the baby if I would just return to HU. I stood my ground and enrolled in a college in Maryland. There comes a time in life when you have to start making your own decisions and be big enough to handle the consequences of your decisions. If you are little fearful about where the decisions you have made are taking you say,

"I've got courage. I've got strength. I am going great places!"

While I was pregnant, as sick as I was, I never stopped going to class. After two years of community college, it was on to the University of Baltimore. My first year there I got pregnant again. Yet again, I never stopped my matriculation.   My education was too important. I didn't see any reason why having a baby or babies should stop me from accomplishing my goals. When others say that something can't be done, when they look at you funny and want to put their labels on you, believe you are a winner. When you experience setbacks, remember what Willie Jolley says, "A setback is a setup for a comeback!" Twenty-one years old, two babies and six years with the same man told me that it was time to get married. Sometimes you've got to encourage yourself. Tell yourself,

THE *Queens'* LEGACY

"I am a winner. I am a champion!"

On July 24th 1993, we tied the knot while still in college. We had a two year old, a five week old, no money, and no jobs. What I did have was something that had been instilled in me from an early age, a positive self image and a "can do" attitude. After living with my parents for six months, our name came up for a Section 8 townhouse in Columbia. Finally we had a place of our own. The babies kept coming. In 1996, we had another boy. In 1998, we had another girl. In 2000, we had yet another girl. Okay, time to get the tubes tied. When you are in situations less than ideal, look to the future and all the great things that will come your way. As you work on improving yourself, things will get better. Shout to the world,

"Every day in every way I'm getting better and better!"

Throughout the child bearing years there was struggle after struggle and God performed miracle after miracle. Our BGE getting turned off would bring someone we barely knew to give us $500. When we were down to almost nothing, a neighbor would ask Kevin to move furniture and pay him $40, just enough to get us through the week. A friend would show up with $100 worth of groceries. Most everyone experiences difficult chapters in their lives. Even then, I knew that my condition was temporary and that I was creating a story that would be used to encourage others.

"I am overtaken with blessings that I freely share with others."

As the years went by, things got better. My husband got a job at Proctor and Gamble in 1998 that paid $28,000. That was a big deal for us at the time. In 1999, I started praying for a house in a nice area with good schools. We started talking to builders and looking at lots even though we didn't have the income to support the dream. That's what you do. You step out on faith and move toward that which you desire. If you wait for the circumstances to be right, you will forever be waiting. When you use faith and take action, you will find that circumstances will align themselves in your favor. God will make it all come together. You don't have to know how he is going to get it done. Just believe that he will. Declare,

"*I believe it*, so that I can *receive* it!"

In January of 2000, we moved in with my parents to save money for the home that we were praying for. We expected to be there for a year. One year turned into five. Five kids in one bedroom, Kevin and I in another, made for tight quarters, but we made it through. I thank God for my parents

114

who allowed us to occupy their home for five years. Thank God for the people in your life who are there when you need them. Verbalize your gratitude to the universe. State cheerfully,

"I am grateful for the abundance of supportive people in my life!"

The years that followed brought more miracles than I can name. It is so exciting to see the Lord at work. You don't always have to see your way through obstacles. Your belief will carry you through. The Bible says that if you have faith the size of a mustard seed, you can say to the mountain, get out of my way and it will move. I am a testimony that this word is true. God has thrown many mountains straight into the sea for us. It isn't because we are so good or perfect, it is because He is faithful and honors the prayers and faith of his people. Shout,

"I am blessed with wealth from the abundant universe today!"

Time went by and we continued to prosper. In 2004, due to the entrepreneurial bug, I started a home-based business. By the end of 2005, we were earning a six figure income and lived in our brand new home built on a beautiful three acre wooded lot in the same neighborhood where I had grown up. AMAZING! I don't have time to share all of the challenges that we overcame during the building process. Just know that in life you must depend on a source higher than yourself. God allowed people to find favor with us, from the landowner selling us the property below market value, to the builder who gave us a great deal, to my parents paying for us to get the brick front on our home. There were deadlines where we needed large sums of money. I didn't have it and I didn't know where I would get it. I went to the Lord and He worked it out. We must remember that God owns it all. Everything in this world he created and there is no limit to His resources. Whatever you need, he will give it to you if you believe. Declare,

"Today, I prosper spiritually, emotionally and financially!"

TRUST. TRUST. TRUST. You've got to trust that God is taking care of you and won't let you stumble or fall. Most people would be devastated if their income of $15,000 per month ended abruptly. When it happened to us, we weren't devastated. I did the only thing I knew to do, I depended on God. The CEO of the company I had a business with didn't like the fact that I was now branching off into other similar businesses and he cut off my income. After building a network of 3,000 representatives and helping so many people, the new lifestyle of financial freedom that our family was finally living came to a halt. We had gone from section 8 housing to living in

a sought-after community in Howard County.   Now it seemed that everything would change.

We knew that in spite of it all, there is one thing never changes and that is God. He is constant. If He has taken care of you in the past, He will continue to take care of you in the future. If He provided for you miraculously in the past, He will provide for you again. Don't doubt him for a minute. Just have faith, trust and believe. We are still in our home and God has moved me into another position. If you've ever wondered where the money would come from proclaim,

"My God shall supply all my needs according to His riches in Glory by Christ Jesus!"

God has your situation under control. There is nothing that you will ever experience, that He won't help you through. Stay connected to the source. Keep thinking the right thoughts and keep talking the right talk. As Brian Tracey puts it, "The quality of your thinking determines the quality of your life, and since there is no limit on how much better you can think, there is no real limit to how much better your life can be." Right now as you live, you are writing your story. I can't wait to read it. Make it great! I will see you at the top!

Bunmi Moore **loves** connecting with people and has a passion to see people achieve, win, and maximize their potential. Each week Bunmi conducts seminars where she encourages others to step out of their comfort zones and experience more of the abundant life that God has for them. She has started a ministry of feeding the homeless in Inner City Baltimore. You can contact Bunmi directly by telephone at 443-864-9440, by e-mail at bunmi.moore@yahoo.com or visit her web site at www.bunmiTV.com.

CHAPTER 17

Worthy Of The Crown

JEWEL DIAMOND TAYLOR

To wear a crown as a "Queen" is not about being a domineering, stuck up, puffed up Diva... I feel like a Queen because I finally found my voice and worth without apology, arrogance, deceit or manipulation.

Have you given your power away to other people?   Are you suffering with emotional scars, shame, secrets and silent screams? Do you hear the voice of your inner critic putting you down?

When you have been told you are no good or when you have felt invisible, incompetent and insignificant, it is like being hypnotized and put under a spell. Once you wake up and snap out of the trance, you begin to realize the truth about your divine, significant, whole, loving and capable self. You can learn to break the trance of low self-esteem and fear. When you can heal emotional scars, you can wear the crown of a Queen...a Queen reigns with grace, faith, courage, love, beauty, brains and purpose. A Queen does not shrink to fit. She is able live with confidence as God guides her to fight the dragons, increase her territory and use her power to practice wisdom and compassion towards those in her life.

THE *Queens'* LEGACY

For many years, I gave my power and peace of mind away to my husband, children, parents and friends because I suffered from the disease to please. I gave pieces of myself away to other people out of a sense of duty, fear, a hunger for attention and conditioning. It was a daily challenge to stay awake from the trance of low self-esteem. I took many hits from "emotional abuse bullets". Being married to a very traditional "old school" guy and birthing two sons, there were many times I felt invisible, exhausted and voiceless. I didn't like confrontation. I was a wounded unprepared "girl" growing up while raising two strong-willed sons. I never felt like a "Queen" in my own home.

When my mother passed away from breast cancer in 1986, I found my crown and my voice. Her death was my wake-up call that life is too short to give your power away. I became determined to break a generational cycle of depression, low self-esteem and a joy-less life. I began to discover who I was without with great joy and fear at the same time. I gradually learned to speak up and stand up for myself without feeling afraid, selfish or powerless. I began to realize that I can only be a happier "me", wife, mother, friend and vessel for the Lord if I learned how to honor my body and dreams. I did not blame others. Instead, I struggled with blaming myself for giving away so much of my power, voice and self-worth.

It is painful enough to be aware of the many tragic crimes against women and girls, locally and globally, historically and politically. So when I think of my personal journey to fully know my worth in God, in the mirror, within my family, in my marriage, in the church, in my race and in the business arena... I shudder to think about the many times I dropped my crown in the past.

To wear a crown as a "Queen" is not about being a domineering, stuck up, puffed up Diva. It is **not** about having a sense of entitlement. I feel like a Queen because I finally found my voice and worth without apology, arrogance, deceit or manipulation.

In fact, once you realize your worth, you don't need a crown. Your self-esteem, courage, body language, attire, words, generosity, inner peace and love speaks louder than any adornment.

Women have been socialized to suppress their boldness, talents, ideas, desires, choices, sexuality, identity and sense of adventure. A long the way, many of us experience an identity theft as we seek to please and accommodate others. My Grandmothers did it. My mother did it. My

Mother-in-law did it. My aunts did it. They were door mats, martyrs, superwomen and silent sufferers. Their suppressed joy and deferred destinies subconsciously taught me not to expect much out of life. Yet as a child I placed them on pedestals admiring them as if they were Queens. I didn't know as a child that their hopes, talents, dreams and freedom were stillborn and some aborted; their depression, anger and exhaustion turned into cancer, multiple marriages, abuse (keep it secret), unfaithful husbands (keep it secret), excessive shopping and a "keep a stiff upper lip" attitude.

Emotional wounds from your childhood, divorce, illness, racism and unhealthy media messages can leave deep self-esteem scars. There are many women, like me, who grew up on childhood fantasies. Stories of the damsel in distress unconsciously shaped our expectations and self-worth. Rapunzel was powerlessly trapped in a dungeon until a man saved her. Cinderella was trapped as a slave in her family, until a prince saved her. We read that Snow White was cast into a deep sleep until kissed by a prince. And let us not forget Dorothy lost and desperately seeking the wizard. He was a fake and told her she had the power all the time. The story ended with Dorothy waking up from a nightmare.

God created women as nurturers, sensitive and compassionate to the others. We are naturally caregivers. Somehow, too many never learned how to take care of self. Society and cultural values have taught women to seek their validation, identity and happiness outside of themselves. In the name of sacrifice, altruism and being a nurturing superwoman, too many women have lost their crowns.

You can rise again after your individuality, spirit and personal power have been crushed. You can learn to be a steel magnolia...strong, yet tender. Self-esteem wellness strengthens your confidence to make decisions. It empowers you to respond effectively in situations where people may take advantage of you. A Queen has boundaries and fights to keep the enemy out of her territory.

Women who have a clear and positive sense of their self worth are better able to communicate to others what they want and need. Because they feel secure with their personal boundaries, beliefs and behavior, they can "give and take" in an appropriate way without compromising their values. They are true to themselves because they don't need another person's approval to feel good about themselves. Approval is nice, but their sense of being a good person does not depend on it.

On the other hand, women who suffer because of abandonment, rejection or failure, often compromise their values to win approval from

others. They either isolate themselves or do things that are unsafe or that violate their own sense of what's right. Women who feel left out or left behind often ask, *"What did I do wrong?"* Their sense of guilt, shame and pain is so overwhelming that this question haunts and torments them. The healthy questions to ask on the road to recovering self-esteem are, *"What can I learn from this experience? What can I do to heal myself? How can I take care of myself without seeking approval from others?"* As you learn to value your peace of mind, self-respect and wellness, you will make wiser choices to decrease the stress, anger and sense of powerlessness and victimization.

We often resist what we need. Change is good. Change gets you out of a rut. Change makes you pay attention to details. Change teaches you to trust the Lord. Change teaches you to trust your instincts. Change teaches you to be flexible. When you are ready to change by reclaiming and re-energizing yourself, you may be called selfish. People around you may feel threatened and may not understand your new strength, courage, voice and choices. An old wise African proverb states, "Around all flowers are insects." You will need self-esteem and courage because there will be "insects" in your life who will be intimidated or insecure about your growth.

If you neglect yourself, others will learn to neglect you.
The way you treat yourself, teaches others how to treat you.

Personal growth happens as you begin to listen to and honor your own voice instead of those who place demands, fear and guilt trips on you. Keeping yourself fulfilled, balanced, emotionally stable, spiritually strong and peaceful is the gift you give yourself. This is not a selfish act or attitude because now you won't blame others for your lack of joy and happiness. You won't expect someone to be the complete source of your joy and happiness. Learn **to *know, love, honor, listen to, understand, trust, accept, respect, protect, believe in, be honest with and take care*** yourself. If you don't, you will spend your life asking, demanding, manipulating, controlling and hoping others will do for you, save you, protect you, support you, validate you, affirm you and believe in you.

I recall a powerful statement from the movie "April in Paris". The young lady depressed about her declining relationship, said with pain, *"I know I'm in here somewhere. I hear myself screaming from a distance."*

It's time to let go of fear, limitation and social conditioning that diminish your joy, progress and success. You have to discover what was lost, denied, forgotten, crushed or stolen. Escaping the pressures of the world and negative conditioning from others is an act of ***self-liberation***. Are you ready to loose yourself? Are you seeking to be free of stress, joyless living, fear, grief and pain in your body or your heart?

You and I can benefit and grow as Queens as we receive the legacies from others in our history pages or family albums. A legacy is something handed down from an ancestor or a predecessor or from the past. I am blessed with a legacy of love and integrity from my two aunts, Janet and Louise. I received the legacy of etiquette, sewing, decorating and the appreciation of beautiful things from my Mother. My mother-in-law gave me the legacy of cooking. My Uncle Rasul left me with the legacy of searching for spiritual truth, cultural pride, teaching and a healthy lifestyle. My father was a gemologist with a jewelry store in Washington D. C. where I was born. He left me with a legacy of the importance of networking, community building and a love for people.

We can stand a little taller as we gain courage from Rosa Parks, political courage from Ida Be. Wells, determination from Harriet Tubman, a thirst for education from Mary McLeod Bethune, mother wit from our Grandmothers, compassion from Mother Teresa, grace and elegance from Judith Jamison, Lena Horne, Nancy Wilson or Dianne Carroll, staying power from Cicely Tyson, creativity from Toni Morrison and Dr. Maya Angelou or the power of song, praise and worship from Mahalia and Shirley Caesar.

I would like to leave you with a legacy of love and self-esteem by sharing one of my poems published in my book "Sisterfriends." published in 1998.

When God Made Me, He Was Just Showing Off *(excerpt)*
"You are caregivers, teachers, leaders and homemakers.
You are artists, students, entrepreneurs and policy makers.
In unity, we are more wiser, richer and stronger.
If we stay in the light, we can't go wrong.
Strength and wisdom...our ancestors continue to send...so SistahQueens, let's
be loyal to the royal within."

As you review the messages in this book again and again, remember you are a miracle. Your life is a precious gift. Be reminded of the teaching in Psalm 90:12, "Teach us to make the most our time so that we may grow in wisdom."

Don't wait to exhale...breeeeathe...shine...glow...grow! Learn the truth that sets you free from doubt, anger, procrastination, limitations and fear.

THE *Queens'* LEGACY

What legacy will you leave? Stand on your holy ground with your crown. Give God the glory for your blessings and "b<u>lessons</u>."

Jewel Diamond Taylor is an Inspirational Speaker, Founder of Women on the Grow, Women's Ministry Leader, Workshop Trainer and Women's Retreat Facilitator ~www.DoNotGiveUp.net

CHAPTER 18

The Beatitudes Of A Widow Queen

JUANITA HARRIS

Blessed are they who mourn, for they shall be comforted.

Today the Lord has instructed me to write about the experience of widowhood from the perspective of the beatitudes. Suspecting this study is more for my growth and reflection I enter into this with fear and excitement. Fear in terms of the meaning of respect for the wisdom of God concerning my life. Excitement, I have never been disappointed by what God has called me to do. What are my qualifications for being called a widow? For 41 years I was someone's wife; Queen of my household to my husband and King. All of a sudden, in a day, I became a widow. There was an identity crisis; who is this person? A widow was an older woman, with gray hair and reading glasses. I do have gray hair and reading glasses but I was not the person I saw in my mind's eye. First Timothy, Chapter 5 verse 9 tells me who I am:

NKJV: 9Do not let a widow under sixty years old be taken into the number, *and not unless* she has been the wife of one man,

One month after my husband's death, I turned sixty. As often as I've read and heard the New Testament, I had never seen that verse. It never pertained to me as it does now.

Who I should be is given in 1st Timothy Chapter 5, verse 5:

NKJV: 5Now she who is really a widow, and left alone, trusts in God and continues in supplications and prayers night and day.

The widow in this passage has no children or grandchildren to care for her. The passage is stating the responsibility of the church to take care of her physical needs. No matter our plight we all need to trust God and pray. For a new season has come, a winter season, cold as snow and sometimes as harsh as a wilderness.

Blessed are the poor in Spirit

To lose a beloved spouse causes one to enter a new spiritual realm. No longer do we have the person who knew us intimately. No longer do we walk proudly as the wife of....

You could say our spirits were one. Paul said that for a married person, their primary cares are for their husband or wife, but for a single person, the primary care is to be for the things of God. My spirit had become poor by one. In essence, the two who became one has been torn apart.

My focus will be from the perspective of a widow, as I have only been a widow and life without a husband is different than life without a wife. I believe one of the reasons for this study is because of my constant concern for financial matters. My husband did not leave me financially well off. I know God is my source and my provider, but having never experienced poverty causes me to struggle to rest in the provision of my Father. This is my failing, not God's failing to provide. Although I am not destitute, I still worry that I'll have enough, and that is not God's will.

There is however, a poor spirit, a humble and unpretentious spirit. What is more humbling than to be stripped of your covering? To not have the one who protected you from the world and sometimes from yourself. Although God does these kinds of things, as humans we often look to other humans for the things that God provides to us in the spiritual realm. Now is the time to know the spiritual is more powerful than the natural. Heaven is my real home and my prayer remains, "Thy will be done on earth as it is in heaven." This becomes more real to me each day. In heaven the angels do not question God, they just glorify Him all the time. In heaven, God is the only focus. God's angels don't have problems, deaths, sickness, poverty or marriage to distract them from their purpose, which is to praise the Lord. It is our purpose also.

To humble myself is my will. Some people are humbled by life's situations and some of us humble ourselves. We perform acts of humility in order to do God's will in our lives. We are independent, self-willed and self-centered in our carnal selves. Only because of the Lord Jesus Christ in us, can we do the will of God.

Ours is the Kingdom of Heaven. In the Kingdom of Heaven we are comforted, provided for, protected and loved by God. We can love Him without concerns about what others will think. We can pour out our deepest hurts and concerns to Him without being ridiculed. He will not reject us in our time of need. He's only a prayer away. We can serve Him and He will not mistreat us. We can give Him our all without the fear of being abused. In the Kingdom of Heaven, we praise, worship and glorify God unashamed. Let it be done on Earth as it is in Heaven.

Blessed are they who mourn, for they shall be Comforted

Mourning is something we do alone. No matter how many people are around or how close you may be to others. No one can mourn for you. Each person mourns in a different way. Some cry and faint; some seem emotionless; however we do mourn. Mourning is feeling or expressing grief or sorrow. For some, we feel more grief than others. The first days of my husband's death were busy and I was numb. I didn't have to feel anything because I was too busy taking care of details. That was my comfort zone and I could keep my mind focused on what I needed to do. Then there are the quiet times when no one calls or comes by and you are completely alone. It is then that we have time to think about our beloved. The little things - it was not the band he gave me, but the wedding band that was on his finger, his fragrance, holding his hand, how he laughed and so many other little things. Some days are overwhelming and if I don't fix my mind on my Lord Jesus, rather than what I have lost, I would go crazy.

My comfort is hope. My hope is that my husband is at peace and in the presence of the Lord Jesus. I find comfort having 41 years with him and that's worth a lot. I think of the good times and forget about the hard times. I think about what he would say in certain situations. The comfort in knowing a person so intimately that you know what they would say or

think is very comforting. My relationship with God is such that I want to know what He thinks or would say about situations in my life. Meditating on His Word gives me insight into what God thinks. I'm not always right, just as I was not always right about what my husband was thinking. Still, it's comforting to believe you know someone so well. We can never know any one so well that we would always know what they think. It's even less likely that we would ever know all of God's thoughts since His thoughts are above our thoughts.

Blessed are the meek for, they shall inherit the earth

The meek are those who quietly submit themselves to God. I accept this season of my life. Now that I must do everything myself, each day is a physical and emotional challenge. I have no excuse for not spending time with God. This is a season for just me and my Lord. He eats with me and sleeps with me, and Oh, how He loves me.

Blessed are they who hunger and thirst for righteousness, for they shall be satisfied

Fasting from food for a period of time to seek the Lord for His will in your life and the life of the body of Christ can teach us how to hunger for God. When my mind is off of what I'm going to eat next, it is an opportunity to seek God. His living water has quenched my thirst so often for those things that would cause me to want more and still feel unsatisfied.

Shopping is fun but I have limited resources. And even if I were a multi-billionaire, things cannot fill the place where a relationship should be, whether with a man or with God. Still, I do feel good when I shop. God, however, has provided me His Word. I can poke around His Word as much as I want and it doesn't cost me anything other than time. I can chew on the meat of His Word for hours and be full of the Spirit when I leave the table. The only thing I gain is satisfaction. My glucose doesn't go up. There are no carbohydrates to turn to sugar and no fat to clog my arteries. Let God prepare a table before you, in the presence of your enemies, loneliness, depression, and extended grief.

Blessed are the merciful, for they shall obtain mercy

Grief may cause us to be short with those we love and others around us. Our cup of mercy may be half full. The angry part of grieving may linger a bit too long. We're mad at the world because things aren't as good as they were. We have no one to share our daily frustrations and triumphs. My husband Richard and I were merciful to each other on a daily basis. That's how you stay married. Have mercy on one another. Of course it doesn't work that way with God because He doesn't need our mercy. As He sees our hearts and the mercy we are willing to give each other, He can shower us with renewed mercy every morning.

Blessed are the pure of heart, for they shall see God

Who are the pure of heart? Can a broken heart be pure? Yes, when we continue to trust and seek God even through our brokenness. God is the comforter and healer of our hearts. Our hearts are being healed as we trust God even the more and see Him everywhere.

Blessed are the peacemakers, for they shall be called the children of God

My idea of a peacemaker is someone who keeps the peace at all cost. Not so in the Kingdom of God. A peacemaker makes things peaceful. We cannot make anything peaceful until we are peaceful. If our insides are turned upside down, we can only cause turmoil and strife. But when we go to "The Peace" as we need to go so often, we can someday give peace to others who go through the stormy days of widowhood. As a child of God I can go to Him every day and say, "You know what I need". He has never disappointed me.

Blessed are they who are persecuted for the sake of righteousness for theirs is the Kingdom of Heaven

Sometimes we may feel persecuted. Maybe it's just me, but it seems I don't have very many married friends any more. As a matter of fact, I don't have too many people to call on the phone, including my family. I travel alone. I eat alone. It seems I have done nothing wrong yet I feel persecuted for being a widow. In this position, I have so much time to go to the Kingdom of Heaven to talk to my Father. The Bible says the widow is to continue in supplications and prayers night and day. Learning to first visit with the Father before allowing my feelings to take me to the land of despair or to the pity party is still an ongoing challenge. Each day I become better at communicating with my Source and my King Jesus.

Juanita has earned a Bachelor's Degree in Business Administration at Southern Illinois University. She expects to pursue a career in a field that will utilize her hard work and accomplishments as a talented and experienced woman of faith. Her goals in life are now on Godly things. On her journey, Juanita has acquired a Masters degree in Christian Counseling and Psychology. As a Life Group Leader and Professional Life Coach, her goal is to reach women who need a partner to walk with for a season and help them to reach their highest potential. With over 20 years serving in ministry, she is still sharing the joy of walking with Jesus.

A widow, after 41 years of marriage with three grown children and two grandchildren, Juanita loves to travel. She has been blessed to travel to Africa, Haiti, and Israel.

Juanita may be contacted at 937-342-0379 or by e-mail at juanitah2000@yahoo.com.

CHAPTER 19

With Faith And Prayer, Miracles Happen

KARLA RAYPON

...in order to attain anything worthwhile, one must pay the price.
Freedom is not free...

All you need is faith the size of a mustard seed and miracles can happen. You must never stop believing and be prayerful during the wintery seasons of your life. That's how you become more appreciative of spring when it arrives. At the same time, you must learn to laugh at yourself and the world. Bring humor to all things and it will lift your spirit and keep your heart young. These are some of the ways that the wonderful woman I am honoring in this chapter has carried herself through her wintery times.

It was October 1984, almost noon, in Balulang, Cagayan de Oro City, in the Philippines. My mom, Teresa, eight months pregnant, was accompanied by my aunts, uncles, my four older siblings and a group of believers. They were told that there was a visionary who proclaimed that an apparition of the Blessed Mother was going to occur in this particular place. They had to cross a lake with waters to their thighs to get to the open field where the apparition would appear. As they all prayed the rosary, my

mom suddenly looked up and exclaimed, "Oh my God, they are going to take me!"

They asked her what she was talking about for no one else saw the vision. They call it the "dancing sun" or the "miracle of the sun" because the sun moves in a zigzag motion and you can look straight into it without hurting your eyes. The Blessed Mother, also known as Our Lady of Miraculous Medal appeared. Beside her was Jesus Christ. Both had their arms reaching toward her, smiling. At the same time, a vision of chariots carrying angels appeared in the clouds. My mom just kept praying and was still in a state of apprehension, awe and wonder during this miraculous event.

She already believed, but had not seen God in person. She knew through His works He existed, without a doubt. This occurrence was a divine confirmation that there is a higher power that is righteous. The Queen Mother Mary, who immaculately conceived our Lord, Jesus Christ left a legacy of eternal love and faith to my mother, Teresa, on that majestic day.

A month after that incident, my mom was in labor in Maria Reyna Hospital, Queen Mary in English. After hours of labor, the doctor told her that the baby was in distress. There was a possibility that if she tried to push, either she or the baby would survive, but not both. They had to act immediately. After four natural childbirths, an emergency Cesarean delivery was performed. At 6:20 p.m. on November 27, 1984, her 5th child was born. It was the 90th feast day of Our Lady of Miraculous Medal. Indeed, it was a miracle. She named her daughter Karla Marie. I am blessed to have been given life and to share this story with you.

As I have stated before, with faith and prayer, miracles happen. And they can happen over and over again. When I attended mass one Sunday at Christ the King Catholic Community, Father Bill said, "Seven days without prayer makes one weak." Upon hearing that, my mom came to mind immediately. She consistently emphasized the power of prayer. If you are at your lowest point, complacent stage or at the pinnacle, pray for guidance and faith. This wisdom was instilled in me since childhood and came from both sides of my family. I can surely attest to this, given the hurdles I have faced and conquered during the short period of time I have spent here on Earth. Prayer is pure magic.

My mom dreamed, envisioned and prayed everyday for an answer to the question of whether going abroad to work and support her children was the right thing to do. God responded. In January 1989, with the help of my maternal grandparents, she immigrated to America. With her back against the wall, as opinions about her decisions were questioned, she sustained herself with prayer. God promised her rewards if she would endure the effects of the tremendous sacrifices necessary to make this change.

My youngest sister, Mary, was only 29 months old when my mom left. When I asked my mom how she could do what she was doing, she told me that although it was heartbreaking to her, she had to erase all fears and doubts because she had a bigger vision for us. She is a true servant and leader. Although we couldn't comprehend what she had in store for us, deep down I knew her unconditional love was the reason why she strove for our betterment. Although she was thousands of miles away from us physically, we were spiritually, emotionally, genetically, and supernaturally connected.

As I wrote this chapter, I spoke with Mom on the phone almost every day to learn more about how she was able to conquer her daily battles. At one point, she stated that the battle of surviving each day while missing her children so much to where it would place her in a state of depression was among the greatest challenges that she faced. She passionately responded to my question by saying, "Prayer is what has kept me strong. We can do all things through Christ who strengthens us." She attempted to visit church every day for that was and **is** her sanctuary. There she is at peace despite the problems that wait for her outside the church doors. On the other end of the phone, I couldn't help but shed many tears. I felt the pain she went through and the unconditional love she had for us. That was an affirmation that if there is no pain, reasonably, there is no gain.

She knew in her heart and soul that she could not give up on the dream of bringing her children to America and providing us a life of unlimited possibilities and opportunities. Accordingly, my mom made no excuses and held fast to that goal. She has passed on to me that willpower to persevere and be persistent with my dreams and goals, no matter what the circumstances.

As my mom worked hard here in America, she paid for most of our tuitions so that we would have the best education. Although we were attending private schools and nourishing our minds, there were many days when food was scarce. We are thankful to God that prayer was instilled in our minds. It got us through the countless thunderstorms that we endured through our lives.

I am amazed at how my mom never gave up and how she kept constant communication with her children though we were continents apart. "Giving up" is definitely not in her vocabulary. She believes with all of her heart that in order to attain anything worthwhile, one must pay the price. Freedom is not free, a philosophy that we hold dear in our hearts and have tattooed in our minds. Growing up in a 3rd world country, seeing the beautiful and the ugly side of it all, we know not to ever take life for granted. The mentality to work persistently for what we want for ourselves and others has been engraved in our very being.

In the book "*The Slight Edge*", Jeff Olson wrote a chapter called "The Secret of a Penny". Everything starts with a penny, "a penny for your thoughts." That one idea my mom had of bringing her children to America, met with action, faith, and prayer, resulted in God's bringing her to the people at that point in her life that would help her make her dream come true. It was a complex process, to legally bring seven children to America. With the help of some Samaritans, along with the assistance of our Creator, on May 30, 1995 my mom's dreams became reality.

I can still smell the air at LAX that evening in May, close to midnight. The plane landed and we were finally through US Customs and the whole nine yards. I can still remember what my mom was wearing. How beautiful she looked, how lovely she smelled. I can still feel the anxiety and the thrill in my heart to finally be able to be in my mommy's arms again. When that happened, I felt so complete.

In America or the Philippines, supporting seven children, or even just one, is a challenge. My three elder siblings were somewhat able to assist with expenses, but my mom took care of most everything. From September 1995-2003, we lived in a two-bedroom apartment in Orange, California. Granted, our place was small, but the love that filled our home was larger than belief. Somehow it was a melting pot for our friends and relatives. They had bigger homes, but I think they enjoyed being in the environment of love. My mom was like their adopted mom and she loved them like her own. God was in our home therefore it was filled with joy most of the time despite, the struggles.

My two brothers shared a room. I, my sisters and my mom shared the master bedroom. We had one king size bed and a queen size bed next to each other. I look back and am thankful for those trying times. I know that they contributed to the bond that was formed, a bond that can never be broken. It positively taught us how to be very tolerable as well.

With a CNA salary, working every night and during the day at times, at three different hospitals, Mom was still able to take us on family trips to amusement parks, Catalina Island, San Francisco, Solvang, and Yosemite. Sometimes I wonder if she had a time-travel machine. Somehow she found time to celebrate our birthdays, attend school recitals, functions and sports activities as well. When I wanted to study violin in junior high school, she bought me a violin. She saw the excitement in my eyes and was determined to allow me to pursue something for which I had a passion.

I'm sincerely convinced that my mom is a super heroine. I don't know that even Wonder Woman is of the same caliber as she. Have you heard of "SupercalifragilisticexpialidociousWoMom?" In short, "SuperWoMom"? Well, that's her alias. Sorry mom, but I had to reveal your true identity. In all seriousness, she continuously sacrifices her entire being to others, and especially her children. She exemplifies complete selflessness. I bet she has a costume and cape under the hospital scrubs that she wears to work. Don't worry because she will be there to save you when you're in trouble. Let me tell you, she has sixth sense for sure.

She is so very much fun and even silly at times. She is the first person to laugh at her own jokes. Actually, her five minute joke turns into a fifteen minute joke because she is laughing her heart out for the first ten minutes, with a laugh that is completely infectious. My siblings and I pick on her like she's our older sister. This keeps her young and makes us wiser. She makes up words by twisting them around to make them her own. Somehow, the manner in which we are connected, we understand what she means. We have countless inside jokes and we will eternally cherish these priceless treasures.

Mom allows us to be who we choose to be, she loves us equally, and operates in fairness at all times. My siblings and I are so similar in so many ways yet completely out-of-this-world diverse. The chameleon that she is enables her to know how to reach out to each of us. So many parents struggle to keep themselves and their children united. She is so special.

My mom's true faith in God, following the path He has laid out for her has resulted with me meeting my husband, Timothy, here in the U.S. We have been blessed with a beautiful daughter, Skarlett, to whom I will pass my mother's legacy. I pray that Skarlett will pass it to many more generations. This has also allowed me to wake up every day with a visible attitude of gratitude.

THE *Queens'* LEGACY

Paul Orfalea stated, "Success is when your kids want to spend time with you once they've grown up!" I yearn and value the time spent with my mom because she completes me. She is beyond wealthy in love and abundant in relationships, which are the only fortunes you may take when your spirit departs earth.

I cannot write enough poems, give her too many warm embraces or kisses, or tell her "thank you" and "I love you" enough to express my heartfelt gratitude toward her for bringing us into this world and allowing us to live our lives to the fullest. She is the valedictorian and the professor with the Ph.D in Motherhood at the University of Life. I will do my best to graduate with the same honors.

God evidently spent a little more time creating her. She is the original **Empoweress**. If my daughter feels just a percentage about me of how I feel toward my mom, Teresa, I have honestly succeeded in life. The financial riches I may acquire along the way cannot compare. For undying love and faith are virtues you cannot buy.

Karla Raypon has operated her own home-based business from the age of 18, while attending Santa Ana Community College for Business and working at a hospital full time. She knew she was born to be an entrepreneur and a purpose-driven servant leader at heart. Her main goal in life is to change the world and her family's legacy, financially and spiritually for generations to come.

Karla coined the word "Empoweress", meaning an Empowering Empress, empowering others while building an empire one person at a time by guiding them to bring out their GREATNESS within.

You can contact Karla directly by visiting her website at www.KarlaRaypon.com or by e-mail at Empoweresslegacy@yahoo.com.

134

CHAPTER 20

Daddy's Little Girl

LAKISHA NEVELS

If I hadn't gone through the storm and the rain, how would I be able to relate to the pain of others?

Entering into this world prematurely, I had to fight for my life. My daddy tells me he remembers it as though it was yesterday; his little girl in an incubator fighting to live.

As I sit here gathering my thoughts, tears are rolling down my cheeks. At this moment, I realize that "daddy's little girl" has never stopped fighting for her life. The battles I face today however are much different. The battle today is to encourage myself and others to move forward in spite of every obstacle before us.

The battles I fight today include showing one little girl or boy who needs to know that they are beautifully made, created perfectly by a loving God, regardless of their disabilities and/or an insecurities. I fight for every woman and man suffering with sickness or disease, and who feel as if the world has turned their backs on them. I fight for anyone who has ever lost a loved one, received horrific news, or has ever been in a depressed state of mind. Finally, the reason I fight is because so many believers fought for me

through their prayers and supplication. Some of whom, I barely knew. Surely I can do the same for another in need.

My story begins sometime mid-year of 2002. I received news from a doctor that suggested that I had Lymph edema, a disease that causes fatigue, swollen limbs and localized fluid accumulation in various areas of the body. It affected my legs and feet and made me self-conscious about wearing skirts or even high heels. There were so many times I cried because I didn't feel beautiful and the stares from others made me feel such uncomfortable. People would constantly ask, "What's wrong with your leg? Why is one bigger than the other?" With pain in my heart and a smile on my face I'd try to explain. I often wore slacks to avoid the questions, the stares and the feeling of being different that devastated me.

This was the most challenging time of my life. Before this, I never had a problem dealing with low self-esteem, even with the fact that I had struggled most of my life with being overweight, I still didn't suffer with self-esteem issues.

Eventually my issues led to depression, hypertension and acid reflex. I developed a hernia and had gallbladder surgery. In 2006, within four months time, I lost my home, my car, and my man. Two days before Thanksgiving, I received a call from my gynecologist and heard what no one is prepared to hear. I had contracted a sexually transmitted disease, Human Papilloma Virus (HPV). This news would suddenly alter the way I lived my life. Now, when I considered dating a man, it involved my telling him and possibly facing his rejection.

My depression deepened. Even though I knew that STD's were not limited to any one person, I couldn't grasp the idea that I had contracted a disease, I was always so careful. I was careful to the point of our being tested for STDs before having sex. I soon found out that science had not yet found a way to test men for HPV and there was no way to have known if my boyfriend at that time gave it to me or I had contracted it prior to our relationship. Devastated about all that was happening to me, I began to survey my life, to try and gain an understanding as to why everything was happening to me. I went as far back to my childhood as I could remember.

Most of my childhood memories are a blur and I can only remember things that occurred after about age eight or nine, which is right around the time that my parent's marriage started to fail. There was always arguing in the house, because my mother was used alcohol as a pain reliever and stress reducer, as a way to quiet the demons of her past. Her dependence on alcohol eventually led to my parent's divorcing.

I stepped up to being the "mommy figure" to my siblings, of six and three years old. A nine year old child in this role was a load to carry and I suppressed my feelings of abandonment and separation to ease the devastation that I and my sisters felt from losing our mother. Although life did eventually move forward for me, it didn't come without the trials and tribulations. By the age of twelve, I had already become a victim of molestation and sexual harassment by both genders. I struggled to find my identity, because deep down in my heart I harvested the pain of my past, which hindered me from being able to have the confidence I needed as a young girl.

All of a sudden I felt violated and I became numb to the world around me. I found myself being afraid to face the very challenges that brought me pain. I didn't know who to talk to and I felt that I couldn't express the hurt to my Dad, because he was doing his best to survive raising three daughters as a single parent. At the time, I hadn't been introduced into a relationship with Jesus Christ, so I began to lean on the only one thing that would listen, 'Mr. Bear'. It sounds funny, but up until about eleven years old, Mr. Bear was my shoulder to cry on, my voice of reasoning and my hope.

Another thing that helped me to deal with the pain of my past was finding that I had the ability to cultivate my emotions through poetry and songs. Writing became my mechanism to communicate everything that I felt I couldn't express verbally, while singing became the avenue for my healing.

My life finally began to change for the best the year when my family moved from Maryland to Virginia. There, I met a woman who I now call my Aunt. She was the woman God used to put the joy and hope back into my life. She was the mother figure that I had longed for my whole life. That year, I also started of my eleventh grade year in high school. Since I had previously attended a predominately black school, going there was a culture shock, but it was what I would need to reach greater heights in life.

Attending a new school didn't come with ease. I was the 'new kid' on the block and I wanted to achieve things that I never before accomplished. So, with prayer and the Lord by my side, I stepped out of my comfort zone, took a quantum leap of faith and I ran for Vice Presidency in our schools student government.

To make a long story short, I did win the election, but I soon got a taste of being racially discriminated against. So, not only was I now the new kid, but I was now the black kid, that wasn't a part of any popularity clicks, nor had I been at this school since the ninth grade like most students who ran.

By the end of my twelfth grade year I was well known by many and I did overcome the racial boundaries that existed. I even recall a sincere apology from my Caucasian running mate, who after getting to know me, instead of my color, was able to be appreciative of my position. As I look forward even beyond high school, into my twenties, I noticed that in many ways I still have to prove myself. When I started working in the construction industry as a human resource professional, once again I was the outcast, the misunderstood woman.

In meetings I would generally be the only woman, better yet, the only black woman in the midst of a round table full of older white men. Immediately, every word that I spoke was put up to a microscope and examined. All ideas that I came up with were debated and most conclusion were overlooked.

It wasn't until one day in our weekly meeting that I had flipped the script from being the "yes sir" woman, to now putting my feelings on the table. I ranted and after I was done telling it like it was, I left the meeting and didn't go back until the following week. Hours after leaving the meeting, I was told that a huge discussion took place and later I received a call of apology. Soon the round table of men was trying to understand and relate to the woman that I am and not who they had perceived me to be.

Today, as I take another look at my life, I realize that my past did hurt and I wouldn't want anyone to endure such pain. However, if I hadn't gone through the storm and the rain, how would I be able to relate to the pain of others? If the obstacles weren't in place to block me from reaching the highest of heights, how would I ever be able to proclaim the victory? A scripture in the word of God says, "For I know the thoughts that I think of you, says the Lord, thoughts of good and not evil, to give you an expected end." (Jer. 29:11)

I'm reminded of the life of Job in the bible. Job was a righteous man and both God and Job loved each other. However, Satan questioned God about Jobs love and in my own words; Satan placed a bet with God to see if Job would still love God through the hardship and pain of losing his land, his money and his family. Before the end of the scriptures, Job did experience hurt and pain. He even wanted to curse the very day that he was born, but he never cursed God. Before long, God told Satan to take his hands off of Job, because Job had gone through enough. God in turn gave Job back everything he lost, but twice as much as he had previously.

So today, I say to everyone and myself. The road we travel just might be the road less travelled. You might not have all the necessities you need, your shoes may get worn out, your water supply may quickly vanish, and you might sweat, get filthy and even cry.

The only thing that will take you through this journey will be your determination and drive. You won't want to give up, because God will show you that life ahead is much greater than the life you left behind. You might feel lonely, afraid and discouraged, but at that very moment you'll hear the whispers of God telling you not to give up.

No matter what your situation is today, recognize that the Queen (or King) in you can rise to the top. Take a stand and tell yourself that you will no longer be subjective or submissive to the pain of your past. You will walk with your head high, you are going to succeed, your life will change for the best and you my Queen (or King) will live out your legacy.

Born in Akron, Ohio this now 30-year old Virginia resident has become a catalyst for change. LaKisha Nevels has been inspired to reach not only the people in her community, but a hurting nation looking to fill a tremendous void in their life.

LaKisha realizes that she is not able to "save the world", but, she is determined to change the mindset of people who have become depressed, oppressed and stressed out about the challenges of life.

The word of God suggests that we being strong ought to bear the infirmities of the weak and not to please ourselves (Romans 15:1). Without being selfish, this young woman is on a mission to become the biggest support system to those who are trying to heal from the wounds of their past, because she too has had to overcome and be healed from some of the very same wounds.

 THE *Queens'* LEGACY

LaKisha plans to leave behind an unforgettable mark in the hearts of many people, through her love, support, and that gentle nudge to move people towards an enjoyable life. Contact LaKisha directly at by mail at PO Box 22722, Alexandria VA 22304, by e-mail at ms_lnevels@hotmail.com or by telephone at 703-861-2302.

CHAPTER 21

Mama, I'll Be Good

LATASHA MCKENNIS

When I was awake, my life seemed like a nightmare, but in my dreams I lived in a perfect world with an abundance of love and joy.

Imagine a utopia where the birds are singing, the sun is vibrant and luminous, the day is calm, love is amid the air, laughter is everywhere, and your very existence is blissful. Then you awaken and discover that your reality is filled with great turmoil, ceaseless negativity, and emotional duress. This is what life was like for me as a child, and before discovering the definition of personal development. When I was awake, my life seemed like a nightmare, but in my dreams I lived in a perfect world with an abundance of love and joy.

I arrived into this world in the late nineteen seventies, first born child of an unwed mother and father. My father was a good man and a hard worker, but had deeply committed relationships with whisky, beer, and other women. My mother was sweet as apple pie and as beautiful as a butterfly, but at some point began to indulge in drugs and became an avid user of cocaine. The combination of the two eventually created an atmosphere of violence and confusion, with me caught in the middle.

There have been countless times when my parents would brawl and I would make efforts to help my mother fight. I would scream at the top

of my lungs, hoping that someone would notice the ruckus of sound traveling from the pit of my belly, crushing my heart, echoing in my head, and escaping from my lips. It may not surprise anyone that eventually, my intimate relationships mirrored that of my parents'. As a result of that "learned behavior," I found myself reenacting exact scenes from my childhood with my significant other. It felt like déjà vu.

By the age of 9, my father became ghost-like in my life and my mother began to take her frustrations out on me. She often referred to me as being black and ugly, told me that I was stupid, and expressed that she wished she'd never had me. There were also several derogatory names she gave me that – none of which were anywhere on my birth certificate, I might add. This caused more mental trauma than any broom being broken across my back. This stung more than the burning sensation that I felt when I sat in the bathtub filled with hot water and Epsom salt after being whipped with an extension cord, tree branch, or some other inappropriate object. Her words were tattooed on my brain, and I thought the pain would last forever.

This malpractice of parenthood and these acts of hatred trickled down to infect the minds of many, and were inevitably tossed into my hands for mental consumption. Realizing that regardless of what I'd endured up to that point, my ability to choose could not be beaten out of me – physically nor verbally – I was given a wonderful opportunity to choose my direction on either path of the fork: 1) keep the ball of negativity moving, or 2) drop that sucker like a hot potato.

Eventually, my mother's harsh treatment led me to become calloused and unemotional towards others. I began to take my pain out on the children at school, and occasionally lashed out at teachers. I commenced to reap punishment by way of school suspension for beating up a kid that said or did something hurtful. I usually only received home punishment from a suspension if I had lost the battle. My mother would literally approach the children and ask them, "Who won?" I don't remember ever losing a fight. Who wants to get beat up twice? I wanted to minimize physical contact with her as much as possible. I was both directly and indirectly <u>taught</u> to use violent and rebellious behaviors to assuage my hurt feelings.

The understanding that I lacked during adolescence was that my mother was doing what had been done to her. As an adult, I have concluded that this had to have been a "learned behavior." There had to have been some outside source – someone or something that she was modeling herself after. These were behaviors that could have only been acquired by experience, meticulous study, and persistent practice. There had to be a more positive and effective ways to instruct, discipline, and communicate with other human beings. Without being consciously aware of it, a search began inside of me to find someone or something better to emulate.

Statistics indicate that 80 to 98 percent of children suffer physical punishment in their homes, with a third or more experiencing severe physical punishment resulting from the use of implements. This simply means that I am not the only one who had this childhood experience.

How thin is the line between discipline and cruel and unusual punishment? When discussing my feelings about this topic, I have been repeatedly advised that if you spare the rod, you spoil the child. I'm not here to tell you how to discipline your children or that you shouldn't "spank" them. I am only here to suggest (based upon my experience) that you try positive actions vs. negative actions. I want to share a few alternative methods of action that I practice with my daughter.

1. I take time out to breathe and calm myself down if I am upset.
2. I go for walks or engage in some type of physical movement or exercise.
3. I discuss my child's actions with her if she is behaving in an unacceptable manner.
4. I LISTEN!!!! Open communication between my child and I is imperative.
5. I offer guidance and direction. I've also sought guidance and direction for myself.
6. I CHOOSE NOT TO USE DRUGS AND LIMIT ALCOHOL USE!!! It impairs judgment.

Today, it is my sincere belief that if my mother had known better she would have done better. She has even openly admitted this to me during some of our deeper conversations. This is why personal development, self-awareness, and self-improvement are an essential part of life for me today. Although I was eagerly determined to prove my mother's theories about me wrong, I also had to learn to let go of the pain and forgive past hurts. This was a "must" if I truly wanted to become successful at building healthy personal and business relationships. I give huge credit to a book called, "The Power Is Within You," by Louise L. Hay for helping me to achieve my personal break-through and gain self-acceptance, as well as a personal Bible study offered by a close business partner. I recommend

these tools to anyone struggling with issues stemming from abuse of any kind.

Thankfully, I was able to transcend a background of constant negativity and abuse, both mental and physical, to a life of positivity, faith in the Almighty, and courage. Developing the ability to continuously subdue thoughts of doubt and self-pity became a daily exercise. I accomplished this by surrounding myself with positive thinkers who referred me to local bookstores and taught me that libraries were free and filled with useful information that could enhance one's quality of life. I didn't like to read at first, so I began to listen to books on CD while I was driving to work every day. The more positive energy I filled my life with, the less room I had for negativity. After taking in information about self- improvement, my desire to help break the vicious cycle of the generational curse of torment induced by self and outside sources became more intense. Seeking to become better daily is the only real cure or solution that I have found thus far. Changing my associations, reading, and listening to audio discs became a positive outlet for me.

After reading and studying new ways to have positive life experiences, I discovered that the most invaluable lesson I learned from watching my parents at war, and being involved in my own personal combats, is that someone is always watching and learning from you. There may be a small child, teenager, or young adult observing you from afar, unconsciously emulating the very vibration of your voice, the movement of your limbs, and the rhythm of your heart. Be it a positive or negative groove, someone is moving to your music. My business mentors taught me that it is okay to be a copycat, as long as you copy the right cat – it is my endeavor to ensure that I am the right cat for my daughter to copy. It may be a good idea to investigate whom you are copying. Think about who may be copying you and what they may be doing.

Everyone has a story and has experienced challenges, hardships, and negativity in some fashion. It is impossible to escape negativity one hundred percent of the time. In many instances, it may feel like our worlds are crumbling right before our very eyes. Maybe you've lost a job or failed in business (I have); experienced the loss of a loved one (I have); been raped or robbed of something (I have); maybe you just feel all alone in the world just as I have. Perhaps everything I just spoke of is incomprehensible to you. Just remember one thing: although you are a product of your past, you do not have to remain a victim of it if you do not wish to. The indelible memories of my past can no longer evoke sorrow within me, because I do not allow them to. The many hardships that I've encountered have created opportunities for growth and an increased burning desire to leave a great legacy for my family. To do this, I must stay engaged in the process of planning and preparing mentally for upcoming events that may feel like tornadoes, earthquakes, and hurricanes.

Through constant prayer, belief in myself, utilizing personal development tools, and by seeking mentors to provide the proper insight, my mother and I are developing a healthy and respectful relationship. She now owns a successful business, drives one of her dream cars, and is a great role model for my sisters and even for me. She has also been off drugs for an extended period of time. We still have our ups, downs, and differences of opinion; however, relationships of all sorts are about continuously growing and improving.

My mother always told me that one day I would thank her. It baffled me as to WHY I would EVER thank her for the way she treated me. Well, despite all we have been through, she taught me how to be a responsible adult. For that I say thanks. She taught me how to be strong and how to be resilient enough to bounce back from anything. She instilled independence within me, and for those things I say thanks.

You see, I understand that I have a choice. I am choosing to focus on the positive results of our relationship while acknowledging and releasing the negative energy from the abuse. I believe that it is easy to turn a negative (-) into a positive, all you have to do is add a line (+), with the added line in this case signifying a shift in the way I view myself. This line may more commonly be known as the proverbial "line in the sand". I view myself as a Queen, which has allowed me to see the Queen in my mother. And for this I am forever grateful.

LaTasha L. McKennis was born and raised in Milwaukee, Wisconsin. As a single parent to one child, and the eldest of four sisters, she holds an obligation and a responsibility to help break the generational curse of physical and mental abuse that has plagued families for centuries. Ms. McKennis has channeled her personal life experiences into a resilience to motivate, mentor, and encourage self-acceptance. In addition to being a motivational speaker, she is the founder and C.E.O. of BDP Media as well as

a promoter with Tempo Management. You can reach LaTasha directly by e-mail at l.mckennis@hotmail.com.

CHAPTER 22

A Queen Whose Time Has Come

LIL JACKSON

Everything that has happened to me continues to happen to others.
I stand in proxy for those who have not yet found their voice.

Can it be okay or even proper to talk about this 'stuff'? It's over, right? It's in the past. Surely I'm over it, right? I'm... functional. Some of this 'stuff' is over 40 years old!

As far as I know, I've never gone into a state of depression; nor have I retaliated or considered revenge. In fact, for many years my family and friends told me I was *living in denial*. Apparently during each episode, I did not display the normal signs of a person dealing with an abundance of drama.

I'm a Christian, for goodness sake! Can I talk about my personal life all out in the open? What kind of example would I be? Do I dare say out loud what really happened? Who really wants to hear about molestation, rape, deception, theft, divorce, child custody battles and Corporate America racism?

Wait... What am I talking about? All of that "*stuff*" can be found on television, 24-hours a day! People are so obsessed with these negative

images, they *TiVo* their favorite tragedy-packed shows. They don't seem to care if it's pretend characters or their neighbors on the six-o'clock news.

But my woes involved others. Must I consider them since 99% of those negative folks are still walking around? I've heard that one person in particular is making an attempt to get their life together. How dare I risk embarrassing him and his family?

The answer is clear and easy. Everything that has happened to me continues to happen to others. I stand in proxy for those who have not yet found their voice. *"Bear ye one another's burdens, and so fulfill the law of Christ."* (Galatians 6:2)

I offer a few mini excerpts from my wonderful life so far; and I DO MEAN WONDERFUL.

My Friendly Housecoat

I may not have been able to stop the body crawling low on the floor into the bedroom. I could not stop him from stretching and reaching up to the bed, slowly feeling for his preferred body part. But, I could stop him from touching my bare body because my bathrobe, a.k.a. "housecoat", helped me feel less of the intrusive touches.

Fortunately for me, my third floor bedroom was much too hot in the summer months.

This allowed me to sleep in my grandmother's air-conditioned bedroom. During each of these frequent visits from the night crawler, my grand mom slept right beside me. I prayed the entire time for her to wake up. Surely she would save me from the horrific, stomach churning, embarrassing visit from the night crawler.

These episodes started at a very young age. That same night crawler started out as a sort of exhibitionist. He would display his private tools and tried, unsuccessfully, to convince me to join him. He progressed with his repulsive antics as the years went on. This all happened often over a period of years.

That pretty, lace trimmed, quilted housecoat got me through a lot of difficult nights when I was younger and living with my grand mom and several other grandchildren. I was the only girl in the house. In addition to the warmth it provided, the quilted fabric was thick enough to provide a barrier between my body and unwanted hands that found their way to my underdeveloped chest and buttocks.

I am also very thankful for a sleeping bag that I received while living with my grand mom. It also was quilted and covered my entire body. The very best thing about my sleeping bag was it had a zipper that I would zip up to the very top, cover my complete body, including my head and for added protection, I would roll over on top of the zipper. I conducted this ritual each and every night. Then, a swollen river gave me a much-needed rest.

Summer 1972

I came up with a brilliant idea. Get rid of my false teeth! Heck, they hurt every time I put them in my mouth. Two fake molars, one glued to each side of a pink plastic thing that was supposed to be a replica of the lower part of my mouth. It had a wire on each side that squeezed around my real teeth to hold it in place. t was awful.

This was a big deal because at 11 or 12 years old, it was the one thing that I knew for sure my "real" dad bought for me. Sentimental or not, the dentures had to go! This was going to be a sneakier undertaking than the time I buried my broken *Julia* doll in the backyard.

Everyone was settling in my grand mom's bedroom; still watching the boring news about a storm named Agnes and the fact that the Susquehanna River was swelling up so high that people were abandoning their homes. I thought with all of this going on, getting rid of my false teeth should be easy enough. I just needed to sneak down to the basement and hide them.

I pretended I wanted a glass of water and made my way downstairs. I turned on the faucet water strong enough to cover the sound of the basement door opening. I quickly tiptoed down the basement steps with my false teeth rolled up in toilet paper and tucked in the front of my underwear. They would not fit in the small pocket of my housecoat. I shoved my false teeth under the carpet that my grand mom bought to make the basement as luxurious as the rest of the house. I raced back up the steps, wet a small glass, dried it with a paper towel and put the glass back into the cupboard.

Mission accomplished! When I made my way back up to my grand mom's bedroom, I was abruptly questioned about my whereabouts. I rolled my eyes at "him" and climbed on my grand mom's bed.

THE *Queens'* LEGACY

The very next morning the river was indeed swollen. We tried to figure out a way to cross the State Street Bridge; but the Pennsylvania National Guard turned us back. We ended up riding in the rear of a *Charles Potato Chip* truck to make it to safety.

As time went by, I wore that housecoat until it was unrecognizable. The pretty pocket finally fell off during a wash cycle. I begged to keep my protective friend, and I cried when it landed in the trashcan.

There was a lapse of time between the flood of 1972 and the next episode of the night crawler. This was due to the fact that we lived in separate houses. Once we stayed under the same roof, it did not take him long to attempt his same malicious moves. This time, I was older and many things had changed. I stood up for myself and mustered up the courage to tell on him.

In answer to my original question, why talk about this now? I recently found out that this perpetrator's list of victims continued to grow – even after I exposed him. Some of them are personally very close to me. I cannot put into words how this affected me. My sleeping bag replaced my housecoat and became my new best friend. When it wore out, I replaced it immediately. Today I am 49 years old and I still have a sleeping bag handy. I finally stopped sleeping in it November of 2007.

Parents take note: Even though an item may seem trivial to you, <u>triple-</u>check with your child <u>before</u> you discard it. That very item may secretly serve as their *"protective friend."*

A Nigger's Heel

One minute, I'm taking dictation from my female boss; the next minute, we are interrupted by the other four Public Relations secretaries who have begun shopping through my boss' unauthorized antique jewelry stash.

One girl asked, "This ring is dull, how do I clean it?"

My boss replied, "Rub it with toothpaste; it'll shine like a nigger's heel."

What?! Did she just say, "rub it with toothpaste; it'll shine like a nigger's heel"?

The only response my 26-year old mind could come up with was to freeze for a second, get up and slowly walk out of her office. As soon as I cleared the door, all the women began to laugh hysterically. I was understandably naïve, although the clues were blatant. My telephone, stapler, work folder and staple remover were all labeled "minority secretary." If that wasn't clear enough, a month after being hired, a friendly co-worker from another department complimented my outfit; she then informed me, "Your boss told us a black secretary was being hired and asked us to donate clothes for you. What was she thinking? Your wardrobe is bigger than mine!"

Sha Na Na

I remember sitting offstage at a carnival watching performances by Pat Benatar, a group of popular WWF wrestling guys, and the rock'n'roll revival group Shan Na Na – the same group that was featured in the movie, *Grease*.

One of the Sha Na Na group members came off stage toward me and said something to the effect of, "Hello, are you enjoying the show?" I responded favorably and continued to watch the show. I was unaware my significant other was watching while this kind, respectful gentleman spoke to me. Later that evening, as we were walking through the carnival, I was strongly interrogated about the earlier 10-second conversation with the singing star. We arrived back at our assigned work trailer and within minutes, I was struck across the face, pounced upon and viciously attacked. The first hit was so swift and brutal – it stunned me. Although I fought back, I was tossed around like a rag doll. My screams went unanswered, I suspect because the trailer was deep in the woods and the sounds of the distant carnival drowned out my plea for help. I was exhausted, beat up and temporarily defeated. I relaxed my body, tuned my ears and thoughts toward the faint sounds of the carnival while I silently endured the remaining unjustified agony. It ended with the foul smell of *burped up*, stale beer and the words, I'm sorry; I didn't mean to hurt you.

To the man that dished out that unprovoked assault, I've long since forgiven you. I offer you the *Holy Word of God*, which tells me that if I forgive men their transgressions, my heavenly father will also, forgive me (Matthew 6:9-15).

"WANTED"

Leap all the way up to the year 2008. What better way to begin the second half of my life than to finally say YES to a longtime friend? My girlfriend advised me, *"Hide your heart so deep in God that a man will have to go through God to find it."* I was not shopping for a husband, but if I were, my particular "Want Ad" would have read something like this:

"WANTED: Husband and spiritual leader with proven skills in hardship. Preferably, one who:

has suffered the loss of close family members (i.e., his father – who served as his pastor and best friend; as well as his niece -- intelligent, gorgeous, 26-year-old, single mom who is suspected of taking her own life);

only 6 weeks after the loss of his niece, withstood a home invasion resulting in FOUR bullets to his body and a long stint in the intensive care unit;

can continue to find purpose in life even though his eldest son was murdered; shot six times, five bullets to the back of his body – at least two while laying face down on the ground – less than THREE hours before his 33rd birthday;

is willing to sustain a healthy body by peddling his bike 10 miles to and from work; and finally

can get mowed down by a car, end up in intensive care (yes, again) one month prior to our wedding...yet still make it down the aisle.

Whew! Thank you LORD!!!

How am I able to persevere? God wakes me up every single day, giving me a choice to start NEW. **Besides, hardship never stopped me from being able to make a mean sweet potato pie!**

High spirited and blessed with versatility, Lil Jackson places herself on the front line of issues relating to and affecting women and children. Her passion and objective is to jump start women right at the point where despair intersects with a true desire for change. As a successful real estate professional, Jackson ranks amongst million dollar plus single-sales agents.

Lil has an Associate's Degree in Mass Communications and is a professional business trainer and speaker. Her entrepreneurial savvy includes retail store ownership, an award winning, competitive baton twirling school and hosting *Your Real Estate Connection* via WDGAradio.com. Currently Jackson shares E-Bay and Craig's List strategies with clients of all skill levels.

You can contact Lil directly by e-mail at liljackson1025@gmail.com or by telephone at 717-979-5429.

CHAPTER 23

The Princess Doesn't Fall Far From The Queen

LORI & HALEY MATHEWS

Praise be to the God and Father of our Lord Jesus Christ, the Father of compassion and the God of all comfort, who comforts us in all our troubles...

It was Memorial Day weekend, May 1998, and I was making a list of things I wanted to take when I was leaving. God seemed to plan things out ever so perfectly for me to plan my escape with the kids. For months, I knew what I needed to do, but was scared. His going to the doctor was the breaking point. He was to quit drinking to preserve his life, not to get worse.

Let me go back to the beginning of my marriage. I was 18 years old and thought I knew everything and it was cool to be getting married. Growing up, many a little girl wants to feel like Cinderella. This was my chance to feel like Cinderella in a big foo-foo wedding dress that I looked beautiful in. I knew my fiancé drank (we'll call him John), but I didn't want to make a big deal of it. I knew he had stress with his family and thought that I could help to make his life better. Little did I know that I was beginning a hellish journey.

THE *Queens'* LEGACY

In the beginning it didn't seem too bad, but as time went on, the control and abuse became stronger. It started with verbal abuse – you know, little things like "you're fat" and "it's your fault". Little by little, my confidence was being broken down. Eventually, I stopped spending much time with my family, because John seemed to have jealousy issues towards them. But we spent time with his family. They were used to having alcohol around and put up with his drunkenness. I didn't want to be around others with him because it was so embarrassing to me. He was a mean and evil drunk, always wanting to fight. The only friends I had were at work.

After being mean to me, he would send me red roses the next day. The first couple of times he sent them, I took his apology seriously. Then I began to recognize the pattern, and the roses meant nothing. Somehow, in his corrupt mind, the roses were supposed to make me feel better for the abuse he had put me through the night before. Verbal abuse doesn't show on the outside. But his words continued to cut me to my core. And from day to day, I had no idea of what to expect. I walked on eggshells.

I was slowly becoming a prisoner inside of my home. The everyday fear of going home was dreadful. There were so many nights I would lie in bed waiting for him to come home. I would worry, hoping he was ok. Then I'd hear his truck coming down the road, and my heart would start to race. As he would walk in, I would act as if I was asleep, hoping that he would leave me alone. Many times, he would wake me, expecting me to have sex with him. There's nothing more disgusting and demeaning to your spirit than having a mean drunk that reeks of alcohol and tobacco, pushing himself on you.

On the night of his grandmother's funeral, we had been with his family and he became very drunk. This was the first time that he threatened to kill me. I was able to call his dad for help, after John broke the glass out of the door. Sometimes after a severe drunken episode like that, he would try to be good for a while. And in that time, I thought that bringing a baby into the picture would make things better. Who was I kidding?! The abuse continued.

He was very controlling and a form of his control was physically holding me down (which he would later do with our kids as well). After having our daughter, I thought he would stay sober longer. The night we brought her home...he got drunk. But Haley became my life. He would threaten to leave and take her, so I always kept her close to me. In my mind, her being close to me kept both her and I safer. I quit work to stay home with her, and while it was a blessing to be with her, it added to my imprisonment. At that point, my only connection to outside life was when my family would visit Haley, or when I would call and talk to my Grandma. It was not long distance to call her, so I would spend a good deal of time talking with her and venting. She had no idea the extent of what I was going through, but she could somewhat relate to the verbal abuse. That helped me to keep a bit of my sanity.

When Haley turned 1 year old, I found out that I was pregnant with our son. My first thought was "how am I going to take care of both kids by myself and live in this turmoil?" During the pregnancy, John continued his abusive behavior. After I had my son, I kept myself as busy as I could with both children and kept John at a distance. The abuse was becoming stronger – not only toward me, but toward the kids as well, and especially our son. And he always abused me in front of them. The older our son became, the more he targeted him by picking on him and holding him down. There were so many nights that I lay in bed and prayed for him to die. It seemed that would make everything easier, the more abuse we endured. Little Haley would do what she could to get his attention when he would become angry and target me or my son.

A Princess' View

Hi, my name is Haley and I am 14 years old. I am Lori's daughter (the one writing this chapter). From a little girl's perspective, I wanted to share my life and what it was like to live in an abusive environment.

I pretty much remember a lot of things my dad constantly did to my mom. He did things right in front of me and my brother, like it didn't matter. He could care less. It makes me angrier each day just to think about all the things he did. As a little girl, it was so hard for me to share what was going on and that it was hurting me. I was scared that if I told and it got back around to him, I would get hurt or killed...not the greatest feeling for a little girl to have.

I remember the abuse getting worse each day and so did his drinking. My dad would hold me and my brother down – especially my brother. I remember my dad choking my brother right in front of me. One night, he got so mad that he punched a hole in the wall. And he would yell at my mom, so I would try to get in the middle to calm him down, so nothing would happen to her...it scared me so much! My mom finally left him, but he was still able to see us.

I remember when I was 6 years old, and my brother and I were at his house and he had passed out because he drank too much. We were really late getting home, so my grandparents came out and found us sitting by him. We didn't know what had happened to him; we were just scared. As a little kid, my feelings were all mixed up, and I didn't know how to share them so I expressed them in a different way. I used to throw things or purposely hit my head on things. All of it was because of my anger towards my dad. I still have major issues towards my dad, but I try not to let them get to me.

I finally thought we were getting a break from his alcoholism when the doctor told him he had to quit or there would be no turning back. Our families became supportive of him and he stayed sober...for 3 days and then became drunker than he ever had before. His eyes were glassed over and he was going through jugs of whiskey every 2-3 days. This time, I KNEW it was time to go. I started making my list on a Friday, and the kids and I left on Monday. When we got to my parents' house, I broke down. They had no idea we were coming, because I had not told anyone. Thank God for my parents! They were our saving grace.

Leaving was a huge step. As the days played out, I found that staying away was almost just as difficult. I wanted to believe his lies....lies of "getting sober" and "getting help". My family constantly had to pour truth into me so that I would not fall back into his trap. I got a protection order against him, which relieved much of the pressure of me having to deal with him, along with the fear that would come up each time I talked with him – after being under someone's control for 9 years, it is very hard to fight the fear that constantly comes up. On the inside, I was still terrified of him....he still had power over me.

A Princess' View

During the fall of 2007 I started to really see my dad again. The first time I saw my dad and was around him I was so scared I felt so sick to my stomach. I started going to a counselor and started getting all of my feelings out. Just recently, there was a boy who verbally abused me. It put my self-esteem down so much because it reminded me of my dad and what he had done. I caught myself feeling sorry for that little Haley again when it was happening to me. I still have flashbacks of everything that happened and it makes me so sad to think that I had to go through all of that.

I'm finding that people like me that have gone through these things or are going through them, wind up being stronger when they get through it. It just seems so hard when you have someone that's violating your personal space and making you feel uncomfortable. You feel like you have to stay stuck in the problem and that you can't tell them "no" or stand up for yourself, or they will get mad at you.

I started seeing a doctor who helped me to get on my healing journey. He introduced me to NET (Neuro-Emotional Technique), a form of releasing charged emotions. This same doctor then introduced me to Treehouse Healing Ministry in St. Louis, along with a counselor who did deep healing work. As the saying goes, "When the student is ready, the teacher will appear." And, boy, was I was ready! Little by little, pieces of my life started to unravel so I could see more of the roots of my issues. And while working with the counselor, I began to realize why it was so easy for me to fall into that abusive relationship.

At age 4, a boy who was 3 ½ years older than me violated my space. I recently read a book called "Boundaries", and it states that those affected by sexual or physical abuse at a young age tend to grow up and be adults who have poor boundaries. At age 4, I felt that what happened was my fault and it laid a foundation of self-doubt, so in my mind it wasn't ok to play freely as a child because I might get hurt. It's amazing how something at such a young age can set us up for years to come.

A Princess' View

Well my counselor tells me I have my rights and when I feel violated, or need to stand up for myself, I should do so. So my focus, right now, is working on me and making "Haley" stronger. At some point I would like to share with him, how his actions and words hurt me. I'm afraid that when I share with him that he will deny everything, which could bring me down, but I'm not going to allow that to happen. I know the truth of what happened. And even though that stuff hurts you and makes you feel bad, you have to be strong. I have to remember to always stay strong, now and for my best days ahead of me.

Over the last 5 years, the "real" me has slowly surfaced, with the assistance of lots of personal work. I've become more of the person God intended me to be. I did not have to stay trapped, just as you don't. What a blessing it has been to look back through my life and see God there with me, always protecting my kids and me! I have learned that what I've gone through isn't about me, but rather about how I can in turn help others. Because of the inner work I've done, I have created a space for my daughter to do her work. 2 Corinthians 1:3,4 states: "Praise be to the God and Father of our Lord Jesus Christ, the Father of compassion and the God of all

comfort, who comforts us in all our troubles, so that we can comfort those in any trouble with the comfort we ourselves have received from God." These words lead me, comfort me, and are now becoming a part of my legacy to leave with others.

Lori Mathews has worked with teenagers and children with special needs for the majority of her adult life. She is also a leader in the youth ministry at her church. Lori is an entrepreneur that builds her business from home and trains and motivates others to do the same. You can reach Lori directly by e-mail at lmathews3@att.net.

CHAPTER 24

The Little Girl Makes The Choice
And The Woman Lives With The Consequences

LYNETTE HARRISON

From the very day we are born we are faced with choices. As we grow older we learn that there are consequences for the choices we make.

We face many choices in our lives. From the very day we are born into this world we are faced with choices. As we grow older we learn that there are consequences for the choices and decisions we make.

Growing up, I had a vivid imagination. As an only child it helped to comfort me and cope with loneliness and boredom. One day while at the neighborhood drug store searching for a comic book or something "interesting" to read, I found a magazine that was very sensual and sexually suggestive. This magazine was a romance novel with a twist, very graphic and depictive of sexual relations although not vulgar in wording, depiction, or sexual content. Coming across this magazine at eleven years of age was not really appropriate, but I read it anyway. Looking back, I see how that magazine touched something in me. It was a tool used by satan to spark

my imagination. It planted seeds of lust, rebellion, forbidden romance and all the illusions that come with that type of knowledge.

I purchased the magazine and read it, reread it, and read it again, making sure to keep it from the eyes of my mother and grandmother. One day as I was reading in the living room my mother came into the house at the same time that my grandmother came downstairs. I went upstairs and my mother stayed in the living room. As she straightened up the magazines that were lying on the coffee table, she found the magazine! Once my grandmother and mother decided that the magazine was not theirs, I was reprimanded for reading it. She ordered me to throw it away and never read it again. As she ranted, my grandmother interrupted her, telling her to leave me alone and to allow me to read the magazines, if that was something that held my interest. I remember their arguing about it. My grandmother didn't have a problem with it. As a result, I never had to sneak to read them again.

I lived with my grandparents from the time I was six years old until I left home at sixteen. The time spent with your children is in their formative years when you train them, correct them, affirm and confirm who they are. These are the years of basic training that lay the groundwork in them and give them the tools they need to make wise choices and decisions. They will not always choose the correct choices but when the right foundation is been laid they will always return to rightful living (Proverbs 22:16). In short, it is in doing the work of parenting that one can fully appreciate the fruit it produces. Even though she never legally gave up her parental rights, my mother gave up her voice and her power for a season. Even though she had begun to make changes in herself she ultimately had no power to do anything because she was not there.

I continued to read the magazines which opened the door for the enemy (satan) to germinate fantasy and illusion in my mind. I grew up in a Christian household and had accepted Christ as my Lord and Savior when I was nine years old. Even so, no one taught me how to deal with the natural God given longings of my soul that wanting to be loved, affirmed, secured and valued. Sadly, while many people hand clap, unlock church doors, usher, sing, and what we call worship; our children are still open prey to the enemy. Don't get me wrong I'm not against ministry and service. On the contrary, I believe in it but Jesus also said that Mary had chosen the good part that wouldn't be taken from her. The good part only comes from spending time with Jesus and being restored in his presence. It's not in the ministry you serve it's only in Christ Jesus.

It was around that time that I had prayed for someone to love me. Someone that would love me and make me feel secure...I was twelve, and I thought I'd met him. He was older and took up time with me. I'd had positive role models in my life and both of my grandfathers played a vital role in my life. They were good providers who took care of my needs and my wants. I wanted for nothing materially. My inner longings were in my soul. My lack of education made it necessary for me to travel down this road and make the mistake I made concerning this boy. It also made it necessary for me to try and find the answers to the longings in my heart and soul in a person.

My lack of knowledge and wisdom made it necessary for me to compromise my precious self for what I thought was an even trade for his love, acceptance and security. My lack of wisdom made it necessary for me to reason and rationalize what was right for what was wrong because I was rendered emotionally cripple from prior issues in my life. How would I have really known? My lack of wisdom made it necessary for this encounter to happen as a means of a continual cycle and repetition. When my lack of wisdom thought it had won, Christ Jesus stepped in! This can happen at any age. For me it was at a very young and impressionable age. For some, it doesn't happen soon enough, however the results are the same: Anger, bitterness, and resentfulness with a main dish of confusion which results in no relationship with God, no effectiveness in the Kingdom of God, no trust in God or in others.

This older boy showed me attention. He looked into my eyes and not at my body. He was very unassuming, charming and attentive. By the time he entered my life I'd spent almost two years fantasizing and living in a dream world. I dreamed about my husband, my children, my house, and even a dog. What I got was raped. Before I knew it my pants were down and I was hollering, pleading, and crying for him to please stop and get off of me...which he didn't do. When it was over, I felt dirty, used, and stupid. I didn't tell anyone. I refused to acknowledge what had happened. I never told a soul and until recently never admitted that I'd been raped. In my case being raped didn't necessarily mean being innocent of guilt.

Sometimes we get so busy with ministry and the things of the church that we miss God entirely. Being in the presence of God is true service and worship. Real ministry is in our everyday lives. True victory and power is obtained as we are obedient to God in our everyday lives. Know this: I am where I am because of the thoughts and the decisions I've made and you are where you are because of the thoughts and the decisions you've made.

THE *Queens* LEGACY

I didn't learn this truth about myself and why things were the way they were in life until twenty years later. Twenty years of denial, lies, and false truths. All because I didn't want to face and confront the hard cold truth of my decisions and choices. Only when I began to invest in myself did I seek more earnestly for the one who created me. I've learned to take responsibility for my actions and to accept what I cannot change and to leave the rest with the Lord.

Lynette Harrison is a native of Washington, D.C. She is a student at Regent University majoring in Religious Studies. Mrs. Harrison is the Founder and President of W.O.M.A.N. (Women of God, On the Move, Making a Difference, Achieving Greatness, Now) a non-profit organization with a mission of empowering women in their walk with Jesus Christ through workshops, conferences, Biblical teaching and radio. Mrs. Harrison is also the Founder and President of G.I.M.A. (God Is My Advantage), LLC, both located in Baltimore, Maryland. She has been married to her high school sweetheart for twenty years and they have six children, three girls and three boys.

You can reach Lynette directly by e-mail at harrisonlynette07@yahoo.com and by telephone at 410-666-8294.

CHAPTER 25

Let Go

MARLANA YVETTE

What will you let go of, to instead leave a Legacy,
One that once you've gone, will impact, all mankind,
So many of us do our sincerest best, to receive and give freedom,
Lead and live positive, constructive, happy lives,
Many of us strive, toil and pursue, what society has shown,
to be the acceptable and successful "good life",
We chase the dreams of others and in turn, make them our own,
Then wonder why, in the process, we face pain and strife,
We fail to ask the question if those dreams and goals are worth achieving,
Or if, for us, are simply best, left alone,
If you are reading this chapter about these queens who've already come,
You realize the King or Queen in you, is ready to reign on YOUR throne,
You're here now, only because, one day you decided,
That you wanted and absolutely must, have change,
You changed your books and Cds, associations, places you went,
But were disappointed believing, overnight, you'd never again, be the same,
The truth of the matter is, it's a process and journey,
We must stay true to the cause, unique purpose, we were placed on this earth,

THE *Queens'* LEGACY

Find and pursue not just goals and dreams, but our true identity,
Through accepting our personal value, gifts, callings, and worth,
Something transmitted by, or received from an ancestor,
or predecessor, from one handed down from the past,
Is the true definition of a Legacy, one someone in the world needs to
receive,
One we've come to share, release, and reveal, together, at last,
To draw each and every reader who picks up a copy,
To read, relate, reflect, and substitute their name,
The good book says there's nothing, that's new under the sun,
What have you overcome? ,
How much of our stories reflect a journey, that for you, is the same,
You are equally as strong, and though we can share and identify,
We must ask if our past must simply be held onto,
Or is it what we have done and are doing with it,
Or most importantly, who we can now lift up,
Who we can encourage, and help now, to pull through,
As you read this chapter and others, understand it's for a reason,
Realize it's your call to receive, release, and Let Go,
Accept you survived the storm, God has so much in store for you,
If your true face and dependence on Him, you're willing to show,
If you can receive and realize, without Him as your guide,
You'll only continue to fight, countless life losing battles,
Continue to find joy mixed with emptiness, waste time with no lasting
rewards,
Never getting around, to that which truly matters,
Our desire and hope, for you, is to read,
Meditate, breakthrough, Walking away, both confident and strong,
Move forward boldly, beginning where you are, start your living Legacy,
And in doing so, find the fulfillment, for which you've so deeply longed,
It's been said that the message, that someone needs to hear,
They can only receive it, when they hear it from you,
So join us in these pages now, hear our hearts, see our true faces, Let Go!
And let the King or Queen deep inside, finally shine through!

You can contact Marlana Yvette by e-mail at marlana@saveonemoreintl.org

CHAPTER 26

Air...Earth...Water...Fire

MEL ROBERSON

Pinkie Liggons was the youngest of 10 children, and she was born a fighter.

Her father was part of the Tuskegee Syphilis Experiment down in Tuskegee, Alabama. I've been told that her one of her brothers was part of it too. African American men were injected with Syphilis and not given treatment. Pinkie Liggons was the youngest of 10 children, and she was born a fighter. Even though she had a gentle spirit, she was strong willed and confident. I guess it was necessary to be that way in the south during the early 1900's if you wanted to survive. It must have been hard to watch your family members die for the sake of an "experiment" that was more like genocide. Even though times were difficult, she always kept her head to the sky.

Pinkie became the "Air" of her family. She was a free spirited thinker. Her positive attitude made her a joy to be around. She had a smile that could light up a whole room. I had the privilege of knowing her... she was my great grandmother. Her life in Tuskegee set the stage for what she would become, and what she would teach her children. She would teach

her four offspring to have a great work ethic, to be flexible, to stay positive, and to always have faith. Not only would she teach that to her children, but to her grandchildren and great grandchildren as well.

One of her four children was Thelma Peters. Born in Alabama, Thelma later moved to Chicago and had six children of her own. Thelma was the "Earth" of her family. She was the foundation... solid as a rock. She had unshakable character. I had the opportunity to know her as well... she was my grandmother. Though earth has characteristics that are solid, it also provides fertile ground that can spring forth a wonderful harvest. Thelma had wonderful food for thought. She would often tell us "If you don't have a horse, ride a mule." I'm sure that her insightful sayings were influenced by her mother, Pinkie. Thelma taught us to be strong and face adversity head on. She had to raise children when civil rights didn't exist. Her strength, along with her mom's flexibility, was passed on to her children. Thelma was the second oldest of her brothers and sisters. Out of the six children that Thelma had, Danella Roberson was the second to be born.

A Chicago native, Danella would take trips to the south in her youth and enjoy picking watermelons from the watermelon patch on her family's land. Danella would take the tenacity and diligence of the south and couple that with the creativity and certitude of the north. She was born creative. Danella became the "Water" of her family. She was soothing, yet strong enough to smooth out stone. Water can be soothing. It can also be powerful enough to wipe out a city. Danella possessed the ability to move around any problem or situation that got in front of her. Born in the mid 1940's, she witnessed the abuse that African Americans took as they fought for equal rights. I know this to be true because she is my mother.

The women in my family have been the caregivers. They have been the ones to record and teach our family history. They have been the ones that have planted the seeds of greatness in us. Though my mom had no daughters to pass the "Queen's Legacy" to directly, she gave my brother and I the tools necessary to start us on the road to success. (My father's story will be told at another time.) The wisdom of the ages has been passed from generation to generation in my family. My mom's fluid-like capabilities showed my brother and I that power doesn't have to come from force. She exemplifies gentleness, being able to get the job done.

Fortunately, my mother does have the chance to teach a princess how to be queen. My two daughters enjoy spending time with my mother. My girls are my "Fire." They keep my heart warm. They are passionate and enthusiastic. They demonstrate strength. Many people think of the destructive characteristics of fire, but fire also represents action, passion, desire, and protection. My oldest daughter made the Varsity Cheerleading team as a freshman. She was the captain of the team by her sophomore year. My youngest daughter was born earlier than expected, and has kept doing everything in life early. She was walking at nine months, talking in complete sentences by two years old, and using words like "extremely" and "cooperative" by the time she was three.

I'm happy to be a Prince in the kingdom of my family. Though the Queens around me represent different characteristics of the elements, they all work together for the greater good of our noble clan. Now that I think about it, they all possess a little of each element. It has been a blessing for me to be able to learn from all of the women in my life. When God made the world, all the elements were put here to create balance. I'm happy that He thought enough of my family to create that same balance for us.

Mel Roberson is an accomplished speaker, actor, spoken word artist, poet, author and model.

For more information, visit www.melrobentertainment.com.

CHAPTER 27

Accepting The Unexpected

MICHELE R. MOSLEY

Not me, I was NOT going to be a baby momma; absolutely not!
That was not MY plan.

Being a single mother was never my life's plan. When I think of it, my life as it stands today was never my original plan. As a young child growing up I wanted the perfect life, as many of us did when we were younger. My parents divorced when I was very young so being raised by a single mother, I vowed that would never happen to me. Not to say that my mother wasn't a good mom, she is a beautiful, strong, courageous African American woman, but I always felt that parenting is a job meant for two people.

I saw her work so hard and struggle to send me to private schools and to give me everything I needed and wanted and I just had no desire to do all of that alone. I had it all planned out; graduate high school, graduate college, marry the perfect man and have the perfect children. Yep that's what I was going to do! It all seemed so simple, boy did I deceive myself!

It's hard when you wake up one day and find that everything you set forth to do is all but a distant memory. I did graduate high school, and at the top of my class I might add, then went to college, but didn't finish; I went to work instead. Working part-time went to working full-time which led to no

time at school. It's very easy to get distracted from your studies when you're young, in need of money and you start making enough money to live comfortably. Growing up I was taught that you go to school to get a good job, so I figured I had a good job, so why did I need school and the student loans that came with it.

I worked hard and played hard. By other people's standard, I was doing really well for myself. I had a nice car, nice apartment and boyfriend; who was I kidding, I was the BOMB! Or so I thought. You couldn't tell me nothing! I was still dating my high school boyfriend, but after six years of dating we had finally grown apart and it was time to end it. If you don't know if you want to spend your life with someone after six years, it's safe to say you don't.

I remember being at church on New Year's Eve 2000 and he came with me, reluctantly. At midnight we were on our knees praying in the New Year and my prayer to God was that if he was not the man for me, please remove him from my life but give me the strength to deal with it. See we ask God for a lot of things but rarely ask Him for the wisdom or strength to handle the outcome. I knew he wasn't for me, but I knew I couldn't break away on my own either. I was with him more out of habit than anything else.

I had a desire to be closer to God and he had no desire to get to know him at all and that was more than enough for me to know he wasn't the one. Eight months after my heartfelt prayer to the Lord, we broke up and although I was devastated, crushed, hurt, angry and every other hurtful emotion you could think of, I kept praying daily without cease and finally one day I woke up and it was gone. The hurt, the pain, the anger, it was all gone; praise God! I tell you, God will answer your prayers, but definitely know what you are praying for!

After six years I was single and loving it! I was free as a bird to the third power so to say, but when my focus should have been more so on Christ, I didn't use my time wisely. I was young and dumb! I sang in a community choir for years and one of my closes friends was a young man in the choir. We would hang out and do different things together all the time. If I was out late with my girlfriends and didn't want to go home or just needed company I would call him. We could lie in bed together laughing and talking until we went to sleep. It was wonderful. He was one of my best friends. I had never experienced friendship at that level from a man before.

After about a year of this I saw him with a girl and noticed I had a slight attitude. Who was I kidding, I was upset! Where did she come from? Why was she there and what was going to happen when I needed him? He couldn't understand why I was feeling like this and neither could I until I realized it was because I really liked him, I wanted to be with him the way she was. Be careful of what you ask for is all I will say.

We started to date and everything was perfect or so I thought. He had a daughter and even though I never really dated guys with children before, I didn't mind with him because he was different. We were moving so fast and although I should have been cautious, I was thinking it was ok, and maybe it was meant to be so why would it need to go slow. Needless to say I was wrapped up in this relationship and lost focus on so many things that were important to me, like God. I should have sought God for everything I needed in the relationship but instead I did it my way; wrong answer!

Within months of us being together I got pregnant. You see because I never put God there in the first place, it was like a car wreck waiting to happen. I couldn't believe it. Not me, I was NOT going to be a baby momma; absolutely not! That was not MY plan. When I told him about the baby he was indifferent, then happy, then not, then indifferent again and although this should have been a major clue as to what I was getting into, I chose to ignore it. Sometimes it's easier to deal with your sense of reality than what the real reality is. He proposed to me and being the optimist that I am I thought we would really be ok, but know when God is not in the midst, it won't!

During my pregnancy I was very sick. I have what is called hyperemesis gravidarum, which generally means persistent nausea and vomiting during the entire pregnancy. It was horrible; I would vomit all day and night and had to quit my job to be on bed rest; I couldn't function in my everyday life and felt like I was dying, literally. This is when things started to change.

When someone can't love you at your worst, how can they love you at your best? He was never really there for me and was all of a sudden distant and mean towards me. He would go days without seeing or calling and when I would finally talk to him he acted like it wasn't a big deal. I would cry myself to sleep most nights because I couldn't understand how someone who had proclaimed to love me could treat me like I didn't matter anymore. I was too ashamed to tell my friends what was really going on so my mom was my rock. She was there for every tear I shed. I truly believe without her I would have gone crazy.

My stepfather took me to every doctor's appointment; my family was my support system. During my entire pregnancy he was back and forth and in

and out of love with me and his exes. At seven months pregnant, I found out that his ex girlfriend had a newborn son by him but a blood test was needed for confirmation. When I confronted him about this he simply said it was none of my business and it didn't concern me. What!?! None of my business, who did he think he was?

Nothing but staying on my knees in constant prayer got me through that time in my life. I had a life growing inside of me but had never felt more alone. See we have to learn to seek God in every situation, not just when we need Him, but to order our steps in every way, even our love lives. Pray for Him to send a man that loves as He does and has His heart because then he will treat you and love you as God does; only if I had known that back then.

We weren't together when I had my daughter but it didn't bother me because my focus was on God and my newborn child. After my daughter was born, he was coming around more often and I figured he wanted to try again and me not really wanting to do this parenting thing alone, figured it couldn't hurt. What was I thinking!?! We played this back and forth game with all these other women in between mixed in with a few baby mommas and new kids and I couldn't believe I was actually putting up with all that drama. It was so unlike me, but the part of me that wanted a family for my child wouldn't let me let him go. That is where my faith was tested.

I always believed I had faith in God but yet I didn't trust him with that part of my life and it was the biggest mistake of my life; it's impossible to please God without faith. I should have trusted that God would deliver me from him and the situation I was in, I should have trusted that God would never put more on me than I could bare, I should have looked to God for everything that I thought I needed him for, but I didn't. I continued to be mistreated, mislead and misused. But I don't blame him because he only did what I allowed him too.

I was raised to never depend on man but God and God alone. I was taught that I was beautiful and smart and that I was a queen, yet I allowed myself to be his slave. I had never felt so unloved, unworthy and unwanted in my life. This went on for a while and I continued to deal with the verbal and mental abuse acting as if I wasn't God's child! Jesus was my daddy but I was acting like an orphan! My pastor said one Sunday that sometimes God will do things in our life to show us that He IS God and He has total control; it was then that I decided to give my life and everything in it back over to Him.

I went to the altar for prayer and after I got off of the floor with tears streaming down my face I felt like a new person. It's amazing what God can do. We often say that He can do anything but it is awesome to see the works of God for yourself. God had shown me what my life could and would be and it was beautiful. I embraced the idea of being a single mother and was happy with that decision and was back to the person I once knew and loved. I finally realized that I was never alone and that God had to put me in 'check'.

You know God will do that, we are His children and every once in a while when we act out, He has to remind us of who He is and who we are to Him! See we all have a plan for our life, but God's plan is what we should pray for; for His will to be done. Opening up my life to God's will to be done has moved me towards being who I was created to be and do what I was created to do.

I have always had a heart to help others and that is what I love to do. I want to help other single parents know that just because you are single does not mean you're alone. God is and will always be with you. Never let your situations become your hindrance, but use them to propel your into your destiny. Just because He doesn't do things in our time, don't worry for His time is not our time and He will do them when He wants!

God is first in my life, I can provide for my daughter everything she needs (and some wants), I'm working towards being the successful entrepreneur I've always dreamed about and I have also had the opportunity to experience love again; real God-sent love from a man who loves me and my daughter and I know my best days are ahead of me. When things don't go the way you planned or the way you expected, pray and hold on to your faith for God will make a way; by any means necessary. God answers prayers!

Michele R. Mosley is a bright, enthusiastic up and coming author and entrepreneur. Writing since the age of 9, it has always been a passion of hers. Michele uses her writing as a way to mend the heart, invigorate the mind and encourage soul. Working in Corporate America since the age of 19, she is quite familiar with unyielding labor, but realized that same labor never helped anyone in the process. Upon that realization, she decided to create her own way to help.

As a single mother herself who knows how difficult it can be at times, she has put into action the steps to assist other single parents on their path to success with parent resources to make strong decisions as they parent alone. Making other women feel good and look good is also her passion and in helping so many other women do just that, a business idea was birth. Michele will launch her beauty and fashion consulting business later this year; At First Glance. Michele wants women to see their natural and true beauty inside and out. Michele is also an Independent Associate with Pre-Paid Legal, Inc.

With so many things going on, Michele still finds the time to spend each and every free moment with her 5-year-old daughter, Reese. She values every moment spent with her little one because everything she does is for her and to secure her future and generations to come.

You can reach Michele directly by e-mail at Michele@michelemosely.com or by visiting her website at www.michelemosley.com.

CHAPTER 28

Queen In The Valley

NADINE MAYE

Trust God and God will take care of you

On May 30, 2003, after 10 ½ years as a probation officer, I resigned. It was a beautiful, sunny, and warm Friday afternoon. I was burned out and ready for change. After spending nearly 15 years mentoring other children and volunteering for various charitable organizations, I wanted to be home with my own two children. I admit I was a little afraid, too. I consider myself an adventurous person, yet I tended to take calculated risks. And I was breaking the rule I'd lived by all my adult life—never leave a job before having another one sealed up. I'd been working jobs since I was 15, and at 38, I could not think of any job I wanted.

I had always worked where I could be of service and help people improve their lives. I'd been blessed in my life, and wanted to be a blessing to others. I enjoyed teaching and speaking and I'd written a couple of articles that had been published. I figured I'd relax and enjoy the summer, and think about how I could build a business around my skills and talents. Although, arguably, I'd committed another faux pas by not having a formal business plan, I felt I was ready. And like Indiana Jones, I could handle anything that came up unexpectedly.

Although I was leaving my "good government salary" behind, financially I was prepared. My husband and I discussed my leaving and he

was supportive. I had paid off what little debt I had (I was a "pay-it-off-in-30-days" credit card user). We didn't live flamboyant lifestyles, so the only debt we had was our mortgage, which was easily manageable. I had 18 months of savings in the bank, as well as investments and my retirement accounts in case an emergency occurred. Yet, I sometimes worried about not having a steady paycheck. God whispered, "Trust me and I will take care of you." Needing reinforcement, I made a sign that read, "Trust God and God will take care of you" and put it in my bathroom, my car and my office to remind me that God was with me. I would soon learn what these words really meant.

Less than a year after I resigned, my husband and I separated. We were not having financial problems, but it was obvious we were not working as partners. We were drifting in different directions, and maybe now that I was home, it was clearer to me than it had been before. My husband moved in with his sister, and although he came to visit the kids almost daily, it wasn't the same. It was too much for me and the kids to take. They cried at night when he left...and so did I. Although I had started going to church again a few months earlier, I had not yet become spiritually strong enough to endure this pain. I begged him to come back, which he reluctantly did. We went to counseling, both with a licensed therapist and the church pastor. It became obvious that I was holding on to a marriage that was dying. Although I was not ready, I had to begin the process of letting go of our 10-year marriage. It was the hardest thing I've ever done in my life.

As I became spiritually stronger, I became more confident in letting go. I had good days and I had days when I cried. My daughter, who was 2 years old at the time, always seemed to know when I needed a hug, and would throw her arms around me real tight, which always made me feel better.

In 2005, I intensified my efforts to rebuild my life. I'd started my company, SpiritWorks Unlimited, Inc. a year and a half earlier to do seminars and workshops to help people improve their lives. I also sold T-shirts with positive messages on them. It was challenging talking to people about having a great life when mine was falling apart. Yet the words I spoke to others were helping me too. Often, I knew they were not my words; they were God's words coming through me. There were times when I was emotionally spent, but still, I pressed on. I did not have the luxury of quitting.

"Trust me, and I will take care of you." I struggled sometimes to hold onto this – particularly when my finances began a downward spiral. Although my husband made timely child support payments, it was not enough to cover all of our expenses. With my excellent credit, I began to borrow a little here and there. And in an effort to keep the kids and me living as we were used to, I failed to cut back on spending. I also made unwise business decisions and investments. My debt mounted, but I continued to spend unwisely. I refinanced my house twice, first to buy out my husband, and second to pay off debt. Yet without stable income from my business, I found myself in the same situation again. Even though, by this time, I had learned to cut back on spending. I'd dug a deep hole. How in the world could I let this happen to me?

"Nadine the Queen" – the intelligent, wise, common sense woman – this could not be happening to me! Yet it was. I finally had to acknowledge to my creditors that I couldn't pay them on time...even my mortgage company. I'd never experienced financial hardship in my life, but now I had creditors calling me. As I walked a mile in the moccasin of financial struggle, I could now understand and empathize with millions of people in similar circumstances.

I didn't know the specifics, but I knew somehow, some way, God would help me get back on my feet again. I stopped trying to use my intellect to fix my life, and I began to listen to the voice of God. I got still, reduced my activities and just began to "let go and let God." This was not easy for me. Yielding control over my life – even to God – felt very uncomfortable at first. But in slowing down, I began to see things in my life more clearly. I began to open myself up to God's love and healing. Sometimes, while my kids were at school, I'd spend the day in complete silence, listening to the beat of my heart or watching the birds fly so gracefully outside my patio door. Other times, I'd go for a walk, or drive to the park and write (writing had always been very therapeutic for me). This was the peace I'd sought after leaving probation. This was the time I'd wanted, to just rest and replenish my soul. This was the gift God wanted to give me all along. But I was too busy running around, trying to keep my family and my business afloat to receive it.

Slowly, my life began to come together. Following God's guidance, I revisited my business mission and got help from a SCORE counselor. I started managing the money I had wisely again. And then God began opening doors. I'd had several articles published, so I started writing more. I wrote a manuscript and started the process of publishing my first book – a goal I'd had for several years. Then I got an e-mail announcing the

opportunity to participate in this awesome Queen's Legacy project. I started getting calls from clients for private classes. My workshops and speaking engagements increased, as did my income. Finally, I could see the light at the end of the tunnel!

My "valley" experience was due to my own unwise choices. God did not put me in the valley. But God did go **with** me into the valley; and it was in that valley that I got to know, love and trust God. I also got to know, love and trust myself. God held me, listened to me without judgment, wiped my tears and healed me. And when I was ready, God led me out of the valley.

I, "Nadine the Queen," went on a 5-year journey that I didn't expect, but God brought me through it. Although we never went hungry, I learned to appreciate food, clothing and shelter. When we said our grace over our meals, I truly understood, "By His hands, we all are fed." I learned to be more patient and empathetic toward those who are experiencing temporary setbacks. I learned to appreciate my children and my family...including my former husband, who is really a great dad. I learned to see how God had been with me my whole life, although I thought I was the one running everything. Most of all, I learned that although we may go through challenges in life, God is always with us and we can trust that God will "never leave or forsake us." The moment we surrender our way to God's way, the healing begins. God led me out of the valley stronger, wiser and better. In the words of Gospel singer Marvin Sapp, "I made it through my storm and my test because God was with me to carry me through my mess!"

Thank you God!

As a Spiritual and Personal Growth Teacher, Speaker, Writer and Entrepreneur, Nadine Maye is President and Founder of SpiritWorks Unlimited, Inc., a dynamic and innovative personal development company. Her mission is to help people awaken to their Spiritual Power and live more abundant lives, creating success in four major areas of life – relationships, work, health and money.

Ms. Maye was reared by her grandmother in a loving home in Washington, D.C. She graduated with honors from Ballou High School, and holds a Bachelor's degree in Criminal Justice from the University of Maryland-College Park. She is the mother of two adorable children. The Maye family currently resides in Maryland.

Nadine Maye has been involved in many community activities, including children's tutoring and mentoring programs, participating in study groups, and in political campaigns. She is a member of Toastmasters International, a lifetime member of the Greater Washington Urban League, and supporter of organizations devoted to helping people improve their lives.

For information on seminars, workshops and speaking engagements, Ms. Maye can be reached by mail at SpiritWorks Unlimited, Inc., 2406 Ewing Avenue Suite #125 Suitland, MD 20746, by phone at (240) 210-0616 or visit her website at www.spiritworksunlimited.com.

CHAPTER 29

Determination vs. Defeat

NANCY SEAGAL

I am exactly where I am supposed to be – living in the light, with the darkness in the past.

By the age of 33, I found myself too exhausted to get out of bed most days. The last seven out of eight years of which I lived in Hawaii, there had been a growing problem with my health. I went from a healthy, energetic person to a person who had been zapped of every ounce of energy, riddled with pain and a multitude of symptoms. My business as a massage therapist and hypnotherapist was slowly growing, while my own health was rapidly declining. What had been sporadic unexplained symptoms throughout those years had now spiraled into an out-of-control nightmare. I found myself desperate for answers.

In the fall of 1997, I was diagnosed with Fibromyalgia. The diagnosis gave me hope that I would get better...yet I continued to feel worse. My symptoms started with unexplained nausea, dizziness, dry heaves, exhaustion, weakness, muscle twitching, stiffness, lack of coordination, wide spread pain that was sharp, like pins and needles, then dull and aching. My legs especially felt this way including weakness, heaviness, hypersensitivity, burning, tingling, and constriction. I had

needle-like pain in my pelvic and throat areas, IBS (Irritable Bowel Syndrome), headaches, dehydration, rashes and hives, hypoglycemia, shortness of breath, visual disturbances (including hallucinations), hypersensitivity to sound, temperature and touch, hair loss, low body temp, low-grade fevers, tremors, insomnia, night sweats, atrophy, bladder problems, Candida, hormonal imbalance, outbursts of anger, irritability, anxiety, jittery, mild depression, impatience, brain fog, confusion, severely slow thought process, long-term and short-term memory loss, difficulty comprehending, and stopping mid-sentence – with my mind completely blank. Then, after a couple months I had paralysis, severe muscle spasms, rigidity and seizures additionally.

Over the later years, before finding the true diagnosis, my symptoms were extreme and intermittent, I found myself often using a wheelchair and a walker. Many times I was afraid to drive, for fear my legs would become paralyzed or I would have muscle spasms and lose control of the car. I became very isolated. The paralysis would not only affect my legs, but it would move into my arms, and sometimes my entire body. The spasms would contract my muscles so severely that it took the full strength of someone to get my leg or arm to bend so that it would break the spasm. I had seizures that left me unable to move with bubbles of saliva coming out of my mouth. After these episodes, I would be completely exhausted. On several occasions my body was on the brink of shutting down and I would surrender to God to take me but then it was as if someone plugged me into a wall socket and I would feel the life force flow through me again.

There were many times when my symptoms exasperated while I was alone. I would lay there sometimes for hours paralyzed unable to move and sometimes in spasms without being able to call someone to help me. A couple times, my apartment door had to be broken down, because I went into full body spasms to the point where I couldn't move at all. I had been able to call for help in time, but was unable to get to the door. The paramedics would find me lying on the floor, unable to talk, because every muscle would seize up. I went from an extremely strong, independent person to someone emotionally and physically as fragile as dangerously thin ice over water, about to crack at any moment, in a matter of just a couple years. When I thought things were getting better, I would get slammed down again – over and over and over...again and again. But I held onto my belief that I would eventually find an answer and prove the doctors wrong.

Shortly after my diagnosis of Fibromyalgia, I visited Japan. While I was there, I was lying down reading a book when suddenly it felt as though

I couldn't move my legs. I chose to ignore it, thinking that it was my imagination and if my legs were paralyzed I did want to believe it. A few days after I came back from Japan, I found myself in the emergency room...with my legs paralyzed. I was hospitalized and after eight days of having myriad tests, they released me. I believed the doctors would discover what was wrong with me. But it turned out that this was the start of another five years of not knowing what was making me so ill. A few weeks afterwards, I was back in the hospital again...this time not only with paralysis, but also with severe spasms and full body rigidity. I spent another week being poked and prodded.

Because all the tests came back negative, the doctors concluded that the problem was "in my head", otherwise known as a conversion reaction disorder or psychosomatic disorder. I suspect that being very open and honest about my traumatic past with the doctors only gave them more reason to diagnose me with this label. As a hypnotherapist, I understood that this could be a possibility, but I didn't believe it to be the case, even though my childhood and younger adult life was full of traumatic events.

My father passed away when I was four years old, leaving my mother to raise nine children, ranging in age from two to twenty. Much of my childhood was without supervision, guidance, structure or support, which led me to become an extremely self-sufficient and independent adult. My mother worked full-time as a cook and left my older siblings to look out for us younger ones. As kids, we were out of control. Verbal and physical abuse amongst the siblings was common place, while my mother tried to keep order in the house. We were dirt poor and often had to rely on charity or state assistance to live. I remember many times we went without food in the fridge or eating mayonnaise and lettuce sandwiches because that's all we had.

Growing up, my oldest sister had all kinds of farm animals. Since we lived in an isolated area, the animals were my only friends where I would spend hours a day playing with them or riding horses. Late one morning, when I was seven, a barn fire started and all the animals perished. A couple years later, at 2 a.m. a man was pounding on our door, warning us that our barn was on fire. Those animals also perished. It was a terrible thing to witness and for years I was left with a fear of fire.

Throughout my younger years, I had been sexually assaulted a few times. As a young adult, I found myself sometimes giving in to overly aggressive guys. This is now commonly known as date rape. It often felt as

if I had me a neon sign over my head that attracted these types of people to me.

At the age of 16, I worried about everything and was very depressed. Along with all the previous traumatic events, my family was now moving hundreds of miles away from the suburbs of Milwaukee to the countryside of Wisconsin where I would spend my senior year of high school. The emotional stress of it all caused me to develop a stomach ulcer. And in a cry for help, I attempted suicide that summer before I went back to school.

Into my adulthood, though not without incident, I continually worked on myself throughout the years, reading self-help books, developing my spirituality, continuously learning new things, and searching for a better life. Had I believed the doctors that told me that it was 'in my head,' I would not be here to tell my story in order to help others. I was focused and determined to find an answer...and I finally found it.

I decided to do several hypnotherapy processes to see if I would get any answers or clues. I worked on my fear, anger, resentment and the physical aspects of my unknown illness, as well as several other related issues. I received some clues in a few of the sessions. When asked what was causing the symptoms, the answer was 'that the doctors hadn't found it yet and that there was definitely something there'. Another answer I got was that it started with the letter 'M'. My conscious mind wanted to believe that it was MS, or Multiple Sclerosis... I would later find out that it was mercury poisoning.

These clues, along with the information from other sessions, were enough for me to know it wasn't a psychosomatic disorder and not to buy into the doctors' misdiagnosis. Knowing how powerful our minds are, and the infinite possibilities we hold within ourselves, it fed my determination to find an answer. Until I found the correct diagnosis, I knew I had to direct my focus on positive and empowering thoughts rather than drowning in anger, self-pity, fear and negativity. I had no clue to what my future held but I constantly searched for what I could do to help heal myself.

Before I left Hawaii, I couldn't work any longer and I closed my business. I exhausted my credit cards and resorted to living on food stamps. I relied on the help of close friends and family for a place to live when I return to the mainland. In Wisconsin, over the next year and a half, I made several trips to the emergency room, where I was hospitalized. There, too, I was passed from doctor to doctor with no answers other than 'it was in my head'. I had another doctor who had good intentions of helping me and to find an answer for me but he misdiagnosed me as well, with stiff person's syndrome.

Finally, I was sent to the renowned clinic in Rockford, MN and was hospitalized. Once again, one of the last doctors that I saw was a doctor of neurology and psychiatry, who labeled me with a conversion reaction psychosomatic disorder. I still refused to believe it. About eight months later, I decided to move to Las Vegas. I still had numerous symptoms plaguing me, but the worst seemed to be over with...until about a year and a half later. One day the spasms and paralysis came back full force. A friend gave me the name of a doctor – who saved my life.

On my first visit with the doctor, after spending two hours with him, he told me to get my dental amalgams removed and then he would test me for mercury poisoning. I returned two weeks later, to get tested. The results came back and indicated the levels of mercury were off the chart – and that wasn't even at my worst! I'd had 12 years of heavy metal poisoning, and it was completely overlooked and misdiagnosed. Finally, I had found the answer!

I realized the source of the mercury poisoning was mostly from eating fish. Looking back, my hindsight is 20/20. I did eat moderate amounts of fish in Hawaii. When I lived in Wisconsin and Las Vegas, I ate less fish, which decreased my symptoms. But when I found a good sushi restaurant, it increased my exposure to mercury and my symptoms exasperated. All the while thinking I was eating healthy, I was not eating the right type of fish. In addition, I believe that my dental amalgams contributed to this, along with the glass thermometer I broke while I was in Hawaii.

Not knowing that mercury goes directly through your skin and settles into your cells – predominantly in your brain and intestines – I used my hands and a paper towel to wipe it up. Mercury separates into beads and is very difficult to handle so I didn't get all of it cleaned up. This happened in my bedroom, where I spent most of my time, so I was continuously exposing myself to it. My symptoms had worsened shortly thereafter.

It was two years before I was rid of the mercury poisoning – without a doubt, it was not easy. The first couple months, my symptoms came back full force, and then gradually I began to feel better. The Fibromyalgia disappeared after about four or five months, as it was the

mercury poisoning causing it all along. I couldn't tell how greatly this affected me until I it was completely eliminated from my body. It's amazing, the amount of energy I have now and how good I feel! I have since discovered that I have some residual issues, but at least now I know what I'm dealing with.

I had been to seven different hospitals and saw well over 70 doctors from 1997 to 2000. I found that I had been tested for heavy metals on my second hospital stay in Hawaii after the diagnosis of mercury poison in 2003, but it showed that the levels were within the normal range. Without a doubt I was not tested properly or the lab screwed up...or both. The answer was there all along...I just had to find the right doctor. I used the power of positive thought to overcome. I'm sure I would be dead right now, if I had given in to the belief that my symptoms were 'in my head'. From the trauma of my childhood to the discovery and healing of mercury poisoning, my life has turned in a new direction. I am exactly where I am supposed to be – living in the light, with the darkness in the past.

Nancy Seagal is a Certified Hypnotherapist, Licensed Massage Therapist, and Real Estate Broker with a background in the restaurant, travel and hospitality industries. Her extraordinary story of survival, conquering adversity, determination and using the power of positive thought, delivers an undeniable message of awareness, empowerment, and the unlimited human potential held within us all. Visit www.NancySeagal.com for more information.

CHAPTER 30

Overcoming The Past

PALONE WILLIAMS

The richness of the human experience would lose something of rewarding joy if there were no limitations to overcome.

Listen to my heart as I tell you my story
Praying and hoping to sustain tomorrow's glory
Struggles of the heart as I try to reclaim
Defeat covers me as I watch them dance in fame
Feeling conquered for years on going
My heart is stressed and tears are running

"The richness of the human experience would lose something of rewarding joy if there were no limitations to overcome." The words of Helen Keller. Can the perception of these words really add value to one's life? Can overcoming the battle of hurt and pain be an illusion by those who never experienced looking at themselves in a mirror; eagerly anticipating another life, another form, another you? As these words stagnate in my mind, I begin to wonder if there is an opportunity for me to overcome. As I remain motionless, I wonder how I got here.

Growing up, I resembled a sponge, soaking in the experiences of those who poured their lives into me. As a people pleaser, the thought of letting people down was not what I was destined to do. I listened and tried to do my best to help them through their battles, while pretending that I didn't have my own. Overtime a wall was formed, each brick representing another unsuccessful attempt at peace and happiness. This barrier provided me the power to smile when I wanted to cry, it nourished my body when food was lacking and helped to overcome the disgust I saw at my mirrored reflection.

I tormented myself with secrets that brought mental, physical and emotional pain. Inconveniencing others with my worries became a fear of how they would look at me. Everyone appeared to be perfectly fine while I felt like a rocking chair, emotionally moving back and forth. Worrying gave me something to do, but I wasn't going anywhere. Continually I prayed for a new way. I wanted to let go of all the pain. If only I was able to love me, then maybe the pain would finally fade away.

Listen to my heart as I tell you my story
Praying and hoping to sustain tomorrow's glory
Protecting my secrets of pain buried inside
As thoughts crossed my head of staying alive
The moment as come when a choice is near
But came a blessing I didn't know I can bare

In 1998, I became pregnant. Overwhelmed with anxiety, I wondered if I had what it takes to love a child. The struggles of my heart pressed hard against my ribs as I wished for a suitable life for my son. Having an empty and sheltered soul was not the behavior I wanted to pass onto my son. The battle continued and with determination I swore that I would not allow him to be alone or feel unwanted. I had to find a way to surround him with people who loved him.

I entered into a relationship with a young man; he was very handsome, was working and loved kids. Within the first year and half things were going well. He loved and cared for my son as though he were his own. As time went on, more of the details about this man were revealed to me. Two and half years into our relationship, we had many uncomfortable moments. I never thought that I would become the target of my significant other and his temper. Having him yell at times at me never bothered me; but when he started to fight me over my own car keys, I felt it best to close myself in again believing that enduring the pain was worth it if my son would have a better life than I did.

190

My soul began to stand still as if I was paralyzed every time I looked at him. Every argument became more furious than the last. No more excuses, I had to find away to make him leave. What should I do? Maybe he will change. Of course he apologized for hurting me and promised it would never happen again. That moment of truth never seemed to last. One Saturday afternoon, I ran from my own home to get away from the pain inflicted by this man. I had bruises on my left shoulder all the way down to my elbow. His fist was imprinted on my thighs and lower back as he hit me for not releasing my cell phone to him.

Leaving my home for a few hours, I returned later that night. Before I went into the house, I had to make sure I would be safe. I drove around my block in search for his vehicle. Under the cover of darkness I entered my home turned on the lights and there he stood. My heart raced and tears formed in my eyes. Of all the pain I experienced, nothing hurt like it did that day as I laid on my bedroom floor, fighting for my last breath. I gasped for air as he sat on my chest and placed pressure around my throat. I could feel his fingers forcefully wrapped around my neck, fiercely squeezing my throat. Begging to be let go, tears rolled down my face as I felt the tingling sensation in my finger tips. All I could think about was my son, how I wanted the opportunity to give him everything his heart desired. As my vision became blurry, the pressure became lighter. He released his grip from around my throat.

The only way out was to leave my own house. I moved and went to stay with my mom for awhile. If he didn't want to leave on his own, I was determined to force him out. I turned off all my power to make living in my house unbearable. A few weeks later, he moved out. Now I had to build the courage to fight the memories and start all over.

> Listen to my heart as I tell you my story
> Praying and hoping to sustain tomorrow's glory
> Fighting for another day wasn't the end
> But now I have my son's heart I have to mend
> What can I do to better my journey?
> As I am thankful I didn't leave on a gurney

There was something I had to do to turn my life around. I needed a change. Though my saga continued, I knew I needed a new beginning and would have to find a way to start by loving myself first. By denying myself my own love, I put my life at risk and nearly sent my son on a journey through this life alone. I realized that it was going to take hard work to overcome all that has happened in my life.

THE *Queens'* LEGACY

The year 2006 marked the beginning of this journey. As a result of being introduced to a business opportunity, I learned that the key for personal and professional success was personal development. I had to work on me. During a three day business convention in Las Vegas, I heard successful people sharing their stories from the stage. There were real people with real life stories; they had the courage to say it was a time for change.

At the end of the convention, one of my mentors held an event where he asked us several questions like, "Why did you get involved with this opportunity?" and "Where do you see yourself in the next 2-5 years?" Never being forced to face my past, I patiently waited for my turn. The middle of my palms became sweaty, my fingertips were numb and my heart felt as though it were going to explode through my chest. I always knew that someday my past would come back to haunt me. I listened as others answered the questions and finally, it was my turn. Pacing myself as slow as a turtle, I made my way up to the front of the room, rocking from side to side as I began to share one of my stories.

Gazing at the top of everyone's head I started to feel a burning sensation in my eyes. Holding them open as wide as I could, I still couldn't stop myself from crying as I shared my story. As I ended, I knew that having released the pain of that incident publicly for the first time ever that I had experienced the best 5-10 minutes of therapy ever. I felt as if my soul wasn't ashamed of me any longer. As I moved back to my seat, I was no longer in a rocking chair. My journey had truly begun.

Listen to my heart as I tell you my story
Praying and hoping to sustain tomorrow's glory
The past was holding me back from it all
With the love for myself I will begin to stand tall
Strength and courage is all I really needed
No longer will the curse of my past keep me defeated

In order for things to change I had to change. It would be untrue for me to say that change is easy. There are days I cry when alone or resort back to my shelter. Beginning with the people that surround me, I had to start all over. My first step was to be around people who wanted more out of life and wanted to live their lives to the fullest. I could no longer allow negative situations and circumstances to control my destiny.

One of my mentors told me the story of a butterfly. Butterflies are known for their life experience. Their beginning starts as an egg, just like humans. Then they move into the cocoon stage which is where the cycle of maturity begins and many changes happen. Their wings then begin to develop on the inside of the larva where they cannot be detected. There are small "wing disks" that are formed, which become enlarged as the wings veins start to develop. The fore and hind wings are developing together. Within hours, the wings form a strong layer around it which makes it hard to damage. Once the larva grows it begins the pupa stage which is the unexpected change. This stage is the change of structure, the final develop where all the stages come together as one and once completed it will lead us to the last stage, the adult. In the adult stage, the wings are no longer connected thereby allowing the wings to open up gracefully and now; the butterfly blesses the world with its beautiful colors.

Do you see yourself as a butterfly? Better yet can you see yourself as a beautiful, successful person? Life has its struggles and without them we cannot become better. These struggles often bring opportunities for change. Do you want more out of life? Do you want to travel the world? Do you want to own your own business? Maybe you just want to be loved and have a big family? In order to have what we want and to leave something for our children and children's children, each one of us has to break down barriers and travel the road leading to our own life's purpose. The only question is how and where we begin. The answer is self love. Every day I look at myself and I say, "I am a strong and a beautiful woman. I love myself unconditionally. I no longer see barriers, just opportunity". In the words of Helen Keller, "The richness of the human experience would lose something of rewarding joy if there were no limitations to overcome."

Palone Williams is a co-founder and C.E.O of her own entertainment company. She has launched her dream business to facilitate new opportunities for change. Ms. Williams has earned her Bachelor's Degree in Business. She calls on her personal experience to inspire not only her son but on others about personal growth, self-development and professional success. She enjoys writing poetry, drawing and dancing. As she continues her journey down the road less traveled she will like to remind everyone that "Your past does not have to equal your future." Ms Williams can be contacted via email palone1920@yahoo.com.

CHAPTER 31

The Crown Of Beauty

QUEEN KELLI

The only way to find out exactly what your inward and outward beauty is and what it's supposed to look like is to ask the One who gave it to you.

All of us are kings and queens. The Bible calls us a royal priesthood and explains that this royal status has been made available to us as our inheritance by the King of Kings. Royalty leaves behind an influence that is durable and permanent, a legacy whose effect remains long after he or she is gone. Now, what you choose to do with it is up to you. What legacy you leave is your choice too. Let me explain a very important feature of a queen's attire and persona called, "The Crown of Beauty".

When we think of a queen, one of the first attributes that comes to mind is "beauty". Not an exterior, earthly beauty, which most often fades with time, but rather an internal beauty, which is eternal. The portion of the definition of the word "beauty" that stands out to me the most is "of superior or excellent quality." Within every person, there is beauty, something that is superior and of excellent quality that God created in you. Each person's beauty is different and as varied as the fingerprint of every individual. No two are alike, no two the same. The only way to find out exactly what your inward and outward beauty is and what it is supposed to look like is to ask the One who gave it to you.

THE *Queens'* LEGACY

I can imagine it being somewhat of an offense to God to take a shortcut to what we think is beauty. Instead of doing what we must do to find out exactly what our natural God-given inner and outer beauty is and what we were intended to look like and be like, we often seek beauty by trying to be like someone else! People do it all the time, especially women, as we brood over "beauty" magazines and studiously scrutinize our 'red carpet' heroes. We subscribe to a certain picture that modern society has painted by which we have deemed certain attributes more acceptable and admirable than others. Then, with our finite thinking, we use that artificial picture to gauge "true beauty" (if there is such a thing) and strive for "it". Or we find someone we respect and/or admire and imitate them. In doing this you do not realize that in the same way you admire someone else, God is admiring the natural beauty He created in you. And you would admire your own beauty too if you would change your perspective and take the time to realize what God has already given you. All He wants is for you to recognize it, appreciate it, and admire the uniqueness of you that He intended.

You will never know true fulfillment in life until you are using your individual beauty (superior, excellent quality) exactly according to the plan or the way God created for you to exhibit it. God said there is a certain posture (conscious behavioral attitude) that comes with wearing the crown of His beauty and being a queen. There are certain things that are to be done and are not to be done. There are certain things that are to be said and are not to be said as we walk in the robe of royalty and display the crown of beauty. I remember the day that my Heavenly Husband placed the robe and the crown on me. I call God my Heavenly Husband because He has been there for me when man would not and has touched me in ways and places man could not. He has proven to be all I need Him to be; therefore, He has become everything to me.

My father and mother divorced when I was nine years old. Their divorce and my father's lack of consistency at spending time with me subsequently left me with a sense of abandonment from the first man I ever loved. I blame neither my father nor my mother for this now. They are both wonderful parents and were undoubtedly handpicked for me by God. We affectionately call my mother, "Queen Mother". She is a queen within her own right and so much of the fulfillment of my destiny is a result of her and my grandmother's example and teachings. I have learned over the years that their divorce, along with many other seemingly disastrous events that have transpired over the course of my life, was meant for evil by the devil, but God has turned these events around for my good. It is those very situations that have helped me become the vessel of honor that He had always intended me to be.

Nevertheless, I had to deal with feelings of abandonment and inadequacy, which plagued me all of my life and followed me into every relationship that I've had with a man, including marriage. Later I found out that for me, both divorce and abandonment were more than a disposition and a feeling. I discovered they were generational curses and an evil familial spirit. Familial means characteristic of a family, appearing in individuals by heredity; such as a familial disease. This familial spirit which came from the enemy of my soul, had plagued my family for years now, had come to torment me. In response, my Heavenly Husband, like a knight in shining armor, was there to deliver, rescue, redeem, liberate, emancipate, and set me free.

What does the crown have to do with this deliverance? God reminded me of the day that He placed the crown of beauty and the robe of royalty on me. It was in His presence, during one of our intimate times spent together, that He told me to look into the full-length mirror on the sliding glass doors to the closet in my bedroom. I could literally see that I was wearing a spiritual robe. The robe was more beautiful than any raiment that I have ever seen. The thing that was different about this robe was that not only was it beautiful, but also as I made the slightest turn from one side to the other it would change colors. Sometimes it would be a crystal, crimson red and at other times, it was a shiny, sparkling purple.

God, knowing my thoughts, then said to me, *"The red represents the blood that Jesus shed on Calvary. The purple represents My royalty. Know assuredly that whether you are in the midst of suffering or at the height of exaltation you will always have on the robe of My royalty."* The tears streamed down my face as I stood there in awe of the moment. The presence of God was so tangible that it felt like I was in the very throne room of God. I felt like I was in the midst of a ceremony, held just for me, in honor of my coronation into an office. The moment was staggeringly spectacular. Then I looked into the mirror again, just in time to see a crown being placed upon my head.

At the same time God began to speak saying, *"Now I place upon you the crown of beauty."* By this time, I lost it ("it" being the strength in my legs to stand and what little composure I was holding on to). I fell to my knees and was utterly broken before Him. I could not stop crying because I could not believe that He, the King of Kings, was crowning me to be His Queen.

This was one of many significant times in my life when God has moved dramatically and vividly during our time alone together. Those times are far too numerous to recount nor would I even choose to. There

THE *Queens* LEGACY

are other times when similar occurrences have transpired. I say similar because no two times are exactly alike, which always keeps me coming back for more of Him. Truthfully, I am absolutely, unreservedly, enthusiastically addicted to His presence. God is wooing you, too, wooing as defined in Webster's Dictionary, meaning inviting you, seeking your favor or affection, or loving you with a view to marriage. And once you decide to say "yes" to His invitation, by spending uninterrupted time in His presence, you will find yourself falling in love and seeking His presence above all else. For me, those dramatic times with the King always happen during a special time that I have chosen to steal away and be alone with Him. Each time is not as theatrical as the coronation was, but it is helpful to remember that neither is each time within the bridal chamber of a human or terrestrial marriage. Need I say more? (Smile)

God also told me that on that day that I was beyond called: I was chosen. He explained to me that everything happens in the Spirit first. On that day, The King chose me and one day, at His appointed time, it will manifest and be apparent for all to see. Then, one day, my earthly king will come crowning me again with his name and the three of us will be one, intended to manifest yet a different facet of His glory.

Please understand that everyone may not have a visitation or vision or some sort of experience like the one I did. Please do not ever think that you have to have spiritual visions in order to be royalty. You are a queen because God's Word says that you are, period. 1 Peter 2:9 says "We are a chosen generation, a royal priesthood, a holy nation, His own special people, that you may proclaim the praises of Him who called you out of darkness into His marvelous light." You are an heir to the throne of the King of Kings because you have Christ's royal blood running through your spiritual veins. That status or spiritual essence has nothing to do with an experience.

One morning God spoke to me a truth that applies to all of us who have suffered from the wounds inflicted by the grasp of the clutches of insecurity, inadequacy, and abandonment, so listen carefully, because, for me, it was life changing:

Insecurity and fear of abandonment are both your thorn and your crown. Insecurity keeps you grounded and rooted and thereby protected from getting the big head (prideful) when people comment and compliment you as you wear the crown of beauty and the gift of glamour I've given you. Queen, always remember that the crown will not be worn on a head that is too big to fit it comfortably. The feelings of abandonment are certainly a painful thorn but a very significant jewel in your crown nonetheless. Keep in mind that what the enemy means for evil I turn around for good. Know that its effects cause you to maintain a passion for intimacy with the King, which can only be filled with a steady diet of My presence within the crucible of solitude.

*Realize that I AM the only one who will never leave you, forsake you, or abandon you. So you can know this truth, Queen, **because** of your thorns, and as a product of going through the process properly. Because it is not enough to go through the process if you do not go through it properly, i.e., complaining, kicking, screaming, and fussing all the way. Rather embrace the pain and suffering. Allow it to produce the character in you that is necessary to walk as royalty, causing you to display the crown of beauty and the robe of humility that glistens brightly and consistently, completely adorning you with the posture (mental, behavioral, physical and spiritual attitude) of royalty, thus "The Posture of A Queen." In other words, no pain, no gain, no cross, no crown.*

Ever since that day, when people compliment me and happen to use the word "beautiful" within their comment, I never tire of hearing that word. It is not because I am vain, but rather because God showed me that whenever I hear that word, it is to remind me that it is the crown they see. They see the crown of beauty that is not visible in the natural realm but is definitely there in the spiritual realm. So as I smile and say "thank you", what they don't know is that in the midst of what may be for me a turbulent day, my Heavenly Husband has just used them to blow me a kiss of His peace, reminding me of who I am, Queen to the King of Kings.

Now, as for you......**ARE YOU SURE YOU WANT A KING......?** Whether celestial or terrestrial; human or Spirit; a king only wants a queen and a queen only has eyes for a king. I had read 1 Peter 2:9, which calls us children of God ROYALTY. It meant one thing when I first read it but yet another after I experienced my visitation, was crowned, and began to spend time within the bridal chamber learning the qualifications of a queen from the King of Kings. As he placed the robe of royalty and the crown of beauty upon me, predestination met revelation and brought about a mentality which transformed my reality as I recognized that we are truly designed for royal representation and intimacy with the King. God told me, "Tell My people I want them to exhibit 'The Posture of A Queen'". Tell them they are royalty and show them how to act like it." The King of Kings is coming whether you want to believe it or not! I have been given the mandate to share the most intimate secrets on my journey to royalty which will influence and inspire you to pursue a deeper relationship with God. As you read <u>The Posture of a Queen</u> in its entirety, you will be captivated by the undeniable presence of God Himself as you are drawn into an intimate encounter with the King that will change your life forever. This king is completely different from the kings in the Bible, kings of the earth, or those you have served as king in your life. Believers have an undisputed, perfect king who requires our ultimate loyalty, allegiance and respect because this king is also GOD.

Are you sure you want a king?

Are you ready for your journey? A journey that will change the way you see

yourself and your life forever?

You will never be the same once you experience...

"The Posture of a Queen"

For products and speaking engagements please contact
Queen Kelli ▪ P.O. Box 93989, Pasadena, CA 91109
626 644-6493 ▪ 626 296-0308
msqueenkelli@yahoo.com
www.queenkelli.com
(Ask for "The Posture of A Queen" spoken word/music CD and
The Posture of a Queen full manuscript)

CHAPTER 32

Dream The Impossible, Think The Unbelievable And Continue To Become

ROSHEA WILLIAMS

"We face tests and exams in life but they count for greater consequences because the results of these tests are indicators of our eternal future."
~Dr. Michael Youssef

As a 19-year old attending Eastern Illinois University, as the first in my family to attend college, I will graduate. My educational goals include pursuing my graduate degree in pharmacy at Howard University. I am eternally grateful to God for the extraordinary opportunities He has provided for me. You may be wondering, how exactly is it that God has blessed me? The favor and divine provision in my life have been a direct gift from God himself. Truly He has remained faithful to His promises. He has strengthened me to maintain my sanity, to remain focused and determined and to excel academically. He has crafted me to be the unique, courageous, sincere, God-fearing young woman that I am today.

Growing up, I witnessed my parent's battle with their drug addictions. Often I longed for at least one of them to put aside their own issues and play a role in raising me. My life was negatively impacted by the irresponsible choices of my parents. As I reflect, I can honestly admit, there has not been one day when I have seen my true parents, without the influence of drugs.

As a preteen, I was emotionally damaged; I longed to have a healthy relationship them. Internally, my heart was infused with pain as I wished I could rescue them from crack cocaine. There were many nights that I cried myself to sleep feeling helpless and alone. As a youth, it was tough to comprehend why my life seemed to be in so many fragmented pieces. As I matured in my walk with Christ, I realized that as long as I remained in the will of God, that He would keep me safe from hurt, harm and danger. Beyond the shadow of a doubt, I am convinced that God is fully able to grant me the desires of my heart. My accomplishments are only by the grace of God. *"For I know the plans I have for you, says the Lord, plans to prosper you, to give you hope and a good future."* (Jeremiah 29:11) My life is indeed a living testimony. Boldly I acknowledge that I have been chosen by God to encourage people around the world to overcome the obstacles of life.

It is often amazing to me, how God speaks to your heart and mind in the midnight hour. Even though I recall hearing my grandparents and pastor say that phrase, as a child, I did not understand exactly what they it. As I grew older, I began to experience the blessings of God for myself. Recently, I sat in my dorm room contemplating the plan of God for my life. As I decided to willingly accept them, tears streamed uncontrollably down my face. I cried until I could cry no more. The prophetic words of Marvin Sapp's single, "You Alone Are God", penetrated the very fiber of my being. I was completely in a daze as this experience literally paralyzed me. I had an encounter with the Holy Spirit like never before. When I reflect on how good God has been in my life, I cannot help but give Him praise. As I sat there, I thought about the obstacles He empowered me to overcome. Despite the fact that my mother and father have been addicted to drugs for the entire 19 years of my life, God has blessed me with a testimony that speaks volumes to his faithfulness.

Fortunately, I was raised by loving, God-fearing grandparents. My grandparents took my younger sister and me in as if we were their very own, and have been the biggest cheerleaders in our lives. Thank God they were willing to step in and take responsibility for us when our parents couldn't or wouldn't. Had it not been for my grandparents love, guidance, strict rules and prayers, I could have ended up homeless, a teenage mother, addicted to drugs, an alcoholic and/or without any sense of direction.

Being blessed with the gifts of God and His calling on my life has meant that I have had to eliminate people from my life; especially those who weren't on fire for Him. As I experience this college life, I have learned that friends will come and go, situations will come to challenge me, and obstacles will be thrown to cause me to stumble. With the help of Jesus, I can stand. I CAN DO THIS and so can YOU! Part of my destiny is to let every person know that they can accomplish the impossible. In spite of what you've been told, you can become the person you were created to be. Release your full potential and know that all hard work brings a profit, but mere talk leads only to poverty (Proverbs 14:23). Regardless of circumstances, you have the ability to set forth a destiny that is in the hand of God. Tell God what you want; He will give you what you need. God has never let me down. His mercy has kept me!! God plans and I plan. His plan is greater than anything I could imagine. My mother, who has been in bondage to drugs for years, has helped me aim for the stars. She advised me to finish school and not make the mistakes that she has made. I love her for that. Over the years, our relationship has progressed. My mother loves me dearly in her heart. How? Every day she talks to me and helps me to understand that some things in this world are just not worth it.

My father has never been an asset in my life. Once a year, he calls and I speak to him kindly since God commands it; I know I will be blessed. It is amazing that some choose not to speak to their parents for whatever reason. Always offer your parents a kind heart; speak with humbleness and show that you have forgiven them for whatever has happened. Holding a grudge will only burden you for years to come. There were times when the kids would ask where my parents were. Out of embarrassment, I couldn't answer. Although I pretended that everything was fine, even walked around with a smile on my face, my insides were a different story. Even with all that was going on, I never allowed confusion and hurt to stop me from excelling academically.

During my junior year at the Medical Academy of Julian High School in the heart of the Southside of Chicago, I set my sights on earning scholarships and internships to the best colleges. One of my instructors told me that for the first time, a student from Chicago Public Schools would be awarded a $25,000 scholarship. The applications required a written essay explaining goals and aspirations that we desired in our lives. I applied. Months passed and I wondered if I would ever hear about this scholarship. God will teach you patience. A week later, I was selected as one of the final five to be awarded the scholarship out of 500 students across Chicago. Two days later, I was the recipient of the scholarship.

Sometimes we wonder why we experience challenges and obstacles in life. Just know that in the end, there will be a great blessing if you persevere. God will always give you the strength to overcome your challenges. There were times when it seemed as if God wasn't listening nor was He trying to help me. Crying out to God didn't change anything. Still, I

had to wait. I know that the obstacles that I have overcome have made me what I am today. God will take you on a journey of distractions to see if you really want what you say you do. You have the power to bounce them back in the direction that they came from. Throw them back with all your strength so that whatever tried to destroy the promise in you is stopped.

As a college student, I have had great opportunities to network with professionals and to get involved with organizations. The most beneficial organization is the Haiti Connection which creates fundraisers to assist the Haitians survival. In December of last year, I went to Haiti and experienced their culture and lifestyle firsthand. I couldn't believe my eyes. There was poverty everywhere. The rich were even living among the poor. Families of 12 were living in small shacks that should only house a family of four. Some of them hadn't eaten in two weeks, while we here in America complain about what we eat. One memorable lady had five children and was pregnant with another. She lived in a shack in the mountains and had Psalms 27 painted in her home. When we talked with her about the hurricane, she shared that she lost her garden, her clothes, and many materials that she needed to survive. She said that at the end of the day, she didn't need any of that anyway; just as long as she had Jesus. Although she had nothing, she still knew that God was faithful and would provide. Many people say that Haiti is a poor country. These people are rich because they have their faith, courage and determination.

Roland Jules was enrolled in an institution in Haiti named Port Au Prince. Education in Haiti is very expensive and extremely limited compared to America. Jules' passion was to learn English, so he was attending school to become a translator; he was100% dedicated to the process. Each day he would arrive early and wait for us to start English class. He never traveled without his notebook and even though the classes were difficult for him, he never gave up. He taught me a lesson. Regardless of how difficult school may become, **KEEP IT GOING!** Don't give up! Many American college students complain about going to class at 8:00a.m. while others, like Jules, would love the opportunity to go, whenever. This trip for me symbolized spirituality, finances, and personal assets. We have to be appreciative of what God gives us and know that He is faithful.

Overall, my advice to you is *to Dream the Impossible, Think the Unbelievable and Continue to Become.* Without God, none of these things are possible. He will give you a strategy to dream, to think and to continue. Attend networking events that will help you maintain a positive spirit. Know that your goals can be accomplished once you decide to pursue them. Be the best you can be. Young people, you can attend and graduate from college. You can visit other countries and impact the lives of those living there. You can accomplish the impossible. God first, know that He is on your side and He loves you.

"The way to gain a good reputation is to endeavor to be what you desire to appear." -Socrates

Roshea graduated Honor Cum Laude from Percy L. Julian High School with outstanding awards and recognitions where she also served as the secretary on the executive board of the National Honor Society. In 2007, Roshea was awarded a $25,000 scholarship from the Enhanced Education Foundation based on her essay, *"Beating the Odds."* She has been featured on ABC News and NBC News, and in *The Daily Southtown* newspaper of Chicago. She is now a sophomore majoring in Business Management, with a minor in Chemistry. You can contact Roshea directly by e-mail at roshea_w@yahoo.com

CHAPTER 33

The Stepping Stones

REGYNA COOPER

What has been will be again, what has been done will be done again;
there is nothing new under the sun." My road of stones, although it has
been traveled before, is uniquely designed for me alone.

"Follow the Yellow Brick Road", these were the famous words spoken to Dorothy on her quest to get home to Auntie Em. Dorothy found herself in a strange land and was sent on a path that anyone in this land could follow to get to the Land of Oz, to get answers from a fake wizard. I have seen this story more times than I care to count though I am blessed to have had women in my life that have shown, by their example, that when your home is built upon the Rock you will always have a place to rest. I have been taught by these women that God alone should order your steps. You can follow your own path or seek the stones God has placed for you to step on. You can choose to follow the yellow brick road like everyone else or you can follow the stepping stones placed by God just for your destiny and purpose.

As a child, I remember walking along paths and noticing, in passing, the different shapes of the stones. No two stones were shaped alike. Some would crumble when stepped on, some hurt when stepped on; some are slippery, while others are secure enough to use as a corner stone. Knowing that my home is to be built on the Rock, I have learned there are stones that

provide the pathway to my purpose. I have also noticed that when I ask God for direction, the stones I should step on are undeniable identifiable.

The Bible says in Ecclesiastes that "What has been will be again, what has been done will be done again; there is nothing new under the sun." My road of stones, although it has been traveled before, is uniquely designed for me alone. I am the only one that will stand on any particular stone at that exact moment in time. This is when my prayer to God to 'order my steps' takes on real meaning. I may travel and cross the paths of my ancestors, but God has given me vision to see my stones glistening as gold. Yes, there are other beautiful stones that may attract my attention. However, to stay on purpose I must step only upon my stones. When I detour from my path, I find myself on side trips that may be fun for a moment, but have ultimately left me stranded. These are the times when I am especially grateful for God's grace, mercy and kick in the pants. Also, I thank God for the women in my life who have taught me the importance of believing that God will do exactly that, order my steps.

As we share our experiences with one another, we began to visualize the elegant tapestry of gems that God shares with us daily. Through shared victories and struggles, we are made aware of stones that should be avoided and those that can enrich our lives. There are many stories shared by the queens in my life, all with one common thread. The only way for your steps to be ordered, is to have your faith and trust in the Lord. I have been blessed to be guided by women with a plan, relentless faith, determination, boldness, dedication to practice, obedience, acceptance and unconditional love.

*The Places you will go with a **Plan***
(Stone of Planning)

My great grandmother Ella Murchison moved to Maryland when she was in her 40s. She had heard that there were better opportunities here in the North and she was up for a change. Of course, it helped that her son had moved here. Grandma never had a driver's license and always used public transportation. As a child, it was fun hopping on a bus to travel with her; the walking wasn't as much fun though. When I turned 16, I would drive my Grandmother around town and she would give me directions from place to place. As I got older and learned my way around the city, it occurred to me that she had been directing me along bus routes. Trips to the mall, that should have taken fifteen minutes, took twice as long because of all the steps it took to get there on public transportation. This was never an inconvenience for Grandma, because she knew the bus schedule. With a plan, she had access to the entire city.

Practice *Makes Perfect*
(Stone of Practice)

My grandmother, Novella Cole, was always happy and serious about God, family, music and practice. I do not ever remember a time in my grandparent's home that someone was not singing or getting ready to practice a piece of music. Grandma grew up singing with her sisters in a Gospel group called, The Young Sisters. She was a gifted musician that never learned to read music. She could hear a piece of music, practice it and it was hers. Church, family, music and practice was the theme. To bring out the purity of their voices, she always had her children practice first without music. I remember sitting with my grandmother in her living room as her children, The Cole Singers, practiced in the kitchen. She would call from the other room, "someone is off, try it again". Harmony was important in her music and all aspects of her life and you practiced until you got it.

One day I was standing in my grandmother's room as she prepared for rehearsal at church. She asked me, "When are you going to start singing?" I was caught off guard. You see, I was a shy child with no desire to be the center of attention. I had no interest in singing in front of the church. In my mind, she was asking me to sing a solo at Carnegie Hall. So I said these crazy words to my Grandmother, "I can't sing". Crazy because I actually thought that answer would get me off that easy. I figured singing on the third row of the Glee Club at school was close enough to fulfilling my family singing obligation. She turned, looked at me and softly said, "You can sing, you just need to practice". Immediately, I knew she was right. To this day, she is still right. She knew how you practiced defines how you play in music and in her life.

Rules *to Live By*
(Stone of Obedience)

Grandma Mary Tabron was a woman full of life. She had routines, rules and as the old people called them, "Sayings". She was a woman of traditions and consistency. When I was young, I went to my grandparent's house every day before and after school. This was my home away from home. In the morning, she would make a cup of instant Maxwell House coffee with Sweet-n-Low. She would always overfill her coffee cup, so that a bit of coffee would spill into the saucer. The overflow was for whichever child was sitting at the table at that time. First, it was me, then my younger

THE *Queens'* LEGACY

brother George took my place. There was always extra sausage or bacon left in a bowl on the center of the stove for anyone passing by to make a sandwich with a slice of Blue Ribbon bread. She only used Niagara spray starch, freshly grated coconut for desserts, kept butter cookies in the cookie jar on top of the fridge and her soap operas started with the Young and the Restless and ended with the Edge of Night. Grandma taught us the importance of eating with your mouth closed, elbows off the table and saying, "Yes Ma'am and No Ma'am" was required. Grandma was consistent and the rules were to be obeyed. I didn't always understand every rule, but I know her rules provided me structure.

Boldness from the Heart
(Stone of Boldness)

My mother-in-law, Anna Mack-Cooper, is truly an example of the grace of God in action. She is a woman who walks in her purpose and does not get caught up in nonsense. She has real life issues, like everyone else, but she has always looked to the Lord for her strength. If you were to meet Ms. Anna today, she would greet you and welcome you in. You would probably think that she was very shy and reserved, but ask her about the Lord and his goodness. She will enthusiastically share her testimony and many words of wisdom. Most importantly, she would share this simple prayer, "Lord Save Me," and the promise that if you seek the Lord He will answer. As I said she is a woman with a purpose. She is an anointed Pastor, Evangelist, and for me an Encourager and these are just a few of her gifting. Ms. Anna's boldness comes from the Lord and will share what she hears from the Lord with one person or a restaurant full of patrons.

All Things are Possible when You're **Determined**
(Stone of Determination)

Unconditional love and the determination to get the most out of every God-given opportunity is one way to describe the richness of my mother's personality. My mother, Mae Allen, is a Super-Mom. She has a passion for people and always has a meal ready to share. As you can imagine, I grew up in a Kool-Aid house with all the neighborhood kids around. I don't know how this happened since we had more rules than anyone else, but everything was fair. My parents would allow you to hang out, my mother would feed you, and take our friends on family trips, as long as you were respectful and followed the rules. Even today, my son Andrew and his friends prefer to hang out at his Nana's house. Everyone loves Ms. Mae because she believes in your dreams and makes you believe that anything is possible. Time after time, in the face of a challenge my mother would say, "Let's try it" and the adventure was on. When I was in the tenth grade, I had a favorite pair of jeans that were fading. This was before faded jeans were in style. I explained my dilemma to my Mom, who said, let's dye them. We went to Woolworths, picked up purple dye and went home to reinvent those jeans. Two days later, I had the coolest pair of purple jeans. I really believe we started the color jeans craze in the late 80's. Now as an adult, I know that it was a lot cheaper to dye those jeans than to buy a new pair, but why tell that to a teenager.

Then there was the time I decided I wanted to go away to college, right after my parents purchased a new larger home. I remember the conversation including these questions, "you want to go where?", "it's how much?", "let's see what we can do". I did not hear about the financial stress it caused until many years after I had graduated from Hampton University, with honors, and my loans were almost paid off. If it was something that could improve your life, Ms. Mae had your back. Not just mine, but all her children, and any friends we ever brought home.

Stepping from Hesitation to Destination

The path we travel is full of twist and turns. After college, I believed my path led to a corporate ladder. However, God has given me new vision to see the steps He has ordered for me are in business, but not how I expected. You see I was following Dorothy's yellow bricks to the traditional land of Corporate America, instead of asking God to order my steps. The women that have gone before me put their faith and trust in God first. In walking in their purpose, they laid testimonial stones for me to walk on. They have shown through planning, practice, obedience, boldness, determination and unconditional love, that anything and everything is possible. As I sharpen my focus on my ultimate destination, the stones that light my path glow brighter and brighter. There are lessons learned on every possible path. These women have taught me even when you make mistakes and go off course, God can turn your adversity around for your good.

As my husband James and I meet with clients as they launch their businesses, we often find many people walking a similar road as Dorothy. They were told to follow a path that anyone could travel to get to entrepreneurial or corporate success, but they have not stopped to ask God to order their steps. Our goal in ministry and business is to assist them in walking in balance and purpose to achieve their success.

Today, I am focusing on the golden stones before me and I am taking time to appreciate the view. My prayer for you is that your path glistens so brightly that it cannot be missed and that you and your family blossom in the abundance of your God given purpose.

Regyna Cooper is a pastor, wife, mother, co-founder and President of Maxser Consulting Group, LLC. Her professional background includes more than 15 years of corporate accounting, management reporting, budgeting and strategic planning experience with leading banks and insurers. These experiences have given her a powerful understanding of the successful strategies used by leading organizations. Regyna retired from Corporate America in November 2005 to begin living her dream and walking in her purpose. ReCoop Production, LLC, an event consulting firm was launched in 2005 to assist Small Business and Non-profit Organizations with meetings and events. In 2007 ReCoop was expanded to become Maxser Consulting Group, LLC with a goal of providing business strategies for entrepreneurs who are launching and growing their vision.

Regyna is an Associate Pastor with Simply Truth International Ministries, a ministry with a mission of bringing the Word to the marketplace all over the world. Regyna's unique blend of corporate process and entrepreneurial drive are perfectly intertwined to assist her in understanding the needs in the marketplace and ministry. Helping organizations, groups and individuals achieve the desired results.

You can reach Regyna by e-mail at info@maxserconsulting.com or on the web at www.maxserconsulting.com.

CHAPTER 34

Excellence Is A VERB

RYAN C. GREENE

All that you know today is not enough to get you through the rest of your life. You must become the person you want to be BEFORE your business card says you are.

A USA Today poll showed that 25% of Americans polled have not read a single book in the last year. I have heard numbers even higher than that. Regardless of your age, all that you know today is not enough to get you through the rest of your life. Even if your mission in life is to simply skate through and do nothing with your life, every day you must learn new ways to survive by being the best worthless bump on a log you can be. I define Personal Development as "increasing your value in the marketplace." When it comes to personal development I live by the mantra "You must become the person you want to be BEFORE your business card says you are."

If you aspire to be a great queen then you must follow the best practices of great queens. You must read the books they read, go to the trainings they go to, do the things they do. You have to become that person in your mind and in your practices before you actually become that person in your position. What good would come out of you being elevated to a position that you were not mentally equipped to fulfill? God will not put more on you than you can bear so if you are not mentally ready to bear the

responsibilities that go with wearing the crown of a queen then you will not be elevated to that position.

Life is not fair, life is JUST. Life gives you what you DESERVE and not what you want. You may *want* to be the Sales Manager at your job but if you do not study your craft, learn to work with others, develop your leadership skills, put in the extra work and grow into that position; then you *deserve* to be just an account executive. You may *want* to earn $250K a year but as long as you demand your company gives you a set salary as opposed to you earning unlimited bonuses, complain about how much life sucks, focus on the problems and not the solutions and get paid for what you do instead of what you know; then you *deserve* to only earn $40K a year. If you want more you have to grow more.

In my first book, *Success Is In Your Hand,* I introduce the "Personal Development Puzzle." For an in depth look at how you can begin making personal development a natural part of your everyday life I would encourage you to purchase that book and work through the exercises. For now I will share some of the bullet points on the Four Keys to the personal development puzzle.

Key #1: Watch what goes into you.

What you let in you is the number one determining factor of what kind of queen you will become. If you keep filling your body with junk foods and sugars you will inevitably become an overweight person. Your attitude on life, the way you treat others and the decisions you make are all signs of what mental foods have gone into you. Remember when your mother use to say "If you don't have anything nice to say then don't say anything at all?" Does it sometimes feel like your mother was the only one that ever taught that?

How often has someone said something negative to you about your dreams, career goals or hobbies and because of their comment you changed your course? Too often we allow people to plant little seeds of discord and doubt in our minds and justify our silence by saying we didn't want to start any trouble. The next time somebody starts a conversation with you with those infamous six words, "I don't mean any harm but..." you need to stop them right there, start some trouble and not let that negativity into your mind. Once you let those negative thoughts in it's sometimes impossible to get them out.

So many people complain about not having enough time to be more than they are when in reality it's just improper management of the time they do have. If every one of us only has 24 hours in each day then why do some people *make* time to prosper while others *waste* time in poverty? It's how you use your 24 hours that makes the difference. If all you have in each day is two hours of free time then you have to choose if you will use that time to better yourself or belittle yourself.

Key #2: Watch what comes out of you.

Once you begin to grow inside there will inevitably be growth on the outside. Personal development is something that, in the beginning, only you know is happening but very soon everyone else sees the fruit of your labor. The following six qualities will help you gauge your development.

Personal Image- The way you dress, the way you talk, the way you walk, your personal confidence and your overall appearance all will change for the better as you continue to develop yourself. It is impossible to grow on the inside and not see a change on the outside. As you begin to grow, your self-esteem will increase, your confidence will increase and your belief level in yourself will also increase. Once your image of yourself changes then you will never be able to let someone else tell you what you can't do. It will be impossible for you to settle for mediocre or average when you know you can achieve greatness.

Attitude- Do people like being around you or not? Your bad day is not a free pass to treat others any kind of way. As you grow you learn to not let your personal issues interfere with your relationships with others. Through your personal development you will learn the power of a positive mindset. Little things that use to get under your skin will not bother you anymore because you will be focused on the big picture. Your success is strongly connected to the relationships you build and the influence you have with others.

Adaptability- Do you go with the flow or do you complain about change? Change is a necessary godsend not evil. Part of the personal development process is understanding that change is good and rather than fight it simply ask how you can help it. Contrary to most of our beliefs, this world will go on with or without us. If we want to have an impact on it then we need to learn to adapt and encourage change. If your life is not what you thought it would be then you need to change some things about your life if you expect something different.

Are you a Taker or a Giver- Do you bring something to a relationship or do you constantly drain from someone else for your own needs? You should

aim to bring more to the table then you take away. Look first to see what you can do for others before you seek what you can get out of a deal. If you spend most of your time trying to reap from the relationships you have and little time sowing into them, eventually, just like a farmer who expects a harvest yet plants no seed you will look up and have nothing. Successful people aren't freeloaders and they do not resort to deceptive tricks to get their way.

Vision- Do you see a brighter tomorrow or are you stuck in yesterday's problems? Successful queens are successful because they focus on the solution and not the problem. They focus on the destination not the twists and turns in the road. If you stay focused and help others see the promised land through your eyes and get them to attach themselves to your vision, you will be amazed at how much more effective you will be. What are you willing to go through to fulfill your vision? People are looking for a cause to fight for, a crusade to embark upon, and a vision to grab hold of to make their own. If your vision is big enough it will draw more than enough people to make you a tremendous queen.

Humility- Do you enlarge others or do you belittle them? So many people allow their ego to get in the way of them achieving success. An ego will not allow anyone else to get credit for something you did. An ego will not allow anyone else to feel good about a small task they did when your task is greater. An ego also will not allow you to be nearly as successful as you could be without one. Being humble, making others feel big about their self and feel like they were even more important than you will pay big dividends when it comes to achieving success. Learning how to empower others will not only make you a more successful queen but it will make the people you lead more successful.

Key #3: The Law of Associations.

The saying goes "You are the average of your five closest friends". Like it or not you are. Think about the cars your friends drive, the places your friends live, the income of your friends, how many children your friends have. If your friends have dreams you probably have dreams. If your friends are positive you're probably positive. If your friends go to church you probably go to church. If your friends curse you probably curse. If your friends have negative lifestyles you probably have a negative lifestyle. If your friends lie, steal and cheat you probably lie, steal and cheat. I think I've made my point. The point is many of us need new friends.

There's another old saying "Guilty by association". Accept it or not, you are judged by the people you hang around. As you begin to grow in your personal development realize one thing, light and dark cannot coexist. Some associations you'll have to limit and others you'll have to break all together. As you grow, your current friends will either grow with you or you will outgrow them. I'll let you know now so you're not surprised when it happens, they probably won't grow with you. So you have to choose what's more important- your current state of reality having just enough to survive or the possibility of abundant success and prosperity in the land of more than enough. Eventually the Talkers will not be able to keep up with the Walkers.

Don't let your "friends" sabotage your dreams with words like "I'm just keeping it real" or "I'm not being negative I'm being realistic." What's real is what's right now; living check to check, working all day everyday to make ends meet, running from creditors, working a job you hate, spending only five hours a day with your family between 6pm and 11pm only to go to sleep and wake up and do it all over again tomorrow, that is today's reality. Who wants to live like that for the rest of their lives? Your dreams of abundant success are not a real possibility to your friends so they feel that it cannot be real for you either. The devil is a liar. If your friends want to "keep it real" by keeping you right where you are then that's a clear indication that that association must be destroyed.

Key #4: Appreciate who you become along the way.

Have you ever been told, "You have so much potential?" I personally hate that. Potential is good but more important than what is in you is how much of that you can get out of you. So many people feel like having potential is all they need in order to be successful, but have you ever seen a tombstone read "COULD HAVE BEEN A LOVING MOTHER" or "WOULD HAVE BEEN A DEDICATED FRIEND"? Of course not! Life and success is not about what you tried, it's about what you DID. From this day on take the saying "At least I tried" out of your vocabulary. That's a submission to failure and it has no place in a successful persons mind.

If trying was all it took to be successful then where would this world be? What if Thomas Edison, Carter G. Woodson, Harriet Tubman, Michael Jordan, Garrett A. Morgan, Madame C.J. Walker, Bill Gates, Sam Walton, Mary Kay Ashe, Rosa Parks or countless other trailblazers all settled for "At least I tried"? It was through learning from failures and giving their best that they overcame obstacles and became great successes in their fields. It

was through those very failures that those individuals grew to the level of notoriety and respect that they are given today.

You have to read now what those who are where you want to be are reading, go where they go, do what they do so when opportunity knocks you're ready to open the door. Natural skill and ability can only get you to the door but you have to grow to a certain level to be able to kick the door in. When you submit to personal development and make it a part of your everyday life, in one week you'll be addicted. In one month you'll start saying things and wonder, "Did that come out of my mouth?" And in one year you'll ask, "How in the world did I get here?"

An excerpt from the song "One Day" to my Queen, Ms Jacqueline M. Kidd

Dear God, what is this some kind of test
Please forgive me while I get this off my chest
Why you always take the good ones and leave us with the rest
I'm sorry that wasn't me talking, blame it on the stress

I've spent so many sleepless nights trying to figure out what to do
It's a good thing I have a relationship with you
Because that's the only thing that can get me through
Knowing that if she ain't here with me then she's in heaven with you

I remember August 10, 2000 like it was just yesterday
As I held my mother's hand while her breath slipped away
It was as if it were her last words and I felt her say
"Baby don't worry. It will be OK"

Someone said "Ryan now you gotta be the man of the family"
But wait I've always been the man of my family
So God tell me how it's supposed to be
That you want me to lift others with all this weight on me

One Day we're gonna fly around heaven together
One Day I'll get to be in your arms forever
One Day the pain that I feel in my heart will end
One Day I'll get to see your smile again

Ryan C. Greene's leadership development began at a very young age. His single mother, Jacqueline, raised Ryan with his younger sister Stacie in the suburbs of Baltimore, MD. Ryan became the man of the house quickly as a "latch-key kid" at the age of eight. He attributes his determination, commitment to succeed and never give up attitude to watching his mother sacrifice her life for the life of her kids. Watching his mother fight to make ends meet, support her family and fight through her sickle cell anemia, gave Ryan the determined resolve to be the one to make a difference in his family.

Ryan C. Greene is an Inspirational Trainer, Entrepreneur and Media Personality. He is the CEO of GreeneHouse Media; a media company whose goal is to provide "Media That Matters" through radio, television, film, music, books and print media. Ryan is the author of four books; *Success Is In Your Hand, My Little Black Book Of Leadership, Lead Wolf vs. Lone Wolf,* and *Success University.* He also hosts his own monthly radio show, "The Ryan C. Greene Show". Ryan graduated from Hampton University with a Bachelors Degree in Marketing and resides in Baltimore, MD.

To book Ryan C. Greene to speak or train at your next event visit www.RyanCGreene.com. To order any of Ryan's books, CDs, trainings and other products visit www.MySuccessfulLifeToday.com
Phone: 410-599-2411
Email: ryan@ryancgreene.com

CHAPTER 35

God Has The Last Say

SHAVON ARLINE

You are UNDEFEATED with God's favor in and around your life.

A life full of miracles...God has continuously shown me, the women in my family and the women He placed in my life, nothing but His favor. No matter what is taken from you or what obstacle has been put in front of you, "God Has the Last Say." A New Jersey native and the child of a burn victim, my life has hit many bumps along the road. But in the end, regardless of my decisions, I have learned from the queens around me that my worth in God and my name makes me the queen that I am.

It was a hot summer day in July of 1978 in Willingboro, NJ; the temperature was in the upper 90's. My older brother (11 ½ years my senior) was out playing around the house as normal, my father had not gotten home and my mother was 9½ months pregnant with a little girl who had decided that coming into the world was not a priority on her timeline. It was a Tuesday evening and the smell of grease, flour and seasoned salt could only mean one thing...fried chicken! My mother was walking back to the kitchen and realized the grease in the frying pan caught fire. Instinctively she threw water on the fire which, now we know, caused the flames to escalate. The grease began to splatter on the floor causing my mother to slip and fall. In order to **protect** her child she grabbed the stove to brace the impact. Doing

THE *Queens'* LEGACY

this caused the frying pan to flip in the air and the hot grease splattered directly on my mother's body while she lay on the kitchen floor.

She was wearing a tank top, apron and her regular eye glasses. The grease landed on her hands, arms, and torso but she never felt a thing. She immediately got herself up off of the floor and began to clean her new curtains behind the stove as only a queen would do. Unknown to her, my mother's body was in shock and the fright in my brother's eyes because of her peeling skin could only mean one thing; something was really wrong! He called 911 and the emergency medical team came and looked at this pregnant woman in horror and immediately covered her with sheets. As they made their way to the hospital, the family was alerted that her body had been mummified to prevent infection.

As the shock wore off the pain began to seep through her body with rage. My mother's pain came from 3rd degree burns that covered her hand and burns on her body from the grease burning through her clothes. The combination of being a burn victim and the full term labor of her unborn child caused excruciating discomfort. She persevered through the pain and pushed until her 9 lb. 5 oz. daughter came into this world with no bruise or marks to show what we they both had just gone through. As the doctors finally examined her entire body and realized what had happened, they concluded that because she wore glasses and braced her fall, she had prevented the blindness that would have resulted from the incident. The words "luck" and "fortune" were used to describe the miracle and all the doctors said to her, "You and your unborn child are lucky to be alive." But as the first queen in my life began to review the experience and as she shares the story with me to this day, we can only conclude....**God has the last say.**

Destinations in My Life

My birth into this world came as an eventful saga; events that could be viewed as a television drama. My life began as a miracle and in only 30 years I have been through things that have shaped me and helped shape my purpose which is to share with others that God's infinite wisdom and love for you puts you in position to meet the "greatness in you" and that His plan for you is divine and will come to pass. A saying that one of my best friends and I have coined is, "You are UNDEFEATED with God's favor in and around your life."

As a child, I grew up in a "Huxtable Home" I had the love and support of both parents (married 42½ years) and a big brother who stood by and stands by me through thick and thin. We grew up learning to love the Lord, maintain an active church life, care for your family and remember where you come from. My mother and her three sisters, whom I would say had a great influence on my life and my personality, would teach me their life lessons. We would openly explore their past struggles to make sure I would do things different and excel as they had done in their lives. There was the pressure to REMEMBER YOUR NAME! Know your worth! Know who you represent when you walk out of this door. I called it pressure because failure for a woman in our family was just not an option. I now understand it was for the glory of true queendom. They were preparing me for a world that tries to take a queen's throne away from her. Oh but as a woman in a family of true queens, it was made clear that no man (or woman) could take anything from me because **God has the last say.**

I excelled in school and in social graces. I was a high school athlete on top of the world in the state of New Jersey with good grades and a bright collegiate future ahead of me until that fateful day when my right ACL was torn. I had fallen awkwardly in a basketball game and knew that my legs were a ticket to college. To my dismay the news of a torn ligament in my right knee made my heart stop as I couldn't catch my breath. The doctor said those words. "You Will Need Surgery and will lose a year to run". Where would I go to college? Would I be the star athlete that I promised to be? My parents took me in for surgery, wondering if my career would be done. After nine months of learning to walk, rehabilitation, tears and pain I won the NJ state title to secure a full track and field scholarship to Tulane University. **God has the last say.**

I flew down to New Orleans, LA as a scholarship athlete prepared to become YES the next "Flo Jo" without the nails and hair! ☺ But God had another plan. I struggled. I ran well sometimes and could not perform at others. I was in a situation where you had to perform or don't eat. (literally) It was important to excel in order to maintain your steady funding for school. The life of a full scholarship athlete is one like no other. But then my sophomore year would change the rest of my life. I would be in excruciating pain trying to run while having three menstrual cycles per month. I finally told my coach there is something wrong with me. I went to many doctors and specialists and I was diagnosed with endometriosis. What is that? I had come to find out the women in my family would suffer with similar ails like fibroid cysts and many of them suffered miscarriages because of this. I thought nothing of fertility and motherhood because I was 19 going on 20 years old. The words from my doctor would alter my path in life; either you keep running for four more years and risk the chance of altering your fertility or you stop. STOP? I was now faced with those same questions from

high school. Where would I go? Can my parents afford to keep me here? Would I be the star athlete that I promised to be?

My coach and the athletic department were very understanding and knew that running track at this level caused my body to react against me. I was granted the rest of my scholarship term as long as I worked for the athletic department and earned my degree within four years. Not only did I complete my degree, I was able to complete my master's degree in 18 months and never applied for a student loan! You see God's plan was not for me to be a star athlete. It was for me to see clearly how only He would be able to work out my personal dilemmas. Making this journey through life and not knowing where I would end up helped come to one conclusion, **God has the last say.**

Wake Up Calls

I worked in New Orleans for another 3 years and had gone through loves' pain. I loved a man I shouldn't have loved and dated a man far away that ended up breaking my heart. I tried to be the woman for men in my "meantime" that didn't deserve the time of day and compromised my morals and values just for love. This coming from a woman who knew her father adored her and on the surface had it all together. You see, I understand now that I allowed my wants and my desires to completely take over me. Let me be clear you should have wants and desires; God made us that way. However, you can't let those desires consume you to the point where now you can no longer make rational decisions. And yes I was there! It took a few years to see that I was headed nowhere fast in my relationships and in my personal life with God. I was living on edge! I was spared from HIV and many other dreaded diseases during this crazy time in my life only because of God's grace and the prayers of the queens in my family and my new extended New Orleans family (sorority sisters, mentors and church sisters)!

So I made a change and decided I needed to leave New Orleans. I moved to Richmond Virginia and excelled. I worked in a government health position, purchased a home and continued just living life. The problem was I had not learned my lesson. I still carried my edge thinking Arline you are invincible! All the while God was just waiting until the right time to show me who was completely in control.

I met a great sister on my new job; we just clicked. We decided about 6 months after we met to go to an old school skating party (note you had to be born in the 60's or 70's to go). That was us! Well the day we were going my parents came down from New Jersey to see me and she decided not to come and pick me up. I was furious! I just wanted to skate and meet some cute guys, but she wanted to make sure I hung out with my family. I didn't hear from her that entire night, and all I wanted was an update on the party. It was Sunday morning and my family and I just returned from early church service. There was a voicemail to call a number immediately. I called and the phone fell from my hand; my mother grabbed the phone knowing that whatever I heard was going to hurt us all. My good friend was killed in a car accident last night. The car I was supposed to ride with her in? The car we were supposed to take to that great party? The car that God spared me from? I fell to my knees. No more to be said... **God has the last say**

"Undefeated"...because of His Last Say

I shared some major milestones in my life as a developing queen to encourage women to embrace the notion that you don't have to worry. There are more destinations that are still too painful for me to write but I think my sisters you are beginning to understand how God moved in this queen's life. The recurring theme seen in the destinations of my life have been made clear. You do not control what happens to you but you do control how you react to those trials and tragedies that come in your life.

The lessons from a young queen are these: (And know I am still preaching to myself and speaking from experience)

1. God requires us to endure life's destinations in faith.
2. Your hard work and perseverance are not in vain.
3. As you continue to live life, your destiny and purpose will be made clear. Walk directly on that path to your open door and to your success.
4. No matter what happens to you and no matter what decisions you make, God Has the Last Say!

I now embrace this. Many don't understand it and at times I don't know why God gives us these assignments in life. I will never be perfect but will strive for perfection. I will continue to pray for the true love I know God has intended for me. I will continue to hold on to the hope of marriage, motherhood and yes, wealth to maintain my lifestyle and to bless others with it! I will continue to hold on to the freedom that I desire; the freedom to be the woman who I know I am! The woman who can wake up, go straight to the gym, who has a husband and children that she adores and cares for and the woman who I know God created me to be. I have no doubts this will come to pass. I have no doubt my freedom will come to

pass. Your destiny and desires will come to past because **God has the last say**.

Shavon Arline is a motivational speaker and has traveled extensively throughout the United States and Caribbean. She also ministers to congregations as an advocate for faith based health initiatives, youth development and spiritual wellness. In January 2009 she received the Young and Powerful Excellence in Leadership Award.

She is a member of the Aerobic and Fitness Association of America and American Public Health Association. She serves on the national program planning and development committee of Delta Sigma Theta Sorority Inc. as co-chair of the physical and mental health subcommittee and chair of the healthcare committee of the Washington DC Branch of the NAACP. Ms. Arline earned her Bachelor of Science degree in Exercise Physiology and Masters of Public Health degree from Tulane University in New Orleans, Louisiana.

Contact Shavon by phone at (866) 381-6825, by e-mail at shavon@shavonarline.com or visit her website at www.shavonarline.com.

CHAPTER 36

The Molestation And The Fear

SHAWNTA BALL

Question: "What Happens to A Dream Deferred?" ~Langston Hughes

Answer: "When the desire cometh, it is a tree of life!" ~King Solomon

For years I have known that insignificant things have irritated me almost always. It could be someone popping and chewing gum, clipping their nails, eating, crunching, smacking or just making dumb noises with objects or stupid sounds with body parts. Even though this may not be things that would get on other's nerves, to me it was magnified. In the back of my mind I knew I had to confront these issues and get over them.

With the Lord being my witness, from childhood to adulthood, I don't recall any sexual encounters before this night that I am about to write about. Therefore, unto this day I cannot explain why as a six year old I would have such affection for a teddy bear. Something could have happened to me long before this event and perhaps, I blocked it out. Maybe it was a longing for affection that I may have lacked during that stage of my life. I'm not sure, but what I know for sure is one evening I was playing around the house (the whole house was home) and like most normal babies of the family you sometimes find yourself playing with your imaginary friends.

THE *Queens'* LEGACY

For some reason that night I was pretending to be the mom, folding clothes and talking to an imaginary somebody. Then I remember being affectionate with my teddy bear and pretending that it was the father. The next thing I recall is someone coming out of hiding and saying if I did not do that to them they were going to snitch on me. At the age of six, I couldn't perceive that if they told on me, I would not have had to continue disgusting acts for the next five years. This is when fear came into my life uninvited and unannounced.

That evening, to stay out of trouble, I was blackmailed into doing things that a six year old should never have to endure. I became a victim of child molestation and grew up thinking it was sort of normal or okay. I had no idea these filthy acts were heinous and would be detrimental to every aspect of my human make-up. Today at age 38, when I recall this traumatic experience in my life, I now realize what effects the molestation has had on my life. It has definitely played a role in the vast poor decisions I have made when it comes to relationships. It has had a tremendous impact on the fear that has gripped me and has literally made me clam up at thought of being confident and secure within myself. I realize that being molested took me down a path of constant confusion, complaining, negativity and insecurity.

This subject was difficult to write because this traumatizing event is the root of my struggles, problems, fears, challenges, bitterness, resentment and incompleteness. From this encounter many of the *issues in my tissues* were born. It is where fear took its hold on me and gripped me tightly. It is where the unexpected experiences and strongholds came into my life uninvited. It is where bitterness got its start and where resentment would spring up from within.

Right here at this rude interruption in my sweet and innocent childhood is where I would pick up such demonic characters that would try to take my life and make it a living hell. Here is where the devil thought he would step in and take over. At the tender age of six years old and unannounced to me is where low self esteem would enter my world. This is where if it had not been for the Lord, the devil would have stolen my life.

Even then the devil was trying to break me down, take control of my mind and demolish me. The devil wanted me to have a terrible outlook on life and men in general and wanted to get me in a place where I would trust nobody. But GOD!!! The devil wanted me to remain tormented in my mind, to be timid, and not speak up for myself. OH BUT GOD!! The devil wanted to rob me of who I am, But GOD!! Uninvited, satan came into my life. I stand here today however, alive and well with a healthy mind and a great outlook on life, on men and family, and more importantly a mind to serve Christ. Therefore, I will no longer live in my past but walk in the vocation that God has called me to also will walk in the liberty that through Him, has made me free. Today I choose to let go and allow Jesus to heal me from all the hurt and wounds that derived from this molestation.

It boggles my mind to think from the time I was six years old until I was eleven, that this demonic behavior would go undetected and I would not tell a soul until I reached seven-teen years of age. Why is it that we would tell someone's inner-most secret at the expense of humiliating them and cause a lot of chaos, confusion, pain and shame; however, when we as children and women, are sexually assaulted, we will not open our mouths to save our very own lives? Why is that? That is elusive to me.

The main culprit is fear. Fear has a grip like none other; it is the root to numerous demonic forces. Fear is a doorway for other demonic spirits to enter and that is why it is so very important to overcome fear. If we get over it, the devil's scare tactics cannot work anymore. The Bible tells me that God did not give me a spirit of fear, but of power, love and a sound mind. Fear is torment, and perfect love casts out all fear.

All these things crept into my life as a child and has been growing with me and showing up in various aspects of my daily living. However, I have proclaimed that I am taking each and every one of these forces head on. No longer will I be a product of someone living life on edge nor beneath my privileges. I am above and not beneath, the head and not the tail. I am more than a conqueror through Christ Jesus who loves me.

What is Fear? Fear, to me is something that shocks the senses and immobilizes one to the point where they are not able to do anything. Most people freeze up when frightened because of something that catches them off guard. I personally think there is a difference between being startled and being afraid. Startled only seems to last for a few seconds whereas fear could last for minutes, hours, months, years or a life time. The Bible tells us that fear is not of God because the Lord loves us and will not cause anything to immobilize us and keep us from going in the way HE wants us to go. Sometimes change can be startling/frightening and could make one not step out on faith. But in this life, I am learning that I must take a risk and meet the challenge. How could we ever know what we are capable of if we never step out on faith?

It's no wonder that when I was about 20, I picked up a terrible drug habit and got addicted to crack cocaine. I even remember reading that poem called "Crazy Horse" and said I would never in my life mess with cocaine. Long story short, I tried it on a dare and was addicted for six years.

As time went on, I was growing tired of chasing the rock and one day while riding in my car with my "get high" partner who was like a sister to me. I said, "I am going get myself together, stop smoking, go to church and join the choir." Instead of her encouraging me, she said, "Why are you going to join the choir? Because you think you can sing?" She skipped over everything else and attacked my ability or inability to sing. In hindsight, I can see that tactic was of an enemy and not at friend.

At that time, when I made that comment, I was speaking from a tired soul and little known to me at the time, I had spoken my new life into existence. I didn't know the Lord and the power of the tongue. Nearly eighteen years ago, the Lord brought it straight to pass and as of this day, September 23, 2008, it has been 13 years, 7 months, 1 day, 23 hours and 16 minutes since I left that tired soul.

Some time ago, I started realizing that many of my dreams and desires had not come to pass and I wasn't getting any younger. I was reading in the book of Proverbs one day and I came upon chapter 13 verse 12, "Hope deferred makes the heart sick; but when the desire cometh, it is a tree of life." Immediately, I thought about the late, Mr. Langston Hughes' poem, "What Happens to a Dream Deferred?" I can't remember the last time I read this poem, but I searched it up on the computer and started analyzing it. I realized that I do not want my life to be a boat load of dreams that shriveled up like dry prunes. Nor do I want my dreams to die and smell of rotten stinking meat. If my dreams die then I will die within. Life would be an empty field of unplanted seeds bearing no fruit. Imagine living the rest of life not on purpose, but unfruitful and being plagued daily by a terrible debilitating disease called the "coulda, woulda, shouldas."

I began to put my thoughts down on paper as far as what I wanted to accomplish, and places I wanted to go. I started jotting down strategies to reach my dreams and desires and this book is one of them. Out of the issues of my life the Lord has helped me birth my first book.

Question: "What Happens to A Dream Deferred?" Langston Hughes-
Answer: "When the desire cometh, it is a tree of life!" King Solomon-

Today, the two go hand in hand in my life because when I start thinking about what things I desire, I pray about it and seek the Lord with my whole heart and let Him be my guide since He knows what is best for me. I know if I have diligently sought Him and seriously put some time into praying and waiting then He has heard my supplication and will deliver the answer sooner or later. And while I am in the waiting, I tune into God and listen to what He has to say. It is so amazing how a Great Big God hears me, listens to me and actually responds! He truly speaks and it baffles me when I try to comprehend Him. The Bible lets us know that God's thoughts are not like ours. Romans 11:33 says, "O the depth of the riches both of the wisdom and knowledge of God! How unsearchable are His judgments, and His ways past finding out!"

I've said all this to say, "I will not allow fear to immobilize me to the point where I am not going to do what the Lord has put in me to do. The desire is burning in my heart and is truly like being impregnated and the baby has come full term. It is close to the time of delivery, the baby is kicking and there is nothing else left to do except let birth take its natural course. Having gone through the child bearing experience, I know what it feels like to have this little creation of God on the inside and it feels like the baby is trying to kick its way out. Just like I felt my little Angel kicking inside of me, I can feel the desire to get this book out of me. It is kicking and saying hey I am over due in here!! It is a beautiful thing. So whether I am happy or sad, whether the sun is shining or it is raining, I will do it if I have to do it afraid!"

John 10:10~ "The thief cometh not, but for to steal, and to kill, and to destroy: I am come that they might have life, and that they might have it more abundantly."

II Timothy 1:7~ "For God hath not given us the spirit of fear; but of power, and of love, and of a sound mind."

I John 4:18~ "There is no fear in love; but perfect love casteth out fear: because fear hath torment. He that feareth is not made in perfect love."

Psalm 37:4~ "Delight thyself also in the LORD: and he shall give thee the desires of thine heart."

Ms. Shawnta M. Ball is a resident of the City of District Heights, Maryland, born and raised in Washington, DC. Shawnta is an author, co-author and entrepreneur and has several ideas being considered for marketing every day household and office items. She is currently working on her first novel entitled, ***"Getting the Issues Out of my Tissues, Memoirs of a Poet."***

THE *Queens'* LEGACY

She has a passion for helping others to reach their potential and to believe in themselves. She has a knack for bringing out the best in others and helping them to realize their dreams and potential. Shawnta is one who stands up for her beliefs and one who looks at a problem optimistically and pursues it head on for a positive outcome. Whether the situation is a broken home, friendship, relationship, office or organization, she strives to be a reliable resource to help mend and restore situations back to its expected order.

Contact Shawnta directly at SMBall Productions and ANGELs Enterprises by visiting her website at www.marykay.com/smball, by e-mail at proverbs_3116@yahoo.com or by telephone at 240-380-6244.

CHAPTER 37

Is Justice Really Justice

SHEILA DATES

"WE WANT THE MONEY," he said. "If you cooperate with us you WILL get out of this alive. If not, you both WILL go out of here in body bags"

The Spirit of GREED unfortunately exists in this world today. Unfortunately, we will NEVER know or understand how anyone could wake up one morning and decide to go on a robbery and murder spree and whatever happens, HAPPENS, IF we get caught we both commit suicide, was the reason for this crime. One black husband and wife did just that. Life was not treating him fairly and he could not give his wife the finer things in life, was his confession when arrested.

The target was a chain of check cashing stores where most of the managers were single moms, with no boyfriends, or dogs to protect them. I was one of those managers followed from my place of employment to my home. They posed as FBI Agents to gain access to my home and to rob the store.

It was nearly impossible to get the money by going to the store because of the security systems in place. Their "Plan A" (rob the store) would NOT WORK and their "Plan B" (rob the customers) was a faltering one. What they did not count on was their first victim being a true "survivor". She had

THE *Queens* LEGACY

overcome sexual molestation by two cousins at age eight; buried her alcoholic grandfather by age 16, her grandmother (stroke) by age 20, mother (lupus) one month short of her 50th birthday by age 30; and CERTAINLY she would survive the attempted murder upon herself.

Nothing in life prepares you for certain things and somehow everything in life has already prepared you...you just don't know it until it's upon you. Whether your child is two days old, two months old, two years old or 21 years old, it does not matter... A parent is NOT SUPPOSED to outlive their children; children are supposed to bury their parents.

On August 31,1999 when the doorbell rang, Regina got up to go downstairs to answer. "Ma," she said, "There are two FBI agents at the door. They wanna talk to you." I looked through the peephole, then I went to the kitchen window to get a better look, and they flashed ID pictures and badges. My store had been robbed and it appeared to be an inside job (one of my employees). It was my day off and I thought they were coming to the house to question me about that robbery. Not to actually ROB the store!

Once they were inside, we were instructed to sit on the sofa downstairs for what appeared to be questioning. Then one of the "agents" pulled out a gun. "WE WANT THE MONEY," he said. "If you cooperate with us you WILL get out of this alive. If not, you both WILL go out of here in body bags." At that moment, time froze; fear, panic, and shock began to set in for both of us. We held each other's hand then we were told to go upstairs. Our hands were tied behind our backs, we were forced to lie face down on the bed, with our feet tied, and Regina's mouth was duct taped. We knew we were going to die at that point.

They wanted the keys to the store, my daughter's car, and the combination to the safe, as well as instructions on how to get into the safe (in that order). After realizing she could not accomplish that by herself, they decided to have me get dressed and she would take me to the store to get the money instead. Leaving my daughter with a man wielding a gun in his hand was the hardest thing I've ever had to do in my life. I've never felt so helpless. I could not protect my daughter from killers.

Forced to drive my daughter's car, once we were in the store, it took three hours before the safe opened. She got $16,000 in cash, plus coins. I was then forced to lie face down on the floor near the safe, with my hands tied behind my back and a cord around my neck. I fought by lifting my head up so the cord was underneath my chin. Had she placed it in the center of my neck I would have been dead in less than two seconds. l fought until I could not fight any longer... then everything just went black. It's now almost 11:30 a.m. and this ordeal started around 7:00 a.m. I was OUT until almost noon when my eyes finally could barely open. My head would barely make it up off the floor, then finally I managed to get my hands untied. ***To this day, I do not know how that happened.*** I dragged myself to the phone to call 911, where I collapsed again on the floor; but still had to drag myself to the door to open it, and through a second door to open it to let help inside to get to me. My eyes were "blood-vessel-busted", blood shot red. I looked like the living dead. After going in and out of consciousness for what seemed like forever, I was finally told my daughter had been murdered. All I could do was breathe and drink water.

I was released into Police Protective Custody. This tragic spree continued into the state of Tennessee where they robbed another bank and got an undetermined amount of money. They also car-jacked and killed another person. That car broke down in Elizabeth, NJ, and while at a hotel waiting for the car to be repaired, the couple was arrested by the real FBI. Belinda Henry went into the bathroom and shot herself in the head, killing herself with the same gun she had pulled on me. I can live with that. Keith Henry surrendered and after three years, I testified against him and he got the death penalty.

But with his many appeals on death row, the Supreme Court ruled that all rulings that had been handed down by a certain judge now had to go back to trial to be decided by a jury, in order for that conviction to stand. So it was my decision to not take myself, my family, and the other families through another trial when so much healing had already taken place; I accepted his attorney's plea of life without the possibility of parole. I can live with that sentence.

How do you survive death? I can't tell you what your process will look like, but the blueprint for my own sanity and healing is as follows:

1. Accept JESUS CHRIST AS YOUR LORD AND SAVIOR! Without Him, depression alone can and will kill you. Romans 10:9-10
2. LEARN HOW TO FORGIVE. You must realize forgiveness is not for the other person, but is rather for YOU in order for *you* to live. It does not happen overnight, and it is a process, but until you forgive your "transgressors", your own forgiveness is blocked. Sin is sin to God; no "little" ones or "big" ones...just SIN. If you want forgiveness, you have to learn HOW to forgive in order to live in the kingdom of God. Each person masters it

THE *Queens'* LEGACY

differently, but if you open your heart and let it in, it eventually comes. Jeremiah 31:34

3. STAND ON THE WORD OF GOD. It's the only thing that kept me from losing my mind. It's a very thin line between sanity and insanity, and unless you have something a whole lot bigger than yourself you can and you will lose it! When the simple, yet profound, Word of God came alive to me ("Father, forgive them; for they know NOT what they do"), I truly started to heal. Luke 23:34

4. CRY, CRY, AND CRY SOME MORE. There is healing in tears. "Those that sow in tears will reap in JOY"; and "JOY does come in the morning". John 16:20-33

5. LAUGH. Laughter is good for the soul. Laughter releases any feelings of guilt. Guilt condemns you, according to Romans 8:1 there is now no condemnation for those who are in Christ Jesus, who live and walk not after the flesh, but after the Sprit. Luke 6:21, Job 8:21-22

6. Forgive yourself, you are not perfect, no one is. Love yourself so that others can love you, for who you are and what you are (human). Allow God to use you, move in you, through you so that he will always get the Glory out of your life.

I had to forgive the man who killed my daughter and the woman who tried to kill me, in order for me to "live and not die". It took GOD seven years of going through the healing process, and being pro active. This meant going to court with other crime victims who had lost a loved one to violent crime. It also meant going into the prisons and ministering to murderers, holding them accountable, and letting them know how much they had destroyed families and how much their crimes affected their victims. It took family, friends, extended family, and receiving love from everyone I came in contact with, being sympathetic to what had happened. It took a support group, a support system, a psychiatrist, a psychologist, and a WILL TO LIVE in order for me to still be here today. Knowing God has a purpose for my life and my time on this earth is not finished yet, my heart had to eventually stop hurting and I had to learn how to process the pain.

Regina is in the arms of the Almighty God, her Lord and Savior Jesus Christ, and I will see her again. She is smiling down from heaven and saying "You go, Mom...You are the BEST!" I had the BEST DAUGHTER I could have possibly had for 21 years, and she touched more people in her 21 years than some people will ever touch in an entire lifetime. So this is dedicated to my Queen, REGINA ZAVETTE DATES ("Regina" means "A

Queen"). We lived. We loved. We laughed at the devil, because WE WON. Now we get to live again in JESUS!

Sheila Dates earned her Bachelor's degree in Social Science from Fort Valley State University in Fort Valley, Georgia. From there, this sweet "Georgia peach" landed herself in Detroit, MI, where she began a long-term career with Delta Air Lines; flew on to Chicago, IL for 15 years; then rounded home plate, returning to her southern roots, making Atlanta, GA her home.

Sheila is President and CEO of Diva Dates Enterprises, where she is living her lifelong dream of entrepreneurship. Through her company, she combines her expertise from the telecommunications industry and Pre-Paid Legal Services.

In her spare time, she enjoys cooking, reading, listening to music and collecting butterflies and black angels. In addition to her late daughter, Regina, Sheila is also the mother of two adult sons, Hanson and Jason.

You can contact Sheila by phone at 404 405-2839, by e-mail at sheiladates@comcast.net or by mail at 31 Jim Goodson Rd, Griffin, Georgia 30223.

CHAPTER 38

Trust The Love That You Are!

SHEILA THOMAS

Just as a seed holds its pattern of perfection within, we hold the internal pattern of our perfection in God

The reality of truth became my life's search when all else had failed my expectations. With great disappointment in life and nowhere else to go and nothing else to try, I began searching for the truth.

I hit ground zero in my life and like a man under water gasping for breath and there is no breath to be found under the water.

Man becomes desperate for that which will sustain his life. The one breath he is and we all are in one Being. The breath I speak of is that of being the core of who I am and my purpose for being here. Where do I come from? What is life? What is real? What is man? Who is God? Where is heaven? What is a soul? What is the reality of truth and love?

Ground zero was my journey to a resurrected life in the reality and enlightenment of the love God created us from.

Life is just an experience in the earth world and we, as souls, are just passing through as a spiritual being embodied in a physical form. Our journey is the path to return through enlightenment of the reality of Love

while still in the earth world. We are to bring healing and restoration to those who accept the limited beliefs that man is evil and not good, that he is a worm and not a king, that he is a failure and not a co-creator with his Creator.

These are all the whispers and teachings of the little mind (ego) edging God out. They are born of anti-love, selfishness, and the getting syndrome. All of this helps to elude us of greatness and of the realization of the powerful beings we already are in divine love. These are the lies that have been told and are of yet.

These things keep us looking away from the reality of who we are at the center of our being. Truth lies within the very breath you breathe. There is one life, one love, one being, one Image that is God and we all are his offspring. We are little expressions of his image.

In this time of great challenge and chaos, there are disappointments and many failures around us with very limited hope. But these challenges present us with one of the greatest opportunities to discover the greatness within our own being. As divine beings, we are the seed of the greatest love ever and we are the co-creators with this power above all powers. Love has no boundaries or limits.

Just as a seed holds its pattern of perfection within, we hold the internal pattern of our perfection in God. This is what we are and it is nothing that can be taken from us. When God see us he sees his truth and this is what we are to him. We are an expression of his love and he holds this truth acknowledged until we notice and acknowledge that he created us in his image and likeness.

Leave behind your limited identity that you are only a finite human being. You are the Heart of God. There is an abundance of things within the core of your being, for the source we are is God or Creator.

Everything we need has already been given and provided by source.

Understanding your energy is Love. Love is a powerful energy that manifests in the physical world what we imagine in our thoughts. It has the power to transcend and transform whatever we desire.

Loving unconditionally will be the biggest leap of faith that anyone will take. One needs to accept and allow that we represent love and are loved in the eyes of God. That love is to be given in expression in everything that we do and think. Love is our service to each other. The answer to life's dilemmas is Love. Take a moment to think on how the world would be different if everyone among us was expressing the love of God from within.

When Jesus healed the sick, he only told them the reality of their truth and they accepted it by the perception of their heart. As a man thinks in his heart, so is he.

Your heart knows your truth when it is not distracted by the logic of the physical world. It will manifest for you the truth of love that transcends all darkness.

Love is not a power that can be reckoned. It has no limits, no boundaries, nor is it controlled by time. It is the authority over all things and all things will bow and cease in its presence. Love is the substance of which all things are made.

Love calls those things that are not as they were and it is so. Love is the substance. It is the nature of God's being, and God is more "real" than anything you can perceive. In truth, the perception of Love, its use and experience, are more powerful than anything you can have in this world.

Love is not something you seek, but it is who you are. In the Beloved, what is within you will manifest outwardly. That which you believe to be your reality is what you will create and attract to you. Keep your focus on your inner world.

Love has not common sense for it is not common, that's the ego.

Trust the love that you are in God. Afford one a freedom that can't be bought and forever hold before you the image of who you really are. Love is your liberty given as a gift by God himself. When we depend on love, hope is found and peace abounds. Peace begins from within.

It takes courage to change and trusting love is what reassures your faith in the everlasting. As you embark upon a day that releases to you the renewed mercies and the compassions of the Almighty, new opportunities are afforded to you and the old ones pass away.

Give not permission of the old to interrupt your now moment in trusting love with all of your might and being.

THE *Queens'* LEGACY

Only you can give power to your yesterday by focusing your attention there. God has already provided everything you need, every promise is yours and everything you are worried about, love has already provided it for you. God himself is the provision for all.

The whole of Love is perfect; absolutely perfect with no exceptions. The whole of Love, being a hologram, is fully alive in all of its parts. Therefore, if there is no interference from a little mind full of things that block the flow of Love and life, the whole will always remember its perfection and will realign or transform to make perfect any and all of its parts.

The whole remembers the perfection of every iota of energy that is alive within it. Therefore, if anything moves out of alignment, the whole of Love simply recreates the part as perfect, glorious, joyous – the expression of the perfection of Love.

So it makes no sense to be struggling to create your good from the world. It is certainly doing things the hard way. It is attempting to visualize that which is your good using the little mind. The little mind by its nature is limited and cannot see the surprising possibilities of God.

Therefore, to affect the transformation that resonates in your hearts is to move into the Reality of Love, to hold the vibration of the Real of Love, to make connection with the unity and the joy, and to trust that the whole then will realign every part. Each expression is perfect as a part of the unified life God is.

God understands how intensely real the drama may seem. I also understand the ego and how it is ever seeking to get attention from you. How it has no overview of the spirit, no sense of the interweaving of great Love, and can only do that which is limited, that which looks at the world as duality, and thus, ultimately has only one part of the whole answer – the perfection of all.

Make the shift. Shift again each moment into the Real and feel. Feel how beautiful the whole is as it sings to you of the great communion of Love that is the whole vibrating the parts back into perfection now.

As you focus into the Real of Love and joy, you also find you have the advantage of the deep communion that you will find with God and with every other movement in the whole of Love. It is this experience of the great heart that you are, of the vibration that is pure and magnificent, of the connection of all life in this unity of love that God is and the sweet interaction of the spirit -- where you can permeate one another and feel Love at work and commune spirit to spirit and heart to glorious heart -- this is where you recognize God at work.

Because Love is always more and God is always giving, you can feel in your heart of hearts that whatever would occur would be better than anything the ego could imagine. Resistance on the level of the ego mind is simply keeping you in separation from this unity where everything is part of the dance of this living hologram of love that God is. This includes the in-breath and the out-breath of God and the appearance and disappearance of seeming forms in the world. What is true always is the continuity of the spirit and the increase of good.

Oh, how we limit ourselves through fear of change and through the inability to perceive with the heart. Sometimes it may seem as though there is a loss until you can view it with some distance or from the Real and see that what seemingly was taken away was simply opening the door to ever more good. It is then you will understand that Love and unity are inseparable and God is only good. If God is your vibration, then you are accepting the exponential increase of Love right now.

Will you say "Yes" and let God place it in your heart and deliver its gift? This gift is the great gift of peace – peace beyond all understanding, peace that transcends duality and ego Peace that comes from trust in the Love and the mending of separation through acknowledging the One and the complete self-renewal of the whole as long as nothing interferes with it?

Attune to the vibration of the great good and the unfolding of ever more Love. Attune to the vibration and memory of trust and let the vibration then bring other things toward you so that you might feel the winds of spirit. Everything always shifts and moves, explodes and dances forth again, dissolving old images. The old world for the New.

When the great rays of light that you are effortlessly penetrate all illusion and find the core, the Love at the center of all that you feel and bring forth the world of Love and only Love that you are helping to build as you experience living the Vertical life. With your permission, with your "Yes," bring forth this essence and allow it to blossom as the bridge world.

Heart perception is a feeling beyond anything that you have ever felt on Earth. It is the radiant light from the Real, the vibration of perfect Love going forth. It now washes through your being and opens up your heart that you might fit more experience of this powerful example of what it means to

be connected and centered in the Real and in the Love. You do this while experiencing the play of light that is the shift and the illusion and by simply opening to the trust and the joy as you truly become the heart of God living here on Earth and connecting exponentially with the Love. Every moment, you are living in this wondrous Love as it bathes you like the sun and removes all shadows.

You can reach Sheila directly by visiting her website at www.TrustLove-TL.Com, by e-mail at Sheila.TrustLove@gmail.com or by phone at 1-800-475-7761.

CHAPTER 39

Gift Of God

SHERRY YATES

My mother's name is Dorothy and it means "Gift of God."

My mother's name is Dorothy and it means "Gift of God". This is my story about the Queen in my life. I look back on my childhood with such fond memories. Great family, friends, palm trees and beautiful beaches; growing up in St. Thomas was fun. Don't get me wrong, there were plenty of challenges. As the daughter of a West Indian father and a Mexican-American mother, I had identity issues. Thank God for the Queen in my life teaching me valuable lessons and making life better.

My father was a small business owner and my mother a school teacher. My mother was very traditional, like most mothers in my generation. She went to work, was home by 3:30pm, helped with homework, cooked dinner and spent time with us. As I grew up, I remember watching and helping my mother make meals from scratch. When she wasn't looking, I helped myself to some of whatever it was that she was making. My mother put her heart into everything that she did for my two brothers and me. Even after my sister died at eight months old from pneumonia, she continued to meet our needs and be present in our lives, all the while teaching us many life principles.

THE *Queens'* LEGACY

My Mother Honored my Father. Until their divorce when I was 16 years old, my parent's marriage was rocky at best. Even with all that happened, my mother continued to honor my father. My father was self-employed and worked every day, including holidays, except Christmas. At Thanksgiving, my mother and I would cook all day long and set out the meal for the family. My mother would let my dad cut into the meat first. As a child I remember thinking, 'wait a minute, I helped all day and he gets to cut the best pieces of the meat first?' One holiday I got up the nerve to actually ask why Dad got to eat first. He had taken all of the ham skin and I really wanted some. "He's your father" was all she said. I will never forget the lesson that my father, the provider, was to be honored even if he didn't help cook. As a wife and mother today, married for 16 years, I too, honor my wonderful husband and teach my children to do the same. It's something that my mother passed on to me and it has helped me in my marriage.

My Mother Let Me Be Me. Growing up bi-racial was not easy. As a child, I had puffy and fluffy hair like Annie from the musical, except my hair was gold. That kind of hair was cute on Annie; it was anything but cute on me. My mother tried her best but didn't really know how to style it. She had straight black hair. In elementary school, one of the girls in my class teased me and told me that I could not get my hair in one ponytail. The next morning, I put about 30 straight black bobby pins in my golden hair until I got that ponytail. It was only a quarter inch long but I did it. You have heard the term "metal mouth", well, this was "metal head". In the hot St. Thomas sun, it looked like I had train tracks on my head. What I so appreciated was that my Mother did not tell me I looked ridiculous. Instead, she let me be me.

My Mother Taught Me to Focus on Inner Beauty. Believe it or not, if I received a bad report card in elementary school, my dad would cut my hair as my punishment. Yes, you read that right. He would sit me on the front porch and cut my hair. How humiliating. Especially since my friends next door would peak from out behind their wall. This one particular day, thank you Jesus, my mother snatched me off the chair just before the scissors came down again, telling my dad how ridiculous it was to cut my hair. Mom took me to a babysitter, saving me and my hair. I don't know what happened after I left, but my dad never cut my hair again.

Around twelve years old I finally started looking cute since my hair was able to grow. My mother had always told me that I was beautiful. But when other people started saying I was pretty, my mother made sure I knew that beauty on the inside is what makes you beautiful on the outside. This is a valuable lesson I work daily to instill in my daughter. There are so many outside influences affecting our young girls and their beliefs about beauty. What my Mother instilled in me, I pass on to my daughter. It bears repeating, inner beauty is much more important than outer beauty; beauty on the inside makes you beautiful on the outside.

My Mother Put No Limits or Expectations on What I Could Be. This is probably one of the most important principles my mother demonstrated for me as a young girl. Growing up, I never once heard my mother tell me what I should be when I grew up. Instead, I was free to pursue my own dreams and visions. Today, as a wife, mother of two children and in business with my husband, I am free to live and work my purpose. Each week my daughter tells me what she wants to be when she grows up. One week it's a doctor, the next week she wants to scoop ice cream, be a business woman like mommy, juggle and the list goes on and on. My answer to her is always the same; "You can do that, just make sure you own it". I further explain to her that you can scoop ice cream, just own the shop. You can be a doctor, just own the practice. We even role play appointments where I am a patient who comes to her practice or a customer at her restaurant. Just as my mother wanted for me, I want her to be free to pursue her dreams and desires and to be who God created her to be.

My Mother Modeled the Importance of Establishing Tradition in Your Family. Sunday was always a day where my mother, my brothers and I went to church. We usually went to brunch afterwards. Going to a Catholic Church, mass started at 7:30am. No matter what you did the night before you had to be at church the next morning. Sunday was also the day that we went to the beach. Afterwards, my parents always fixed a special Sunday meal. As a woman today, I still prepare a wonderful Sunday meal for my family to enjoy. When I look back on my childhood, I remember the importance of tradition even in the smallest things.

My Mother Did Not Overact at My Mistakes. My mother is a very smart woman. I wonder if she was a private investigator because she surely knew how to get information out of me. One day she found a note in my room from a boy saying he was going to send me a picture of himself naked. There were other things in the letter that were innocent. As she read the letter out loud, I was dying a slow death, waiting for her to get to the 'naked' part. When she read the 'naked' part, instead of getting upset, she laughed and asked me; "So, did he send you the picture"? Although she was simmering inside, in that instance, my mother taught me that to get information, sometimes you must stay calm.

My Mother was the First to Talk to Me About Important Issues.
When I was about 12 years old, my mother and I visited the Christian bookstore and got a book about sex and its place in marriage. Because my mother was first to tell me about the 'birds and the bees', I remained a virgin through my school years. She also let me know that there was nothing shameful about being a virgin.

My Mother Taught Me to Be Early, Not on Time. My mother did not believe in being on time for anything. She believed in being early for everything and I mean everything. Can you imagine, school starts at 7:45am and you get dropped off at 7:00am? The gates to my Catholic School weren't even open half the time. We had to be ready and out of the door at 6:30am for school that started at 7:45am. Sometimes my brothers and I would literally have to run up the hill, and I mean hill, to catch my mother who had already pulled off. Now this principle, I am still working on.

My mother is truly an amazing woman who followed her dream of being a school teacher all the way from California to St. Thomas. She is a Queen who has left a lifetime of legacy for me to pass on to my own children. I am so thankful to God for the gift of my Mother. Because she still lives in St. Thomas and I live in Maryland, I don't get to see her as often as I'd like. Her legacy shines through my life on a daily basis. Her quiet strength still supporting me in everything I do. I love my mother with all my heart. She truly is my gift from God.

Sherry is a wife, mother and entrepreneur. She retired from Corporate America in 2003 to take over operations of Circle of Champions Seminars and later launched the Women in Business Network of America, as its President, with her husband. You can reach Sherry by e-mail at sherry@wibna.com, by telephone at 301-218-2188 or by visiting her website at www.wibna.com

CHAPTER 40

She Hath Done What She Could

DR. STAN HARRIS

A Tribute to my Mom and my Queen - Thelma Jean Gessler

The Holy Bible, a divine library known to some as "Basic Instructions Before Leaving Earth," tells a powerful story of a woman who took an alabaster box of a very precious ointment, broke it and poured it on Jesus. ~Mark 14:3-9 KJV

Some criticized Mary, because they felt this oil could have been sold to feed the poor and was being wasted on this person whom they had come was a fraud and a fool. Jesus said, "Let her alone. 'She hath done what she could.'" Jesus also stated, "Truly, I say to you, wherever this gospel is preached ... what she hath done shall be spoken of in memory of her." Wow! What a powerful declaration! This text was the basis of what I preached at my Mom's home-going service on June 19th 1991.

I believe that my Mother, like Mary, left a legacy. "She hath done what she could." She gave it her best. I believe the Lord said to her, "Well done. Thou good and faithful servant, thou hast been faithful in a *'few things*.' I will make thee ruler over many..."   ~ Matthew 25:23 KJV

THE *Queens* LEGACY

For many years I believed that I had to get everything just right and be perfect. This belief left me overwhelmed and frustrated time after time. It was not until I understood this passage about the "*few things*," that I was released from the bondage of perfection. The "few things" that we do, even if we don't do them perfectly can and do make a difference in the world. My Mother wasn't perfect but she was an excellent role model for the "*few things*" that make a difference.

Three simple truths that Mother held to will perhaps result in someone speaking and/or writing about *your* legacy that you leave behind:

1. "She hath done what she could," to be **perceptive**.

The woman in the text recognized Jesus for who he was and she somehow knew that the end was at hand. V.9 Jesus said, "She is come afore-hand to anoint my body to the burying."

Some have the gift of sensing and perceiving things before they come to pass. My mother sensed that if I wasn't disciplined, it would in time, lead to my ruin. She consistently applied discipline to my upbringing. I remember her once telling me that if I ever went to the playground without her permission, she would beat me all the way home. I tested her of course, only to find her at the playground, belt in hand and in keeping with her promise, she whipped me the whole way home. I don't advocate abuse of any kind, but the lack of discipline, especially in child rearing, may well be the worst type of abuse. The departure from a wholesome discipline is evidenced by what we read each day in the newspapers and hear on daily newscasts.

Some people perceive their role as a parent as being a friend to their children rather than a mom or dad. "*Self Discipline the Silver Bullet of Success*" is a workshop that I run regularly. It is available on compact disc. The workshop outlines a structured and consistent model for self-discipline that can be applied to families, civic organizations or to self. I firmly believe that self-discipline is the core of attaining and retaining one's heart's desire in this life.

I recently co-authored a best-selling book with Brian Tracy, Jack Canfield, Bob Proctor and Loral Langemeier titled *Walking with the Wise to Overcoming Obstacles*. An important principle covered in *Walking with the Wise* is **"The ability to apply self-discipline to delay short-term gratification in order to enjoy greater rewards in the long term is the indispensable prerequisite for success."**

Perhaps that is one reason why Mom took me with her when she won a free month of Shotokan Karate lessons. She wanted me to see first-hand the result of hard work, training and a commitment to self-discipline. After her free month of lessons, she continued train and study. The day came when she became a skilled Karate student. One day when she and her boyfriend became engaged in a physical fight. I watched her deliver a side snap kick to his jaw that knocked him out cold!

I soon got involved in a popular form of Martial Arts known as Isshin 'ryu Karate. That was forty years ago. Out of nearly seven billion people in the world that train and practice Isshin 'ryu, I am one of only a hundred to achieve the 10th Degree Black Belt. I have been inducted into the Black Belt Hall of Fame, an honor that I humbly owe to my Lord and Savior through the example of my dear mother and the self-discipline inspired by her. A basis for an important concept that I teach is, "If while you practice, you don't want to quit, you haven't really practiced. Our bodies are forged in the fires of our wills." ~Anonymous

Mom worked two jobs so we didn't have to go on welfare. She believed that her sons would learn a work ethic through her example. If she were to "work the system" and take advantage of the benefits that offered an existence of a dependence on the government and charity, what would inspire her sons to do any better? During that time African Americans had initiative but few opportunities.

Someone with true initiative will create opportunities. Without true initiative learned through self-discipline, opportunities that present themselves are ignored.

2. "She hath done what she could to be **persistent**."

Some criticized the Woman in the text, as some criticized my Mom, but like the late Dr. B.R. Lakin said years ago, "If you want people to get after you, just do three things, have more, know more and do more, and if you want people to leave you alone, just have nothing, know nothing and do nothing."

Scripture indicates that all who were around to see Mary anoint Jesus were murmuring and condemning her. Scripture also indicates that she didn't care what they said. She was determined to complete what was in her heart. How many times have you allowed the murmuring of others to stop or put a damper on what you intended to do? Jesus said, "She hath done," not that she would do or might do. Therefore, have the courage to complete the desires of your heart in spite of any obstacles or messages that you receive from critics.

THE *Queens'* LEGACY

Calvin Coolidge said, "Nothing in the world can take the place of Persistence. Talent will not; nothing is more common than unsuccessful men with talent. Genius will not; unrewarded genius is almost a proverb. Education will not; the world is full of educated derelicts. Persistence and determination alone are omnipotent. The slogan 'Press On' has solved and always will solve the problems of the human race."

My mother had it rough in life but she never gave up. She embraced the idea that what doesn't kill you, will only makes you stronger. Although small in stature, she was one of the strongest women I have ever known. My dad left when I was three, my brother Ronald was 2 and Lonnie was 1 (yes we are like stair steps). She moved back to Harrisburg, Pennsylvania from Baltimore, Maryland with no husband, three babies and started over.

My mother's example of persistence taught me more than I learned in college. As a matter of fact, I would never have made it to college without learning the valuable lessons learned from my mom. Interestingly enough, after doing my post graduate work and becoming a professor, on one of the many occasions that I had the opportunity to address thousands of students and other professors, I spoke on the topic, "Things My Mother Taught Me without Saying a Word." I tell people constantly, "Your walk talks, and your talk talks, but your walk talks louder than your talk talks. As a matter of fact, your talk speaks so loud that I can't hear a word that you say."
 "You are writing the gospel, a page each day;
By the things that you do and the words that you say;
People read what you write whether faithless or true;
Say, 'What is the gospel according to you?'"

The gospel according to Mom was "Don't quit. Don't throw in the towel." These are two important rules that I try to live by. If everyone lived by these rules there would be no suicides, fewer divorces and less situations of abandonment, including abortion. How many times have we given up on our ideas, dreams, goals and hopes because they didn't happen soon enough? What if we would have just persisted and held on to our dreams? Who can say what would have happened if we never gave up and never quit? Just tell yourself, "I won't give up." Quit wanting to quit and focus your energy on being persistent as "My Queen," my mother did.

Another quote of my own that I use frequently to help people shift their mindset is "When I make up my mind to do something, circumstances align themselves in my favor. When I say I can't, my mind stops trying. But when I say, 'How can I?' My mind keeps searching until it finds a way. There is a way and I will find it, and if not, I will invent it."

Remember the old saying, "Necessity is the mother of invention?"
~ Anonymous

I know that this is true because there were many times growing up that my family didn't have food. The Volunteers of America provided hot dogs, potato chips and a coke for a quarter. Often we had to move because Mom didn't have the money to pay the rent and many times, the lights were turned off. Mom stuck it out and readers, you can too. Don't ever give up no matter what. "Keep on keeping on."

3. "She hath done what she could" to be **Positive**.

Mom understood what few realize. Adversity is inevitable, but misery is optional. Date-raped by a minister and becoming pregnant with my older brother Keith, who eventually came to live with us didn't stop her from believing. My dad visited from time to time while we were growing up, but never helped with the bills. Mom worked every day and survived on three or four hours of sleep each day. Despite the adversity that was often overwhelming, she kept a positive attitude and took care of her boys.

Another important quality that I learned from my mother is rooted in how she never criticized or blamed our dad for her situation. Once I had a job, owned a car and was able to visit my father in Baltimore, I learned that I had a lot of half brothers and one half-sister. The half-sister was only two months younger than my brother Lonnie. I learned that my dad had left Mom for a teenage girl who was pregnant with his baby. I maintain that we were not born winners or losers, but choosers. Thus we can choose to win and be happy.

Acts 26:2, "I think myself happy."

Mom never told me her secret, but it was obvious that she saw herself as happy. She was determined to keep focused on pleasant and positive things. We can think about our problems and be depressed, or we can think on the promises and feel blessed.

The documentary film, "The Secret," was a huge hit but I teach people <u>it's not a secret, it's a scripture.</u> Proverbs 23 verse 7 "For as a man thinketh, so shall he be." We understand from the Word, that our thoughts determine our destiny.

Henry Ford said it another way, "There are two types of people, those who believe they can, and those who believe they can't and both are right."

Every coin has two sides. Mom always looked at the heads instead of the tails. No one's life is all good or all bad. I've learned that what you focus on the longest becomes the strongest. My friend Zig Ziglar whom I've spoken for on numerous occasions and co-authored a best-selling book entitled, <u>Walking with the Wise</u>, states "It's your attitude, not your aptitude that determines your altitude."

As a boy I got into a lot of trouble, it wasn't long before I got kicked out of School. I'll never forget coming home that day. Mom was sleeping as she was on night shift. When she woke up, she asked what I was doing home. I told her that I had gotten jumped by the two guys at school and I had beaten them up. I was suspended from school because I had earned a reputation of a troublemaker. With tears in her eyes, she said, "I've been doing the best I can. It just doesn't seem to be working." Then she said, as she wiped away the tears and with a slight grin on her face, "I know that one day you will make me proud."

I will never forget her words they transformed my life and attitude. I vowed that I would never make her cry again, and that I would make her proud of me!

Today, some of my accomplishments include authoring books, becoming a Karate champion and Evangelist who has spoken in all 50 States and 27 Countries, I've been heard on radio and seen on numerous TV programs. I have fulfilled my mother's teary wish of so many years ago. She once told me how honored she felt to know a man of my caliber. I told her that I was only the result of her influence. Her words of so many years ago fell upon fertile soil.

If you are a parent, be sure to plant positive seeds (words) that will one day bring forth a powerful harvest.

On June 13, 2008 I received a call from the Harrisburg State Hospital in Pennsylvania. It was about 11:45 p.m. Central Time. I was living in Gary, Indiana. The caller said my Mom had fallen while at work, hit her head and was being hospitalized. I asked, "Is it serious and do I need to get there immediately?" Their response: "The ambulance was taking her to the Polyclinic Hospital and she should be okay."

Immediately I called Pastor Mike Golden, a young man whom I had taught in Bible College who was now my mother's pastor. It was almost 1:00 a.m. Eastern Standard Time. I asked Pastor Golden if he could go visit Mom. Twenty minutes later the phone rang. Pastor Golden said, "I'm at the hospital, I hate to tell you this, but she is gone." "Gone where?" I asked. "Did they take her to Harrisburg Hospital, or Holy Spirit Hospital?" "No, he said she went to Heaven."

"What, how can this be? They said she should be okay."

I thought to myself, this can't be, who will pray for me now? Well, after getting to Harrisburg the next day and speaking to the coroner who said, "Young man, I can't explain what happened. I've had had two instances like this in my 30 year career. Your mother had organs like a thirty-year old. She was in great health. For some reason her heart took a wrong beat and stopped."

"I know what happened. James 4:14 says, 'For what is your life, it is even a vapor that appeareth for a little time and then vanisheth away.'"

God called Mom home at His appointed time for her. I found her Bible among her things and on the inside cover she had written, "Just an ole sinner saved by the grace of God, moved out for renovation and repairs." These words are written on her headstone today. At her Home Going service twenty-one people received Christ as their Savior. How about you? Where will you spend eternity?

My brothers said, "Stan, thank you." To which I responded, "For what?"

"We'll miss Mom, but it was you who told her how to be saved and you who have lead all of us to the Lord. We will see her again one day in Heaven."

Friend, if you have never received Christ please do so now. Romans Chapter 6: 23 "For the wages of sin is death, but the gift of God is eternal life through Jesus Christ our Lord."

I am blessed and highly favored just like you! I'm too blessed to be depressed, too blessed to be stressed, to glad to be sad, and too anointed to be disappointed!

Christ has "done what He could to save you." Now it's up to you to receive Him. I want to help you, please E-Mail DrStanHarris@aol.com, or call 717-275-3508.

Now, I trust that you will do what you can to be **perceptive**, to be **persistent** and to be **positive**! You don't have to do what others have done, or even what my Mother has done, just be sure to do what <u>you</u> can do, and let it be said about you, "They have done what they could." I have a <u>free gift for every reader</u>, just go to www.FreeFromDrBreakThrough.com and get then while supplies last!

CHAPTER 41

Show Me How To Live

TANYA NORWOOD

As I learn to make Him Lord over every area of my life, He is with me and I will not fear or be dismayed.

I lay on the futon unable to move. There is darkness all around me. If I had a gun, I would shoot myself. That won't work. Even if I had a gun, I'm too scared to pull the trigger. If I had a knife, I would slit my wrist. That won't work either. What if I am not able to cut deep enough and don't bleed to death? If I had some pills, I would surely overdose. That won't work either. What if I don't take enough, I'm found, and my life is saved? Oh, the shame of it all. Oh God, help me. I want to die. This black hole is blacker than ever; there is no light. At 40, I just can't live like this.

My mother was a single parent during the 1960's. She worked to provide for me and my twin sister, Tracy. During elementary school, we would come home at lunch time and let ourselves in with the key we kept tucked inside our shirts on strings around our necks. We'd eat lunch, clean up after ourselves, lock the door and go back to school. The same drill applied after school. Go home, no one was allowed to come in the house with us. We'd change our clothes and go out and play. We loved to play and play we did play. It was never long until Mommy would round the corner; as soon as we saw her sky blue car, we'd take off running and leave our friends

behind. We would run as fast as we could to meet her at our house. She could barely get out of the car without our jumping all over her. We'd hug her and she would hug us back. Truly, we loved one other.

Mommy got sick when I was 9. I'm not quite sure what happened. My older sisters said she had a stroke. Tracy and I couldn't see her right away but eventually we went to visit her in the hospital. The moment she saw us she smiled. She couldn't talk very well. The doctors said she was paralyzed on one side. Eventually Mommy left the hospital. We stayed with our oldest sister until Mommy was well enough to go home. We were so happy to go home to our own house and be with Mommy. After the stroke, Mommy was not able to return to her job. She regained mobility, but lost her independence. I would hear her crying sometimes. Was it because her health had failed or was it the loss of her independence and the resulting dependence on others? I was left to wonder.

Children were seen and not heard. When mommy cried I would go to her and we would hug. I wanted to comfort her, yet she continued to cry. I felt so sad. God let my mom get better over time. I knew there was a God because Mommy always talked to Him and made reference to Him. She took us to church or sent us on our own when she didn't go. We always went to vacation Bible school in the summer time. There was a kid's club in our neighborhood that included lessons about Jesus and the many days spent under the summer sun on Mrs. Baynard's lawn learning about Jesus. I invited Jesus into my life as Savior at the Kid's Club.

One morning Tracy and I woke up and heard a strange noise. It was Mommy. We found her in the bathroom, slumped over the bathtub. We called our older sister who lived down the street. Our neighbor came over and tried to get her to breathe. I kept thinking, "Why is the ambulance taking so long?" It's all a blur after that. Mommy died. I know she didn't mean to or want to leave us, but she did. Daddy showed up for the funeral. At 12, I thought it strange that he was there. Although they were still married, he hadn't been there much, I'm sure he loved her at some point.

I believe today that God had a plan for Mommy. He took her to be with Him in Heaven where there are no tears; only peace and happiness. My mom didn't take her life, and neither should I. God will come for me when He is ready.

After the funeral, Tracy and I went to live with our oldest sister. It worked out okay for awhile. Then I started dating older boys. I suppose in some way I was looking for my daddy in them. My twin, Tracy and I spent one summer with my dad. It was an attempt to keep me from my older boyfriend, which didn't work. He drove up to see me. It was an adjustment being with my dad; however, having Tracy with me helped. When summer ended, we returned to my oldest sister's.

It still wasn't working out real well. My oldest sister then wanted to send us to another sister in Hawaii. I was in junior in high school and didn't want to leave my boyfriend or my friends. I refused to go and went to stay with a friend. I later ended up in foster care and still had to transfer high schools during my junior year. My twin sister ended up going to Hawaii.

My foster parents loved the Lord and gave me a good home. It was an adjustment having a man who wanted to have an active part in my life. God always knows what we need and provides. Tracy, my twin sister came back from Hawaii for our senior year of high school which made me very happy. I had missed her so much. Every week, it seemed, I asked my foster parents if she could come and stay with us. Upon graduation from high school in 1978, it was off to North Carolina to college. My foster parents drove me down and left me on campus with my bike. It was yet another experience and adjustment.

Something began to happen during my first year of college. I started to not want to get out of bed. I would miss classes day after day. I didn't eat and found myself in a lethargic and very depressed state of mind. At the end of the first semester of my sophomore year of college, I had dropped all but two classes. I then decided to leave school altogether. I wasn't coping very well and I was continuing to have days where I just could not bring myself to function. Before I left school, I found a job and stayed in North Carolina. The Lord has always provided for me. I returned home in April of 1982.

When I returned home, a few months later I married my childhood sweetheart. I had no idea what marriage entailed and was I headed for trouble especially with no premarital counseling. I was still missing days out of my life and not understanding why. I saw a counselor for a time, but things just didn't get better. I had so many insecurities and hang-ups going into the marriage that I made many poor choices.

Physical abuse began in my marriage. After 10 years of marriage, we separated. Two years later I was divorced. I, through my faith in God was able to forgive him and more importantly, myself. I healed slowly by talking to God, reading my Bible, reading self help books, and going to church. I knew there was a God. He was real and I knew that He loved me. I continued to seek out a counselor that could help me understand why I was

losing days and sometimes a whole week. I wanted to get out of bed, but didn't have the will to do so.

I was determined to get better. I knew deep within that I was called to live an abundant life. Complete wholeness of mind, emotions, physical and spiritual well-being was to be mine. I chose to do self inspection which was hard. I looked at who I was – my beliefs, values, biases, expectations and behaviors. I learned to change my internal self talk and listen to God's voice.

During the two years of separation from my ex-husband and four years after the divorce, I chose to not even date. A relationship, I felt, would have only clouded my focus. I wanted to be clear on what I was leaving behind, who I was becoming, what I wanted and where I was going.

Time truly does heal all. Eventually, I was able to move on with my life and I knew I was getting better. I was healthier in mind, body and spirit. God had refreshed me. After taking various classes, God provided the idea for my first business. *Today Realize Your Dreams* became a reality in the early 90's with God's help. I was able to leave corporate America and become a consultant, speaking and training on the power of goal setting. In 2000, the Lord also blessed me to start my home-based business, *Prepaid Legal Services, Inc.* I have been engaged in this business for eight years.

I started to date again, but decided to not have sex before marriage this time around. I chose to save myself and to be obedient to what God called me to do. I presented my body as a living sacrifice, holy and acceptable unto God, in order to receive the best God intended for my life. I wanted to follow God's plan to abstain. I didn't know when, but knew that I wanted to marry again and to be a part of a team. He who finds a wife finds a good thing. My current husband, Jerome found me. We dated for two years, no sex or vacations away. Jerome and I have been married for twelve years now and I thank God for him. While I dated Jerome and after marrying, I was still seeking out a counselor to help me with the time I was losing from my life by the bouts of debilitating depression that I continued to experience. I was better, but still not healed from this condition.

I found a therapist that suggested that I might have a chemical imbalance in my brain. She worked with me and referred me to a psychiatrist, a doctor who can diagnose and treat mental disorders. "I'm not crazy," I told myself but I went because I wanted to experience the abundance in my life promised, by the word of God.

I remember sitting in the doctor's office and his asking a few questions. I broke down and cried uncontrollably. He asked why I was crying and I couldn't answer him. I truly didn't know. I just knew that his questions triggered emotions and that crying was my natural response. The doctor prescribed Paxil and while I was initially resistant to taking the medication, I took it and eventually began to feel better.

I knew I would not have to remain on medication for the rest of my life. After 1½ years, I, under the direction of a doctor, weaned myself from it. There is a scripture that says whom God sets free, is free indeed. My therapist continued to work with me and teach me coping mechanisms along with an understanding of clinical depression. I know and believe that God didn't create me to live depressed. Deep within, I heard Him say, "Tanya, I know the plans I have for you. These plans are not for evil, but for good, to give you hope, a future, and an expected end. I have not given you a spirit of fear, but of love, power and a sound mind."

Today at 48 I am still working through symptoms of depression during my menstrual cycle, much like others who might have migraines, become emotional, or have cravings. I am not, however depressed. I have been delivered from that feeling of hopelessness and despair. Since God would not let me die, I asked Him to show me how to live. As a result of really tapping back into my faith, I decided to make a sincere effort to activate my faith -- my corresponding, suitable and appropriate action for what I 'm believing God for out of His word.

He is showing me how to live. He is the one who goes ahead of me. He is helping me to come back stronger in spite of the setbacks that continue to surface in everyday life. As I learn to make Him Lord over every area of my life, He is with me and I will not fear or be dismayed. In the strength of His might I'll stand and fight until the battle is over and done. I live Victorious in Christ.

Tanya Norwood is an Independent Associate with *Prepaid Legal Services, Inc. (NYSE)* her home based business where she educates and protects individuals against Identity Theft, gives individuals and families equal

THE *Queens'* LEGACY

access to justice under the law, and provides economic empowerment. Tanya is also the founder of *"Today Realize Your Dreams" (T.R.Y. DREAMS)*. T.R.Y. Dreams was created to show individuals how to take control of their own destiny through the goal setting process.

Tanya is a keynote speaker who presents seminars and trainings on the goal setting process and her business opportunity. Over the past 10 years as a motivational speaker, her clients have included Drexel University through Mentoring Partnerships, Inc., Youth Services, Inc., The West Philadelphia Enterprise Center, Junior Achievement as well as various businesses and schools. Tanya has also been mentored by motivational speaker and trainer, Les Brown.

You can reach Tanya directly by e-mail at trydreams@hotmail.com, by phone at 856-667-1990 or by visiting her website at www.prepaidlegal.com/hub/tnorwood.

CHAPTER 42

No More Excuses

TAWANA WILLIAMS

If you don't want to be successful, keep making excuses

I could've given a million legitimate excuses for not living my dreams; but I was born to a mother that told me, **"There was nothing that I could not do"**, so excuses were not allowed in our house.

I'm Tawana Williams, your messenger of **Hope** and **Inspiration**. I've overcome the devastating adversity of being born without arms. I was gang-raped during a home invasion, raped by my stepfather, addicted to crack and cocaine for ten years, and I've experienced abortion as well as motherhood. Oh yes, I beat the odds! That's why I'm **"Unarmed But Dangerous"**...so what's your excuse?

What are some of the things that have happened to you that you've allowed to defeat you, control you, stop you, or to give you a false definition of who you really are? Whatever those things are, get ready to remove them because it's time for you to live a "no excuse" lifestyle! What are some of your excuses? Is it your job, your mate, your family or friends, your finances, your children, or is it simply **YOU**? James Lane Allen said: **"You are the handicap you must face. You are the one who must choose your place"**. So what place do you choose? If you want to make it in this life, then don't give yourself any excuse not to make it. In life, you're either going to have excuses or results...you can't have both.

THE *Queens* LEGACY

George Washington Carver said, **"99% of all failures come from people who have the habit of making excuses"**.

Your life is in your hands; you are the keeper of your life. It's now up to you, because everything starts in the mind. Every book that's been written, every choice that's been made, every business that's been started, every invention that's been invented, all started in someone's mind. So, if you tell yourself that you can't, you won't. Henry Ford said: **"Whether you think you can do a thing or you think you can't do a thing, you're right"**.

Our greatest power is the power to choose. Neglect to use that great power, and you automatically grant permission for others to choose for you. Every person, sooner or later, comes to the realization that all conditions – good or bad – are self-created, and started in the mind. So change your mindset, and you change your life...that simple! **Only the owner can deal with such a mind; he has to unlock himself.** So...**no more excuses**...you've got come-back power! You've got more on the inside than you realize; so tap into your unlimited potential, and make it happen for yourself. Get your mind into a place where you choose to make a difference.

I started my business with a vision, $300.00, a computer, a telephone, and business cards. I'd send out 40-50 emails a day...I called strangers to open doors for me. When I realized that the world wouldn't give me a job, I decided to create my own job. I'm now the CEO of Tawana Williams Outreach, Inc. Remember, in life you're going to have excuses or results. George Washington Carver said: **"Do what you can, where you are, with what you have, and never be satisfied"**. You see, I was not satisfied with my life and where I was, so I decided to use what I had to continue to move, and things began to happen for me...and they'll happen for you too.

As I looked at my life, and all of the time and energy that I wasted making excuses about my situation, guess what? My situation never changed...and yours won't either. I can't even begin to tell you all of the moments of frustration, disappointment, and the set-backs that I've had; the trials and errors that I've gone through just trying to do something new, trying to learn something different; trying to do something that I was told I could not do. But I was so determined, so driven, that I refused to give up, and I did it. You'll find that in yourself too. Things in life can make you bitter or better; it's been said that **"bitterness is like drinking poison and expecting someone else to get sick"**.

I've elected myself to be the Captain of my own ship. I stopped ruling things out for myself, and began to speak to myself. I told myself that I could do it, and I did it, and you've got that power too. I want you to learn how to remove or stop that negative self-talk that we all tend to have. You know how it goes: **"I can't do it"**, **"It will never happen for me"**, **"I don't have a college degree/the money/the resources"**, **"I don't know the right people"**, and so on. Stop ruling things out for yourself...oh yes, you can do it! Remember that there are 3 kinds of people in the world:

1. **Instigators** (those who talk about things happening).
2. **Spectators** (those who watch things happen) and;
3. **Participators** (those who make things happen).

What determines which category a person falls into is the **"ME Factor**.

We need to learn to identify our **foes** (those we can**not** celebrate our accomplishments with). I've come to realize that everybody's not happy with my success, and you'll find that in your life too. There are "haters" in this world; people will smile in your face and stab you in your back. Remove those negative people from your space, immediately. Learn to surround yourself with people who will **celebrate** you, not **tolerate** you. Harold R. McAlindon said: **"Do not follow where the path may lead; Go instead where there is no path and leave a trail"**.

Where will your trail lead? What legacy will you leave behind? What statue will be erected in your name? Or will you continue to make excuses for the things that you don't have? It's time to stop "excusing" your life away. If you want something to happen for you, then don't give yourself any excuse for not making it happen.

Focus and balance are essential to accomplishing anything you want. Here are some suggestions to bring **FOCUS** and **BALANCE** to your life:

1. **Stop whining and complaining**; No one cares about your sorrows, stop the pity party!
2. **Position yourself around positive people**; hang around those who have what you want (i.e., get a mentor).
3. **Take responsibility and control of your life**; hold yourself accountable for what you want, stop depending and waiting on others to do things for you...**it's YOUR LIFE**.
4. **"Upgrade" your relationships and knowledge**; hang around people that are smarter than you, invest in yourself, read books, listen to motivational and positive messages.
5. **"Upgrade" your determination**; you must see yourself doing it – encourage yourself daily, give yourself positive affirmations, pat yourself on the back. You don't need anyone to validate who you are...validate yourself!

THE *Queens'* LEGACY

You must understand **the major key to your success or failure in life is YOU**. Set standards for yourself. Some of us go through life complaining about everything, signing up to be volunteer victims.

I've been a professional Motivational Speaker since 1996; traveling around the country, speaking life into dry bones, awakening the dead, believing in others until their belief in themselves kicked in. Many times I was promised to be paid, and when I arrived they didn't pay me; and that will happen to you too. It's been said **"that your passion is something you love so much, that you'll do it for free, and you'll do it so well that people will begin to pay you to do it"**. Many times, people have tried to pass me off as a freak show, and I knew what they were doing, but I also knew what *I* had to accomplish. So keep your head up, keep the faith, and when you fall, get up again...and again...and again!

The only way that I was able to be a guest on the Jerry Springer Show in 1993 ("Beating the Odds"); the only way that I was able to join the Les Brown Platinum Speakers Network in 2004; the only way I was a Mentor on the Judge Hatchett Show in 2005, had phone interviews with Oprah's Producers and Montel Williams Show Producers, was featured in 4 national magazines in 2007, on Total Christian Television in 2008 (worldwide), The WORD Network (worldwide) in 2008; is that **I saw myself doing those things. You've got to speak those things that are not, as though they ARE.**

I encourage you to find someone positive; find someone doing what you desire to do, and learn from them, watch them, take notes, pay attention and "follow the leader." Get some structure, some leadership, and some balance to your life, and things will begin to happen for you. You've got to **"be willing to do the things today that others won't do, in order to have the things tomorrow that others won't have"**. Oliver Goldsmith said: **"People seldom improve when they have no other model but themselves to copy"**.

Remember this: **your past has brought you to where you are right now, and what you do from this point forward, will dictate your future...** So live full & die empty!!!

This has been Tawana Williams, your messenger of hope & inspiration. I want you to hold on to these words until we meet again (I know that I will...even without arms):

When you were conceived, you were given all that you need. Nothing's missing.

"NO MORE EXCUSES!"

Tawana Williams was born without arms and she has a powerful and uplifting message for people of all walks of life. Her compelling story is one of triumph, perseverance, and determination. She has overcome many obstacles, and has never let her disability stop her.

Tawana has an incredible number of accomplishments to be proud of: a guest on the Jerry Springer Show in 1993 ("Beating the Odds"); guest Mentor on the Judge Hatchett Show, in 2005; phone interviews by Oprah's Producers, as well as The Montel Williams Show Producers; being featured, with her husband Toby in Homes of Color magazine, in March 2007; Hope for Women magazine, in Spring 2007, and Epitome Magazine in July 2007; as well as myriad other accomplishments that many people dream about, but most never give themselves a chance to do. Among these, producing her own radio show, lobbying Congress, being featured as a Keynote Speaker, and receiving countless awards, certificates, and being featured in numerous articles.

Tawana lives in Wilson, North Carolina with her husband Keither "Toby" Williams, her daughter, April and 2 grandsons, Jalen and Noah. Her Latest Book **"Unarmed But Dangerous"** is now available!!!

To book Tawana for your next event, Call Angela Young (301) 883-8425 or (202) 256-1834, www.tawanawilliams.com, www.tawana.mentorsclub.com motivationalspeaker2003@yahoo.com.

CHAPTER 43

My Black Is Beautiful

TERESA ANN HAILEY

*After working all day and tired, we returned to the van, where
we were met by five Ku Klux Klan members dressed in full KKK regalia.*

All of my life I have been very interested in the Civil Rights
Movement (the "Movement"). Being raised in a middle class family afforded
me an opportunity to participate in events, travel and activities around the
Movement. My parents taught me to work hard for everything that I
wanted. Everything that is worth having does not come easy. **<u>Greatness
comes with a price</u>.** I was often discriminated against within my own race.
I would often see and hear light skinned girls attain different privileges,
whether they earned them or not. Often, I was teased because of my dark
skin, big nose and lips. It took me a long time to realize, understand and
believe that as Black as I am, the sun cannot shine one day without shining
on me.

Experiencing the pain that my parents and our leaders
experienced, I believed, would help in order to have a better understanding
and appreciation for the Civil Rights Movement. In 1980, I was the Co-Chair
person of the Martin Luther King, Jr. events, in Denver, Colorado. Martin
Luther King, III was our guest speaker. Later that year, I moved to Atlanta,

Georgia where I volunteered at the Martin Luther King Center for a year. What an incredible experience. I met a number of people including kings, queens, elected officials, local and national civil right leaders, entertainers and so many more.   While at the King Center I saw some of Dr. King's clothing. Surprisingly, he was a small man. I had the opportunity to read some of Dr. King's handwritten letters. One gains great insight from reading Dr. King's own words versus someone else telling the story.

Many days I would find a reason, any reason, to visit Ebenzer Baptist Church located next to the King Center. I wanted to see "Daddy King", Dr. King's father.   For the most part, I would find him in the same place. It was such an honor to talk to him. He was so completely filled with knowledge and wisdom.   I believe that education is very important and attaining good grades is a must. Daddy King shared A+ information.

Being hired to work at the organization that Dr. King founded, the Southern Christian Leadership Conference (S.C.L.C.), was my greatest experience.   At that time, the S.C.L.C. was under the leadership of Dr. Joseph Lowry. I participated in many events including, boycotts, sit-ins, marches, get out the vote drives, S.C.L.C. conventions and I met a lot of people who marched and went to jail with Dr. King and other leaders in the Movement.

One event that stands out for me was when the S.C.L.C. was boycotting a major food chain. They started out talking and meeting. When that did not work, the S.C.L.C. organized a state boycott. If I remember correctly, the chain refused to promote Blacks and minorities to management positions. We boycotted for months. Then one November, the day before Thanksgiving, when a lot of people were doing their last minute shopping and the stores were very busy, Dr. Lowry selected a store and decided that at a specific time, we would block the doors so that people could not get in or out. I was very surprised at the number of Blacks that were willing to cross the picket lines.   After all, we were fighting for them.

Because we were not allowing people in or out of the store, the store manager called the police. When the police came, at first, they refused to take us to jail. I remember them repeatedly asking us to move. Finally they called for backup and about 20 of us went to jail. ***I was so excited***. When we got to jail they put the ladies on one side of the jail and the men on the other. They would not let us in a cell with the other people that were in jail for other reasons. They cleared out a big cell for the ladies and one for the men. There must have been about 10 ladies arrested with us, including Mrs. Lowry and her daughter. We prayed, talked, and everyone was given an opportunity to express their concerns and feelings. We basically spent all of Thanksgiving in jail, fighting for the rights of others. It was nothing like when Dr. King went to jail. The jail employees were very nice and accommodating. They made sure that Dr. Lowry had everything he needed.

Just as the store management felt that it was over for the day, another group of people came singing and demonstrating. Once again, they blocked the doors, this time Dr. King's children, Martin Luther King, III and Bernice King went to jail. The boycott went on for months. I am proud to say that the store now promotes blacks and other minorities to management positions.

Another highlight was attending a meeting where it was announced that Rev. Jesse Jackson was going to run for the President of the United States. I very much wanted to work on his campaign. I did not want to pass up that opportunity. So I started going to the office every day, either before school or after work. Once again, working on that campaign was an awesome experience. One day a group of us went to small cities in Georgia, (I don't remember the names) to register people to vote and to offer them a ride to the poll. After working all day and tired, we returned to the van, where we were met by five Ku Klux Klan members dressed in full KKK regalia. I don't know why, but I was not scared. I told everyone not to pay them any attention and to get in the van. I do believe that it was my leadership and the ability to keep everyone calm that saved our lives.

When we returned back to the office, the talk was out. I was introduced to Rev. Hosea Williams. At the time I had no idea, who he was or the powerhouse that he was. I was invited to his office where I saw pictures of him being beaten by the police. I saw pictures of him on the balcony with Dr. King the day that Dr. King was shot and killed. Some pictures I remembered seeing in Jet and Ebony magazines. At the time, Rev. Williams was a State Representative and one of the only elected officials who was reelected while in jail. My first day meeting him I was scared to death of him. He was on the phone yelling at the secretary to the President of the United States. I remember thinking, 'this man has lost his mind.'

Rev. Williams announced that he was running for Congress and I was hired to work on his campaign. I would arrive at the office around 8:30am or 9:00am and would not stop working until 9:00pm or 10:00pm. Sometimes I was given an opportunity to travel with him. Part of my job was to help him get to places on time and to be prepared for the event that we were attending. People would always stop him, and tell him their problems, asking him for help. Rev. Williams was always fighting to get someone's job back, fighting with a major company, or helping a mother get

THE *Queens* LEGACY

her son out of jail. That is why it is so important that every African American realize and understand that you are able to drive your pretty car, live in your beautiful home, sit in your air conditioned office because someone went to jail, fought and died so that you can have the American dream. I am saddened when I hear that thousands of kids drop out of school every year because they are bored or when I see kids wearing their pants three sizes too big and hanging off of them; disrespecting their parents and teachers; and too often more concerned with the designer name on their clothes rather than their education.

Rev. Williams and I travelled to Forsyth, Georgia for a Martin Luther King, Jr. March (the "March") that was organized by a young White guy trying to bring about a change. The people in that community did not want us there, nor did they want the March to go on. They threw bricks, bottles and other things. Later I learned that Blacks and minorities were not allowed to live in Forsyth, Georgia. **No Blacks** lived in Forsyth, Georgia. None. The news media heard about what happened and the story went national in minutes. Oprah Winfrey produced a show from Forsyth in front of an all White audience. There were White's that Oprah interviewed that could not refrain from using the "N" word. It was known, if you were Black, you better not let the sun go down and still be in Forsyth. You would not make it out alive. Within days of this happening, Rev. Williams organized a march the likes that Georgia has never seen. There were so many people in attendance that they didn't fit in the city. It was something to see. People came from all over the United States. Local and national civil rights leaders and others from the Movement were there. The march was broadcast live on TV. Sometimes I wonder if the town is still all White, especially after that march.

The time I spent with Rev. Williams helped me to develop leadership skills, the ability to organize, and the ability to stand firm and true to my beliefs. He taught me that when you are confident in your purpose, there is no need to be fearful of men nor external personal conflicts that attempt to hinder you. You know, with confidence, that sooner or later every trial, every hindering situation and every opposing person and thing in your life will eventually and inevitably bow and submit to God's plan and purpose. It's just a matter of time and circumstance. There were times when Rev. Williams would do things that I felt was wild and crazy. He would always tell me, "you have to get a person's attention and make them take you serious. They have to understand that you mean business."

From time to time, Rev. Williams and others who were involved in the Movement would sit and talk about their experiences working with Dr. King, going to jail and all the wrongs that they saw. At that time, everyone knew someone who had been beaten by the police, gone to jail unjustly or was discriminated against. Our children have no idea how many people were beaten and died just to give them the right to higher education. How dare they drop out of school and not take their education seriously. The Civil Rights Movement will always have a special place in my heart.

Family unity is another subject that is dear to me. Too many family members are not speaking to each other. It is very important that you resolve your differences. One of the ways that we can minimize fighting within the family is to make sure that we have a clear plan for our loved ones when we leave this world. It is our responsibility to make sure that our final arrangements, including life insurance, funeral expenses and our last will and testament are in place. Again, it is our responsibility to cover the cost of our own funerals, not your loved ones.

We also need to have two people in place to serve as our guardian should we be incapacitated; maybe an attorney, your pastor or someone else that you trust. Put your wishes and desires in writing, from what song you want played at your funeral all the way down to what you want to wear. Your guardians will then be responsible for making sure that your wishes are carried out. *Your wishes* should be carried out and not you're brothers, sisters and loved ones fighting over their wishes for your funeral. Every family has that one person who believes they are entitled to everything and won't mind stealing to get it.

When my mother passed, my brother and I spent over $50,000.00 of our inheritance to pay an attorney, fighting over what my mother had left for us. Please don't allow this to happen in your family. This is a must if you have kids under the age of 18. You do not want your children to become wards of the state. Family is all that you have, do your part in keeping your family together.

Teresa Ann Hailey has founded many organizations and charities during her lifetime including the Denver Youth Chapter of the NAACP where she served as President until 1983. Teresa was selected as one of the <u>Outstanding Young Women in America</u> and has worked in political campaigns from the State Representative level up to the Presidential level. Teresa travelled throughout the state working on the Rev. Jesse Jackson's 1984 Presidential Campaign.

In April 1990, Teresa was appointed Colorado State Director of the Miss Black Colorado USA pageant and shortly thereafter, she purchased the rights to the International Pageant System. Ushering the new century, Teresa was crowned Ms. Texas North America in February 2000. On September 1, 2007 Teresa opened Mary's Manor Banquet Hall in honor of her mother who passed in 2006 from lung cancer.

You can contact Teresa directly by e-mail at missblackintl@hotmail.com or by telephone at 713 430 6376.

CHAPTER 44

Pearls Of The Pursuit

TIFFANY LYMON

You truly are a Queen and you have a legacy, but if you avoid the process all you will leave behind is your empty shell.
The world needs your Pearl. The Queens need your legacy.

Women of all ages and walks of life seem to universally embrace a string of pearls as something classic, elegant, traditional, and feminine. Adding a string of pearls to a well-tailored suit seems to adorn a woman with an extra sense of class, strength, and stature. Perhaps it is because many of us women can relate to the pearl. Created uniquely out of a process characterized by pain, sacrifice and struggle the pearl emerges strong, with beautiful iridescence.

To create a pearl, an irritant gets trapped within the oyster's shell and in an attempt to get rid of the irritant, the oyster produces secretions and even releases parts of its own flesh in a continuous process to remove or reduce the impact of the irritant. This process over time develops the small irritant into a pearl – eventually even after the oyster is dead the pearl remains. The sand, the secretions, and the flesh seamlessly unite to form something of value.

THE *Queens'* LEGACY

The story of the pearl is the story of many women I know. Some causes, issues, missions, and people that cause pain for some women nationwide, find their way into their hearts, their spirits and their beings. They are so deeply affected that they are willing to sacrifice blood, sweat and tears for something good and tolerable to come out of their pain. I call the results of these women's struggle "The Pearls of Pursuit." We all have these pearls, or the potential to develop them. We also have the capability to wear or share our pearls. Strike that comment. We have the <u>responsibility</u> to wear and share our pearls.

When women grow strong enough, resilient enough and transparent enough to display their pearls it makes them even more attractive and more powerful. Just like a string of pearls, The Pearls of Pursuit are not developed to be hidden, but to be displayed, shared and worn for enhancement. In this chapter, I want to share with you a portion of the pursuit I am on and committed to; and how I see the process as only the birth and development of a "Pearl of Pursuit."

My overall life's pursuit is to reach my life's mission; to Educate, Empower, and Enrich. In this pursuit, I learned about the Pearl of Passion. The passion pearl is enticing and appealing, yet painful and life-altering. When you wear your passion pearl, people notice! The pearl is so alluring, that sometimes people forget what it takes to earn it. This pursuit has led me through many disappointments, heartaches, and through the wilderness of change.

The most current leg of my pursuit began in 2004. I was going through the final stages of a divorce, which was a very a draining process in every aspect of my existence. At the same time, I was trying to cultivate a healthy, new relationship (with my current husband) and make every effort to shelter my two children from the turmoil that was going on in my life. I felt very frustrated with the state of my life at the time, I felt like all the work I had done, the degrees, the prayers, the sacrifices were all in vain and that there was no more hope of a normal life...in short, I felt frustrated.

Frustration and irritation are likely to be the same feelings the oyster has when it is trying to get rid of that foreign particle in its shell....and thus the process begins! It was at this crossroad that my life could have gone in one of two ways. I could have settled for life as it was...not terrible when put in a proper perspective but below where my dreams lived... OR I could have taken all the frustration and irritation and used it to fuel to my journey. I chose the latter.

Many of you reading this can probably relate...maybe you are in the frustration part of the pursuit where you are conceiving how life could be "if," this or that. You fill in the blank. Perhaps you are in the wilderness stage – where all you know for certain is that you are not where you were nor where you are going; or maybe you are sitting at the end of a pursuit reminiscing about how it all went down...even still you might have taken the other path and settled and are now reflecting on how life could have been. In any case, I hope that you are able to relate to something here because there is power in sharing there is release in association and there is freedom in knowing that where you are and where others have walked.

I decided to take that frustration and put it into my pursuit as a business owner and trainer. Honestly, the frustration that I felt within this pursuit has far outweighed the frustration that has led to the pursuit...but once you start it's as hard to turn back as it is to go forward. Here is a point of awe within the pursuit...It starts out with a small irritant or frustration...but if you stop and take inventory in the middle of the pursuit you will find that what you walked into was far more frustrating than where you started. I will use my journey as an example.

When I started the pursuit, I felt empty, unfulfilled, unloved, had very low self-esteem. I felt like a failure. But in the grand scheme of things, being gainfully employed, raising two beautiful children in a relationship with a loving man and dedicated father, had earned my bachelors and masters degrees and had a lot of potential. Sort of like that 80/20 rule. The 20 percent that was bad was really bad, but the other 80 percent was pretty favorable. As the story goes, my focus and line of sight was limited only to the 20 percent. I then begin this pursuit to reduce the frustration in my life.

Through my journey, my life purpose between 2004 and the current day I have been laid off twice in a 12 month period, filed bankruptcy, been diagnosed with stress-induced migraines, sabotaged my marriage, depleted my life savings, experienced tear-filled days and sleepless nights and roller coaster evenings in between. I came within days of car repossessions, house foreclosure and dealt with more than my fair share of misfortune. So let's analyze this...I let a relatively small irritant drive me to create an even larger irritant.

Apparently logic isn't one of the pearls of pursuit. But isn't that the process that the oyster follows? It adds more and more of its secretions and its being to surround tiny foreign particle just to make bigger. Logic would say, "Doesn't that sound like it would be even more irritating?" That

is like taking a hair that is in your eye and instead of removing it with your finger, replacing with a finger. That in my view is what passion does, it forces you to keep going despite how it feels or seems. In the long run you will reap if you faint not. I don't advocate giving or and feeling pessimistic, but I hope to arm you readers with reality. To prepare you for when this happens to you, you have the wisdom to brush it off as normal and keep going. I was surrounded, in the beginning, by a lot of people that were on the other side of the journey but were too proud to admit the pain and failure along the way. My sisters, we are killing dreams and destinies. When we do this, even the Bible tells us simply that we are freed by our testimonies. When we are transparent we free ourselves and others.

The journey to now made me feel like I was certifiably crazy at times. I made however, and I know it's still not over. My journey to this point has yielded a life where I am simultaneously still recovering from the last leg of the pursuit – wondering what the next leg has to offer. I now have a wonderful, supportive husband, 4 children and two businesses. The first business – Mind Over Money, LLC – started out as a financial education organization and was transformed into a business development firm.

During the 5 years that I spent trying to promote and build that business as a financial education and services firm, I acquired a wealth of knowledge and skills as they relates to operating efficiency, marketing strategies and professional development. This time around I have already had international exposure– who knew? The other business - The Lymon Financial Group merges the vision of the original company with the some strategies learned at one of the companies that laid me off. At the Lymon Financial Group I provide financial services and education to individuals and business owners seeking comprehensive strategies to help them reach their financial goals. The beauty is that I can relate to people in just about any financial situation because, in my pursuit, I have experienced many spectrums. Because of my warehouse experience I strive to do it as professionally and efficiently as the big name companies that exclude so many people that many of them couldn't be their own clients (but that is another book).

Do you see the Pearl of Passion is the pearl that allows you to push your way through what you can't see your way through? It becomes so addicting you stay up all night to feed it, you see it in everything you do and it literally becomes an extension of you...just like the pearl. The creation of this pearl will force you to shed parts of yourself, and it is the shedding of these parts that allow you to proceed. When you get rid of the guilt, the low-self esteem, the mediocrity, the fear...you will be surprise at the beauty that comes out.   Maybe I will be a multi-billion dollar trainer one day, maybe I won't but I know that the baggage I have shed and the beauty that has evolved in this process is more valuable than riches.

My goal with this chapter was to touch the heart of the woman that feels like she must be a failure because of what she is experiencing...and tell her to just keep shedding you are making your pearl; to the woman who can't understand why nothing she does seems to work but has a vision of how it could...I say don't stop your pearl is just being hardened; to the woman that is wondering if she is working in vain, wondering if her work will ever bear fruit...I tell you don't fret, your pearl will bear fruit for your benefit and its splendor will also add to the lives of others.   Embrace your pursuit...Embrace the process...It is worth it and the results are eternal...even the mistakes can be passed on to stop other generations from making the same mistakes you have made.   Nothing is in vain if you learn from it, even the biggest failures can become pearls.

When I first got this revelation about the analogy of pearls and what we experience in life, I started to read as much as I can about pearls. I think that the most interesting fact that I have found was that pearls created naturally have an iridescence – a glow, an attraction – that cannot be created artificially and that is one of the ways you can differentiate them from counterfeits. WOW! What revelation that was for me and hopefully for you. Imagine if First Lady Michelle Obama didn't earn her pearls, or if Oprah didn't earn her pearls, or Rosa Parks or your grandmother or mother or YOU...would we, as women, be the unique, beautiful queens we are today?

I will leave you with this: Wherever you are in life make the most of it; be transparent; share your pearls; you can save a life if you let go of the ego and wear your pearls – your experiences and lessons learned – with a humble pride. You truly are a Queen and you have a legacy, but if you avoid the process all you will leave behind is your empty shell. The world needs your Pearl. The Queens need your legacy. You can do all things through Christ who strengthens you...Phil 4:13

THE *Queens'* LEGACY

Tiffany is known for her ability to take complex concepts make them practical and applicable, Tiffany Lymon is always striving to deliver her mission – Educate Individuals, Empower Communities and Enrich Nations - with excellence. As the owner of two businesses, Mind Over Money, LLC and The Lymon Financial Group, Mrs. Lymon has the opportunity to partner with business owners and individuals to help navigate through the process of achieving their professional and financial goals. Mrs. Lymon has had the privilege of providing her dynamic training and services to youth, individuals, business owners and leaders at national and international conferences.

Personally, Mrs. Lymon is a wife and a proud mother of four. She enjoys spending time with her family and traveling as her way of gaining life's balance. Her personal mantra is "And This Too Shall Pass"...It keeps her humble in good times and hopeful in bad.

Tiffany Lymon can be reached by e-mail at tlymon@mindovermoneyllc.com or visit her website at www.mindovermoneyllc.com.

CHAPTER 45

A Letter To My Daughter-
The Keys To The Kingdom

VERA CORNISH

My hope for you is quite simple, live a life more abundantly than you can imagine. The "Keys To The Kingdom" are on the table by the door.

Dear Alana,

I remember like it was yesterday the first time I handed you the keys to the car. Exhilaration spilled from every pore in your body. Undaunted by the fact it was an older model stick shift with four on the floor, you claimed your rightful seat, ready to take the world by storm. Quickly, you came to the realization this was going to be a process and not necessarily easy. However, you knew beyond a shadow of a doubt that if you didn't give in to the frustration and difficulties, you could go anywhere in the world. There is no greater gift that I can give you than the Keys to the Kingdom and to encourage you to once again claim your rightful seat in the world. Unlocking the doors to life has been a journey full of amazing events, some joyful and some painful. Without any of them, I wouldn't have arrived at the point of realization that I am truly part of a royal family.

The truth is your mom was always a little different, a little peculiar and some even say strange. Why wouldn't I be? Think about it, I was the

daughter of June and Johnny a.k.a. "Fast Black" and "June Bug". In their mind, they were King and Queen of the Hill District in Pittsburgh, Pennsylvania. They were "living the life", entertaining and enjoying the music of Ray Charles and Louie Armstrong. My godfather was "Billy D". Not the movie star, but just as handsome. In their world life was great, at least on the surface. As the story is told, my birth was the answer to a difficult period in their life. However, there is a difference between fantasy and reality.

The reality was a baby didn't match their lifestyle, no matter how cute. Where do you put a baby in a pink Cadillac? When do you fit in feedings and diaper changes and where was the house with the white picket fence? There were hard decisions to be made. Enter Grandma Delia and Aunt Minnie. Grandma Delia was a Pentecostal Evangelist. Aunt Minnie, my father's sister, was willing to open her heart and home. These two women became my guardian angels. The decision was made, and at the age of nine months, I went to live with Grandma.

For ten years, this was the collision of two different worlds, two different mindsets. Within Johnny dwelled the power to influence, strong enough to change the direction of June's life. Walking away from everything that formed her foundation, she left high school in her senior year to stand firmly by his side. The reality of their lifestyle involved drugs, alcohol, the numbers and more. To their child, they gave the gift of endless possibilities; releasing her to the person that held the Keys to the Kingdom.

Delia was a woman that knew that nothing was impossible for God. Devout in her belief, she had her own struggles, the loss of her husband, the loss of her home, dwindling health and yet a resiliency that only Faith could bring. Reflecting, Delia knew she was the daughter of the King and that every twist and turn would work together to give Him the glory. She had been entrusted to raise his child.

Delia had a comfortable home on Watt Lane in the Burg, with a pantry attached to a small kitchen overlooking the back yard. The sister could cook. Memories of yeast raised rolls and aromas of home cooking filled the air, paired with bar-b-q from the local pit and fried chicken that sometimes came in a brown paper bag, compliments of Johnny. I was a child relishing cruising in the pink Caddy with Dad straight to Islay's for ice-cream, gliding through the park barely able to see over the dashboard. I embraced those rare visits from June and she was always bearing gifts. Life was great, except for the volcanic eruptions when the worlds collided.

Quietly there is an untold part of the love story. The hurt and pain of love, of bad decisions, of the devastation that heroin reeks on the mind, body and spirit of a man and the toll it takes on the woman that loved him. There is a harsh realism to falling into a pit so deep and dark that the only way out is a miracle.

Life suddenly changed. James, my Grandfather passed on and Delia lost her home. We moved so many times I lost count. Delia was committed to protecting me from the dark side of my parent's life. For all the comfort I perceived, the reality was now poverty. Undaunted, Grandma still produced meals that were memories. Breakfast was an event, homemade pancakes served outside seated at a small table in the backyard covered with a checkered table cloth. More moves, food lines, waiting for the surplus cheese, the canned jellied pork and never a complaint from Grandma. She was still praising God and holding Vacation Bible School complete with taffy pulls made from black strap molasses.

I lost Grandma at the age of nine and moved to Wilkes-Barre, Pennsylvania with Mom. Trust me, it's all about food and friendship when you're ten years old. I entered the world of perogies and kibbee. Life had changed. I had gone from the Hill to the valley surrounded by beautiful Pocono Mountains. This was yet another door opening in the journey of a lifetime.

Still as sultry as ever and alone, June is yet unprepared to raise a family and now has two children. Enter Kathleen. I'm now the one asking, what do you do with a baby? The memories are chaotic; times of laughter peppered with anger and rage. June clearly had lost the Keys to the Kingdom and was searching desperately for love. The influences were strong and seemingly right for the moment yet unravel into situations that caused her children to live in fear. It still amazes me how deeply rooted fear can be.

At the points of deepest desperation, I would call my guardian angel, Aunt Minnie. At the speed of light, I would find myself in either North Philly sitting on the stoop or back in the Burg with Dad. Summers in the city became the norm as was going to the Uptown Theatre listening to Martha Reeves and the Vandellas or having my hair pressed on Centre Ave. and catching a little Bar-B-Q.

The years passed quickly, the friendships were amazing. I loved learning. Grandma had taught me to read exceptionally well and we did it daily. Of course there was only one book to read, the Bible. That foundation

launched me into a craving for knowledge. This was against the backdrop of June's life unraveling. School and after school activities became my home away from home. High school became my playground. In many ways I excelled. Trust me, high school has all the influences necessary to destroy the best dreams and I was a dreamer. I now know the key to my success was the foundation set by a praying Grandmother. Her prayers shielded me from a life ending in prostitution, drugs and alcohol. It is truly amazing how darkness lurks at the edge of dreams, always there, never giving up, ready to destroy and always creating a false reality.

In my junior year, I met the love of my life Lenny Cornish. We were both cantankerous and opinionated from the beginning. Pepper that with Big Dreams and we were meant for each other. Home was still worsening as the time flew by. Only by God's grace, I donned cap and gown and graduated high school with Penn State my next stop. Let's be very clear. By now I was not Christ-centered, however the journey dictated church every Sunday morning regardless of what you did Saturday night. Again, God was there guiding and protecting me even when I didn't realize it.

Penn State was wonderful. Lenny and I got an apartment together, shared great times and graduated. Both families were overjoyed. Make no mistake about it; no one was happy we had decided to live together. For all the mistakes they had made, they didn't want us to repeat the patterns of the past. In the midst of the Penn State years, there was the unpacked baggage of the past; fear, anger, deception, alcohol and more. Through it all, I now know God had his hand on my life.

Fast forward, we married shortly after graduation. What a celebration! Aggie, your Grandmother, nine Aunts and an Uncle rounded out my new family. What we hadn't found were the Keys to Marriage God's Way. So while the years passed and life seemed wonderful, twenty some years later and one beautiful daughter; the baggage was still sitting in the corner unpacked and full of all the things that destroy two nice people. Hidden from sight lurked fear, frustration, anger, deception and turmoil. Surrounded by great friends we made our own rules for living. Young and misguided, our relationships were interwoven with dysfunction. In some surrealistic way we believed all we needed was each other and the end of the rainbow would be a life of happiness. Even suicide and death couldn't convince us differently. It's amazing how darkness can confuse even the most astute people.

God's plan continued without fail. I went to work as a teacher, lived on a beautiful eighty acre horse farm, worked as a college administrator, served in the office of three college presidents and started my own business. Best of all, I gave birth to you. That's the short version of the latter part of twenty some years of life. The pattern was still the same, great opportunities, fantastic experiences and the baggage still sitting in the corner unpacked.

What I thought was the perfect job opportunity turned out to be God's plan for me returning to the roots of my childhood, returning to Him. How did it happen? Someone prayed with me, not for me and invited me to church. I will never forget that first day, literally walking back into more light than I had experienced in years. I will never forget the sermon that changed my life, "Master of Disaster". Need I say more? That was the turning point! From that time on God continued to peel the onion, healing my mind, my spirit, my heart, and my very soul. The journey continues, leaving behind fear, frustration, anger, rage, hurt and pain. One of the most precious Keys was learning to trust God, open the baggage, take out the lessons, and leave the rest behind.

Now, so many years have passed and only God would know that every single experience could be used to give hope to others. I am so thankful that I found the Keys To The Kingdom. I am thankful for each person that was placed in my path as a beacon of light; it is so easy to wander in darkness, looking for a way out. As a young person, I believed life went through clearly defined phases. Later I began to call each phase a season. I now know each season is really a door leading to yet another wonderful deeper understanding of life and purpose.

The journey has created an amazing platform that assists others to find their way and live a life of hope. Now I know nothing is impossible for God. Your Legacy? Cornish & Associates Inc., a newspaper, a radio show, training programs, workshops, personal coaching, corporate consulting and the seeds of entrepreneurship to sow into the future of others. When people share their hopes and dreams, often clouded by difficult circumstances, I simply ask; "How can assist you?" With a quiet smile, I think to myself, if you only knew my *entire* story.

Grandma was right; the greatest key of all is accepting Jesus Christ as "your personal" Lord and Savior. The rest is walking through door after door deeper into the Kingdom and coming to the realization that you are a daughter of the King. It is with great honor in this season of my life, that I take my seat as a Queen, a member of the royal family. I now know that abuse of any type, even by those who say they love you, is not of God and the key to true freedom is forgiveness. Johnny, June and Delia are now

THE *Queens'* LEGACY

gone. Amazingly, Johnny is hopefully with Delia. I can only hope the same for June. The couple of the week are now divorced and rebuilding their lives. The love they had for each other is now manifested in you.

Always remember how much I love you. My hope for you is quite simple, live a life more abundantly than you can imagine. The "Keys To The Kingdom" are on the table by the door. Use them wisely and always guard them with your heart. You are the Living Legacy of the Queen.

Love,
Mom

P.S. Keep a spare set for someone else who may just want to meet the King!

Vera Cornish is dedicated to "Conducting the Business of Life" therefore assisting individuals, entrepreneurs, small businesses and corporations in personal and professional growth and development. Vera is known as an astute trainer, inspirational speaker, insightful facilitator and lifestyle coach. She is the publisher of *The Urban Connection* a newspaper targeting diverse markets and co-founder of *Profiling Excellence* a magazine that features *Success in Diversity*. Vera is also the host of the radio show, Make the Connection, The Women's Empowerment Hour and founder of The Empowerment Mansion.

Vera is a firm believer in the power of the human spirit and is committed to assisting you in taking both business and life to the next level. Her presentations include You Are The Brand, Overcoming Fear and Change Your Mind: Change Your Life.

You may contact Vera by phone at 717-545-0299 or visit her website at www.CornishandAssociates.com. She would love to hear from you.

CHAPTER 46

A Tribute To Dr. Dorothy Height

WANDA MUIR-OLIVER

The torch is being handed to us, now we must pass it on, keeping it alive by dream givers who want the flame to continue lighting the way. We must continue the legacy of these great leading ladies.

Throughout our lives, we often reflect on the person who has taught us well. Dr. Dorothy Irene Height is a Queen, who is leaving a legacy, while leading by example. We often call her Queen Mother; she truly is a gift to us. We are blessed to have her with us. At 97 years old, she still possesses a quiet and gentle spirit.

Dr. Height's leadership role began with the YWCA in Harlem as a social worker. In 1937, Dorothy Height met Mary McLeod Bethune, founder and president of the National Council of Negro Women (NCNW), as she was escorting Eleanor Roosevelt into one of the group's meetings at the YMCA, shortly after Dr. Height began volunteering with the organization. Dr. Height joined others in advocating for equal rights, and full equal employment, pay and education.

In 1947, Dr. Height was elected as National President of Delta Sigma Theta Inc. She led the sorority to a new level of organization. She was instrumental in the Ride Wing Project; a mobile library that was dispatched

to black communities. During segregation, there were not many libraries that blacks could go to and read, so this program gave them the opportunity to visit a library in their own community.

Dr. Height established Delta Volunteer for community service and the Jobs Opportunity Project. After Dr. Height's presidency with the sorority ended in 1956, she took over as the 4th elected President of NCNW. Dr. Height has done so much for this organization and has kept Mary McCloud Bethune's last will and testament alive. NCNW helps women of African descent to become knowledgeable concerning their health and personal needs. It promotes leadership among members and helps to improve communities. Dr. Height often says that we still have a lot to do.

In 1986, Dr. Height founded the yearly event, Black Family Reunion in Washington, DC. The reunion offers many opportunities to children and families. There are educational events, entertainment, and health awareness just to name a few activities. Dr. Height erected a Statue of Mary McLeod Bethune in a Federal Park with the funds raised by thousands of women. It was the first statue of any woman in Washington, DC. Every July 10th, there is a program in the park celebrating Mary McCloud Bethune's birthday. There I met a dear friend, Dr. Evelyn Bethune, granddaughter of Mary McCloud Bethune. Her stories about her family enriched me greatly.

Dr. Height also founded the Bethune Museum and Archives for Black Women. It was the first institution devoted to black women's history, and established the Council House as a national historic site. Dr. Height's Civil Rights Wednesdays in Mississippi brought black and white women together to communicate, and to help out at the freedom schools and voter registration drives in the south. Dr. Height worked tirelessly with Dr. Martin Luther King and others to work towards integration for blacks in America. She often says that progress has been made, and we have accomplished much, but we still have a long way to go.

Dr. Height had a dream as President of NCNW. She believed the organization needed to own its own building. She planned and organized a unity drive among the NCNW sections, and she recruited her friends and family in the effort. NCNW was able to purchase a building and payoff its mortgage. The NCNW National Headquarters, known as the Dorothy I. Height building is located at 633 Pennsylvania Avenue, NW, between the White House and the Capital. It is the only African American-owned building on Pennsylvania Avenue. The building has seen a lot of history over the years. Slaves were sold on the corner, President Lincoln received haircuts there, and Harriett Bleacher Stowe wrote Uncle Tom's Cabin in the building.

When we attend a meeting at the Dorothy Height Building, we are aware that we are coming together for a common purpose. During our President's Roundtable meetings, we come to roll up our sleeves and work on accomplishing various things between the regional sections and the national office. We are still working on unfinished business that Mary McCloud Bethune set out for us to do. It gives me great pride to know that we are helping to improve humanity in some way. Sometimes our Executive Director, Alfreda Davis, or Dr. Height will come to the meetings and give their input on our discussions. We are able to learn from each other.

I attended my first NCNW Black Family Reunion in Washington, DC in 1987. I was visiting from Virginia with family members. Everyone was excited about seeing the exhibits, mingling with one another, and having interesting conversations with various people from across the country. It was then that a family member introduced Dr. Height to me. I shared with Dr. Height how much I enjoyed the family reunion. She told me she was glad that I was enjoying myself, and invited me back to the reunion. I assured her that I would come back.

In 1999, I was living in Maryland and some friends began discussing the National Council of Negro Women. I told them of my earlier visit to the Family Reunion. My friends were urging me to join, but I was too busy with family, Delta and other things, so I kept putting it off. Finally, I joined and I was invited to attend my first tea with GBS NCNW at the Alpha Phi Alpha house in Baltimore, and the occasion was simply beautiful. Dr. Height was the invited guest.

At a Section meeting at GBS NCNW, I was elected 1st Vice President and became very busy within the organization volunteering with the section and then with National. Dr. Height asked me to come back. She made me feel that the organization needed me, ignited my interest and inspired me to become involved at a greater level. Dr. Height became my "reflector." She helps me see a little better. She gives me another eye that improves my vision and allows me to gain a clearer focus on things.

It was a beautiful day and I had an appointment to meet with Dr. Height in her office, I always looked forward to being in her presence, because I knew that during the course of our conversation, I would gain some wisdom. Dr. Height had a way of keeping me hungry for learning. Dr. Height would

refresh my memory of the 13th, 14th and 15th amendments. We have talked about our youth and the importance of getting them involved in their communities. When we involve ourselves with our youth within the Sections, we are building their character and confidence.

Janis Ferebee of the Bethune Program partnered with Social Services to create a workshop that would teach young people the realities of what it takes to live today. She invited children from NCNW Sections to participate. Several members volunteered, along with the director. The children were given interviews and a life skills test. They were given mock occupations and salaries that they had to use for rent, a house, health care and anything else required to sustain them. We enjoyed interviewing the children. After the interviews, we watched to see how much they would spend. The children expressed how much the seminar helped them to have a better understanding about economics.

The new generation needs to be continuously empowered and mentored. This really can make a difference in helping a child to move in a positive direction. Human beings need to be stimulated – some more than others – which is why Dr. Height created the Dorothy Height Institute. This institute provides information concerning the organization as well as personal growth in leadership. The Institute had its opening during the last National Convention where Dr. Thelma T. Daley gave a powerful seminar. Everyone walked away from the Institute feeling positively empowered.

In 1998, Dr. Height became President Emeritus of our organization. However, she comes to the office everyday to work on matters with which the organization is involved. You can learn more of the history of Dr. Dorothy Irene Height by reading her book "Open Wide the Freedom Gates" with a foreword by Maya Angelou.

Join NCNW.org

Dr. Height, I love you. You have dedicated your life to serving others and promoting extraordinary leadership. There are not enough words to describe how awesome you are as an individual. I respect you for your honesty, integrity and sincerity. Your talks with me have enriched me greatly and will be a part of my spirit as long as I shall live. Thank you for taking time to share your wisdom with me. I am blessed to have met you. You are a strong vibrant woman that is full of great purpose.

Wanda Muir Oliver

Wanda Muir-Oliver is an author/poet, educator, activist, actress, and most recently a motivational speaker and mentor to children and teens. Wanda earned a B.S. degree in Liberal Arts with a concentration in three disciplines – Psychology, Social Work and Special Education. She is working towards certification in Special Education, while pursuing a Master's Degree in Counseling.

She is currently working on a re-release of her poetry book *Realities of Life* with a foreword by Dorothy I. Height.

Wanda Muir-Oliver currently serves on the Executive Board of the National Council of Negro Women's Eastern Region 'Presidents Roundtable." She is also Parliamentarian at National Headquarters in Washington, DC. She is a member of the Bethune Recognition Program Committee and also serves on the Arts & Letters Committee for Delta Sigma Theta Inc.

Having received a mayoral citation in recognition for her community service, she has worked and is excited to work with the homeless, the needy and those looking for a better opportunity in life. You can contact Wanda by email at marrshollywood@yahoo.com or visit her website at www.wandamuiroliver.com

CHAPTER 47

Swimming With The Dolphins

YOLONDA D. COLEMAN

I started crying but still refused to give up. This is not the day. Mommy, this is not the day, I whispered in my head hoping that through telepathy she'd hear me.

"Your hands are magic, Girl. You should go into business," Mom said as I rubbed the Keri lotion on her legs.

"Yeh, Ma! That's what the fellaz tell me too," I said and chuckled.

Days before Mom died, six of her sisters and brothers showered her with attention. Her best friend left her "good government job" for a moment to engage in girly banter. Cousins flew from the north to talk about old times. Each of them in their forties, Mom reflected on the memories and then sadness set around her.

"Not that I wish it on them, but why me?" she asked.

"I know, Mom. I know. You just wish things were as easy as growing up. But guess what?"

"What?" she asked me.

"You're still my pretty girl."

"Aw, thank you." Her smile lit up the room in her Florida home.

Nurses changed shifts throughout the day. One was less experienced than the others. The day shift nurse wrapped gauze around Mom's incision in her stomach. It was a bit over the top. The mound was standing tall around the doctor's poor attempt to put in the Gastrostomy Tube (G-Tube). Puss was oozing like a river. The gauze was supposed to catch it. That it did, but as Mom said, "I look pregnant."

"I told you to go ahead and drop that load," I said jokingly.

"Yeh, well I wish I was pregnant. At least I know I'd be out of pain in 9 months."

"I know that's right, Mom."

Nurses changed shifts again. One was more sensitive than the others. A new day shift nurse ate and cried with the family. However, when Mom started passing blood through her urine and rectum, the nurse went into panic mode.

"This is usually a tale, tale sign of the end," the sensitive nurse mustered to say through blood shot eyes. Her eyes were wet with sorrowful tears.

I started crying but still refused to give up. *This is not the day. Mommy, this is not the day,* I whispered in my head hoping that through telepathy she'd hear me. She did. Mom held on and was a trooper in between vomiting and fighting for her life.

Nurses changed shifts again. One was more experienced than the others. The night shift brought in an angel. She never broke bread with the family, and we were somehow prejudiced in our thinking. She had a limp and cane. It was later explained to us that she survived a cliff hanger--- literally.

Once, the nurse was in her car and almost drove off a cliff. God saved her so that she could be Mom's guardian. She prayed for Mom, put her on the prayer list at church, and brought in a lute, or was it a ukulele? It was a stringed instrument that allowed her to play, *How great thou art.* Mom sang along as I was spread across the bed watching and listening.

Mom was at peace, in minimal pain, and the singing put her to sleep. God uses people no matter their condition. The night shift nurse was a blessing. A new day was waiting on us. Slumber was our friend.

"Happy Birthday," slowly seeped through Mom's brownish, pink lips on the side of her bed. It was exactly one week and one day before I would turn 29. She had just given me a present prior to the Emergency Medical Technicians rolling her into the ambulance.

"See, I've been saving. That's just between you and me," she said.

"Okay, Mom." I tucked away my stash with bewildering questions running through my head. *Are you trying to tell me something, Mom? What does this mean? Will you not be here for my birthday?* I kept my thoughts inside. I was afraid of the answers.

Mom never let us see her sweat. She constantly kept a smile on her face regardless of how weak she became over time. Even after her doctors were nowhere to be found and the pain was unbearable, Mom proclaimed, "I want to live."

When the hospice doctor came in to speak with Mom, he was puzzled.

"Why are you here? Why did they perform that procedure? Tell me everything that went on?"

He asked the questions we had been seeking answers to as well. Somehow, those whose expertise it was to help restore Mom's health somehow skipped town without any transferred files, and all of us were clueless. Nevertheless, her spirits remained high---higher than those of us not suffering from cancer, blocked intestines, gang green forming in the abdominal area, and a bleeding urethra. At 43, she fought with prayer and faith.

Passion of the Christ was the last movie request. She watched it on a mini DVD player for Easter. She shared her last supper with me and a neighborhood friend. Ice cream. She couldn't digest it, but that's what she wanted. It went in her mouth, out of the G-tube, and into her bag. Radiation and chemotherapy destroyed her digestive system. We worked with what was left of it. The caramel, whipped cream, vanilla scoops, and cherry went down just fine. She was happy, so I was happy I could make that wish come true.

After a week of spending time with mom, I resigned from my job. On a Tuesday night, I played with my best friend, my only living direct connection, my kindred spirit, my mom.

"I want to see you walk again," I said to her.

"I told you I did it the other night," Mom said expressively.

"I know, but I wasn't here so it doesn't count. I have my camera. I'll be right back."

"Oh, gurl!" Mom sighed as she was used to me forgetting and remembering things all in the same moment. I imagined her saying to herself, *That girl is going to get it together someday.*

"Okay, I've got power. I'm recording!"

"One two three. One two three. One two three." Mom was out of the bed with the assistance of a hospice care nurse. She had to count her way through drastic movements.

"One two three. One two three. One two three." She walked over to the chair in small steps.

"One two three. One two three. One two three." Mom did it! She got up, walked, and sat in a chair. The Olympic crowd gives her a 10 with a star. I was so proud of her. Then, I had another bright idea.

"Let's talk to the camera," I suggested.

"Oh! You can see what you're recording. That's not good," Mom said as she looked at the LCD on the camera.

"Hey, Ma? Guess what?" I asked to divert her attention.

"What's up?"

"You're the best Mommy ever!"

"Oh, thanks. You're such a sweetie pie," she said.

"I love you."

"I love you too."

"Okay, let's sign off," I said.

"Alright, peace." With two fingers, Mom ended our talk show. It was the show I could not take credit for producing. God orchestrated every move of that evening. I took a nap and waited for another tomorrow to arrive.

It was 6:30 a.m., March 30, 2005 when I decided to get Mom a Mother's Day card. It was the day before my birthday and I wanted her to have her "flowers" while she was still around.

After leaving the drug store with a newspaper and Mom's purple card with flowers on it, I stopped by a friend's house to grab a few more hours of sleep. However, the quiet of the day worried me. Stillness was my alarm. My phone had not been ringing. I hurried to my car to locate it. It was buried under my driver's seat. I had several missed calls from "Momc" (mom's cell phone). I called back.

"Where have you been? The doctor needs to speak with both of us," my dad frantically spoke on the other end.

I still wasn't worried but found myself in a place that I remembered just 5 years, three weeks, and two days earlier. It was an unusually beautiful spring day. It was the day my biological father died. March 7th. Remembering, it was March 7th Mom was rushed to the hospital. It was March 13th we buried my father. It was March 14th they gave Mom two weeks to live. Every day was becoming the Ides of March for me. Where was my soothsayer, Shakespeare?"

"Do you want us to make her comfortable or make her aware that you're here?" Dr. So and So asked. I became numb. I was still seeing Mom and I walking around the cul-de-sac talking about the knucklehead men we used to date and her constant reminders to me that *A man does not make you whole---love yourself first.* The night prior was our way of making progress. It wasn't supposed to come to us making a decision to *make her comfortable* or *make her aware.* Leave it to me: Make her well again.

Of all the crazy emotions surrounding my world, *make her comfortable* was the final answer. I really don't remember how I arrived at that decision and why it was my choice at all. I just nodded a lot and tried to digest it all. In and out of room 250, I quoted John 3:16 in Mom's ear. It was

her favorite scripture. I then made a silent request, *God I just want to hear my mother's voice again.*" And you know what? I did. She cried out, *Jesus.*

Still hopeful, I got on the yahoo group to keep my sorority sisters posted. Family and friends were informed of Mom's fight. I studied broadcast journalism and became Mom's correspondent around the country. It really was an up to the minute email broadcast. Just as I hit send to an email going out to a college classmate, my stepfather walked into the family room.

"We're losing her," he cried.

Not today. Not now. Not exactly in the position I was when I found out my father died. I had just shut off my computer from an Instant Message session with Mom...talking about my father's condition before he died. Talk about being here before. I slowly rose from my chair and walked to the room. There, in room 250, surrounded by nurses, was my mommy at rest. She was lifeless but very much alive with her eyes and mouth agape trying to speak to me from the other side. Tears formed in my eyes and I had to speak to her spirit.

"Mommy, I love you. I'm going to make you proud. I'm going to go to Afrika for you. Tell our loved ones before you I said hello---"

At that moment, I flat-lined but my heart was still beating. I was living off her strength, her courage just as she wanted. The nurse closed her eyes. Almost two months after her Home Going Celebration, Mom's energy was still present. She asked us a long time ago to cremate her remains and spread them in the ocean. She wanted to swim with the dolphins. In granting her last wish, my aunt and uncle took a cruise to Cozumel, Mexico with me and Dad.

At midnight, May 20, 2005 we each took her ashes and let them blow in the wind and into the ocean blue. I was last and called out those who love her and those she had yet to meet---son-in-law I know she and God are working on for me and grand children. Two days later, I was sitting on the deck with Auntie who said, *It would be nice to see some dolphins. That would make the trip complete.* Not even 15 minutes later, we noticed something popping up in the ocean. Just to the right of the wake from the ship, one, two, three, four, five heads popped out of the water trying to catch up with the ship. They were dolphins.

"That's your mom!" Auntie exclaimed while pointing in the direction of the dolphins.

I waved with excitement and whispered, "Hi Mom. You're swimming with the dolphins just like you wanted."

Forever gone in the physical but forever living in my spirit, Mom remains my hero. Mom gave me life the moment she took her last breath. I wasn't prepared for her departure, but I know her strength was transferred into my spirit. Thoughts of Mom's resilience are my reasons to live without regrets. When stillness surrounds me and there is only space and God, I cry silent tears to the beat of my thumping heart and movement of my heaving chest. I miss Mom, but I know as her legacy I have to walk in peace and enjoy my journey as a queen...just as she did.

Yolonda D. Coleman was born and reared in Washington, D.C. One of the original Posse Members on BET's *Teen Summit* from 1989 to 1994, Coleman has made appearances on CNN and News Channel 8. She finished in the top of her graduating classes at Benjamin Banneker H.S. in Washington, DC and Hampton University in Hampton, VA.

Coleman was first published at the age of 15. Her most recent release, *Sugar Rush: Love's Elevation*, is national best seller. As she continues to inspire and motivate others, Coleman is just waiting to see what adventures life will bring her way. In the meantime, she is committing her life to her passions: writing, and helping to serve as a mentor to other dreamers.

For more information on Yolonda visit www.coffeedreamz.com/ecard.